marco pierre white
THE DEVIL IN
THE KITCHEN

THE AUTOBIOGRAPHY

An Orion paperback

First published in Great Britain in 2006
by Orion
This paperback edition published in 2007
by Orion Books Ltd,
Orion House, 5 Upper St Martin's Lane,
London WC2H 9EA

An Hachette Livre UK company

10 9 8 7 6 5

ISBN 978-0-7528-8161-4

Printed and bound by Mackays of Chatham plc, Chatham, Kent

The Orion Publishing Group's policy is to use papers that
are natural, renewable and recyclable products and made
from wood grown in sustainable forests. The logging
and manufacturing processes are expected to conform to
the environmental regulations of the country of origin.

www.orionbooks.co.uk

Picture credits: The Estate of Bob Carlos Clarke viii–ix, 66, 83, 96, 129, 144, 153, 175, 207, 226,
250, 293; Terry O'Neill 275; Storm 124; Marco Pierre White 2, 7 16, 28, 278, 283, 301.

'A dash or two of introspection and a few great big dollops of raw honesty appear to have done wonders for the psyche of our once most irascible chef' *Telegraph*

'Inspirational' *Sunday Times*

'If you really want to know what the chefs get up to in the privacy of their own pantries, pick up [*The Devil in the Kitchen*], a tale of violence, genius and sex among the pans' *Scotsman*

'Marco Pierre White was the original rock-star chef – the guy who all of us wanted to be. From the moment my chef pals and I got a look at his first cookbook – and at photos of the Man Himself, in all his haggard, debauched-looking, obsessively driven glory – we dreamed of nothing more than to be just like him. He made history'

Anthony Bourdain, author of *Kitchen Confidential*

'Marco will always remain the epitome of the wicked, talented, flamboyant chef – the archetype made flesh. And, really, would we want him any other way?' *Independent*

'The original enfant terrible of the kitchen . . . One can feel White's influence not only in his gastronomic legacy, but also in the wild-boy posturing of the volatile celebrity chefs who now populate our televisions'

Guardian

'A mighty achievement . . . this highly readable book will be a source for the historian of social mobility in the 1980s and 90s, as well as those more interested in how chefs of that era teased and tortured the food on our plates' *Times Literary Supplement*

'The first half of this book is one of the most inspiring memoirs I have ever read – the story of how a motherless, uneducated boy raised himself by hard work and determination to the very top of his profession'

Lynn Barber, *Telegraph*

'Strangely fascinating' *Mail on Sunday*

'A three-star memoir . . . bubbles over with pot-hurling, star-chasing antics' *Vanity Fair*

Marco Pierre White was born in Leeds in 1961. After training with the likes of Michael Lawson, Albert Roux, Nico Ladenis, Pierre Koffmann and Raymond Blanc, he opened Harveys, which became the most talked about restaurant of the late eighties, and won him two Michelin stars. He went on to build a gastronomic empire which included the Canteen, Mirabelle, Quo Vadis, Criterion, Marco Pierre White at the Hyde Park Hotel, and the Oak Room. He inspired award-winning chefs including Gordon Ramsay, Heston Blumenthal and Jean-Christophe Novelli.

In 1999 he retired from the kitchen and handed back his three Michelin stars, but he continues to launch restaurants. Recent ventures include Frankie's, in partnership with jockey Frankie Dettori, as well as Luciano, with Sir Rocco Forte.

He lives in West London, with his Spanish-born wife, Mati, and their three children, Luciano, Marco and Mirabelle. He has another daughter, Lettie, by his first wife.

Described by Piers Morgan as 'the world's most mischievous journalist', James Steen cut his teeth on gossip columns in the late eighties (when he met Marco). His career has included editing *Punch*, where he learned how to lunch and fight legal battles. He is married to journalist Louise Gannon and they have three children, Charlie, Billy and Daisy.

For my mother.
And for Mati, the woman who finished the job
my mother started.

Acknowledgements

SINCERE thanks are due to the following special people who helped create this book.

The literary agent: Jonathan Lloyd, of Curtis Brown, and his assistant, Camilla Goslett.

The memory-joggers and insight-providers: These included Piers Adam, Heston Blumenthal, Martin Blunos, Peter Burrell, Eric Chavot, Adam Helliker, Keith Floyd, Simon and Rena Gueller, Mr Ishii, Nicky and Juanita Kerman, Bernard Lawson, Rex Leyland, Charlie Methven, Nick Munier (now of Bon Appetit in Malahide, Co. Dublin), Jean-Christophe Novelli, Neil Reading, Andrew Regan, Morfudd Richards, Egon Ronay, Kate Sissons, Deborah Sherwood.

The publishers: The Orion team, led by the unflappable Ian Marshall, included Shauna Bartlett, Lorraine Baxter, Lucy Henson and Hannah Whitaker. Craig Fraser produced the jacket design; Helen Ewing designed the inside pages.

The meticulous lawyer: Roy Furness.

Loved ones and authors who played the role of 'readers' and dished out advice: Fletch Dhew, Paul Donnelley, Shirley Flack, Chris Hutchins, Dean Keyworth, Dominic Midgley and Stephanie Smith.

Others who got in on the action: Gideon Benaim of Schillings, and Mark Thompson, for many years my solicitor. Beverley Nunnery, of the eponymously-named company of shorthand writers, kindly gave permission to publish transcripts of my High Court action against the *New York Times* and *International Herald Tribune*. The guidebook, *Helping Children With Loss* (published by Speechmark) was invaluable reading before tackling the childhood years.

The ghost-writer's wife: Louise, for being patient (and the Steen brigade, Charlie, Billy and Daisy).

Five guys who played a significant role in my life: Albert Roux gave me my big break in London; Raymond Blanc inspired my palate; Michael Caine took me across the Thames and introduced me to Sir Rocco Forte; Sir Rocco gave me the restaurant where I'd win my three Michelin stars; and Michael Winner encouraged me to marry Mati.

Importantly, I owe a debt of gratitude to every member of staff who has worked with me over the years. And I truly appreciate J-C Slowik, my long-time restaurant manager. He taught the staff, 'Rule number one – the boss is always right. Rule number two – if the boss is wrong, go back to rule number one.'

And finally: A salute to the kitchen porters – you guys never get the recognition you deserve.

The first photograph Bob Carlos Clarke took of me, in 1986.

Contents

For Starters

ONE OF the purposes of this book was to recount the joys of working in a professional kitchen: a very long, tiring day of sweat, toil, aggro and bollockings (and that's just when service was running smoothly). I mentioned in the hardback edition of this book (published as *White Slave*) that after retiring from the kitchen in December 1999 I did not miss cooking but really missed the adrenaline of serving the finest food. I was a happier man, I said, for removing the apron and stepping away from the stove. Knowing what my life is like, it would have been peculiar if that had been the end of the matter.

So I suppose I wasn't really surprised when, within a few weeks of publication, I received two offers of work which, if accepted, would mean I'd have to put on the apron again and return to the kitchen. I accepted both invitations.

The first job seemed uncomplicated enough and (given my experience) undemanding. I was asked if I would go to France to do a cooking demonstration for fifteen ladies in the kitchens of Sir Rocco Forte's hotel, Château de Bagnols, which is just outside Lyon.

The women were all guests at the hotel. Their husbands would be spending the day wine-tasting at the Montrachet vineyard, while I'd be at the stove doing my demo. When I arrived at the hotel, a smartly dressed man dashed up to me, held out his hand for a shake and said, 'Hello, Darko.'

I was a bit irritated that he couldn't get my name right and said, 'No, it's Marco.'

Again he said, 'Hello, Darko.'

Again I said, 'No, it's Marco. It's Marco with an "M".'

'No,' he said, 'I'm Darko, Marco. I'm the host.' I felt a bit of an idiot (and after that I was very polite to Darko) but not half as stupid as I did the following day, when it was time to do the demo.

The plan was to cook three dishes in one hour, or rather rustle up three dishes that each took a mere twenty minutes to do. These dishes had to be quite effortless and ones that the ladies could easily cook at home, so this is what I decided to serve: grilled lobster with parsley and chervil and a béarnaise mousseline; turbot with citrus fruits, a little coriander and some fennel; then sea bass à la niçoise. It was while cooking the last one – the sea bass dish – that I came unstuck ... or rather stuck to a plate.

The sea bass à la niçoise is the most simple of dishes, in which the tomatoes are put under the grill so that the water content evaporates under the heat. You're getting rid of the acidity, basically, and bringing out the sweetness. Once grilled, the tomatoes are thrown into a pan that contains olive oil, lemon juice, coriander and basil. While the grilling process was going on, I somehow got dragged into a bit of chitchat with the ladies, which was disastrous because the distraction meant that I lost my timings. There I was, bantering, laughing and cracking jokes, when suddenly I remembered the plate of tomatoes under the grill. As I grabbed the plate I felt the most excruciating pain in my hand and realised that the searing heat of the dish had welded my thumb to the porcelain. My entire body must have flinched. Yet the gaggle of smiling ladies – my happy pupils – didn't seem to notice that their cookery teacher was being cooked.

I told myself I had two options: firstly, I can either be professional and pretend nothing is happening, even though I cannot remember the last time I had so much pain inflicted upon me; secondly, I can succumb to the agony, cave in, drop the plate and scream so loud and for so long that I shake the foundations of Rocco's château.

I went for the first option. In my head there was this mantra: take the pain, take the pain, just take the bleeding pain. I must tell you, that plate came out of the grill faster than any plate has ever come out of a grill. Normally, I would have got a spoon and scraped the tomatoes from the plate and into the pan, but because of the agony I was enduring there wasn't time for the spoon and I found myself tossing the sliced tomatoes from the hot plate into the air, and then it just so happened that they landed in the pan, neatly on top of the herbs and the olive oil and lemon juice. It looked like a circus trick and afterwards the kitchen chef came up to me and said, 'Wow, you are so quick.'

I should have said to him, 'It helps if you're handling a plate that feels like molten lava.' But I didn't.

———

Back in London, and while learning how to live with a grilled thumb, I got my second offer to return to the kitchen. It was a call from the *Hell's Kitchen* people, asking me if I'd like to do their show on ITV.

In these memoirs, you'll find me giving an opinion about chefs who would rather be in front of the camera than behind the stove. As far as I'm concerned, if someone is paying a huge amount of money to come to your restaurant and eat your food then you have a duty to be in the kitchen. When I was a lad working at Le Gavroche, if Albert wasn't there for the service, there was a difference. Maybe the food didn't come out quite as quickly, but things just strayed. The foot had been taken off the pedal. Is it hypocritical of me to do Hell's Kitchen? No, I don't think so, because I am not a chef. I do not claim to be in the kitchen. When punters come to my restaurants they do not expect me to be in the kitchen (and anyway, chances are they'll see me in the dining room, front of house).

Now, this wasn't the first time I'd been approached by Granada to do *Hell's Kitchen*. They asked me to do it a few years ago. I said no, and since then many TV production companies have come to see me, to talk through ideas for this and that, and invariably the projects haven't been right. This time round the Granada people said, 'Can we come for a cup of tea and talk about *Hell's Kitchen*?' We ended up having lunch, and then we met again and did another lunch, and I found myself sitting there thinking, I can work with these people.

In between the two lunches, I had started to consider the prospect of stepping back into the ring and the idea appealed to me. Sometimes in life we have something to prove to ourselves. I want to prove to myself that I'm not over the hill and that I still have a lot to give to my industry. So I accepted the deal: I'll do the show in September and every night for two weeks I'll be seen trying to show ten celebrities how to cook.

Maybe it's good for my kids to see me working in that environment – something to remember their dad by; an insight, in a crazy way, into my world – and it'll be wonderful to be reunited with some of the guys from the old days. In the kitchen I'll have Tim Payne, who started with me at Harveys, as well as Matt Brown, who worked with me at the Hyde Park, and Paul Buckey, who as a lad worked at the Canteen and is now pastry chef at the Yew Tree. Front of house, the maître d' will be Nicolas Munier.

You'll read about Nic in the pages of this book. He was my restaurant manager at the Hyde Park Hotel and at the Oak Room, and he's one of the best in the business. I may as well tell you the story about the time, back in the nineties, when Nic and I headed off for a spot of fishing with Eduardo, aka Eddie the barman. We were driving from London to the South Coast, with Nic at the wheel, when suddenly – bang – our car collided with a van.

The crash wasn't a nasty one and none of us was injured, and I clambered out of our car and ran to the van to see a woman in the driver's seat, and her dog sharing the passenger seat with a few bouquets of flowers. Wouldn't have taken Sherlock Holmes to deduce that she was a florist. 'Are you all right?' I asked the woman. She said she was fine, and she seemed okay, so I got back into the car and said to Nicolas, 'Let's go fishing.' Three miles down the road, there was a police road block. There were five police cars and loads of coppers looking for some guys who had left the scene of an accident: us.

The police were convinced, inexplicably, that I had been driving the car (which I had not) and they kept calling me 'Mop Head'. Then they got annoyed when they came to make a note of our names. They said, 'What's your name?'

'Marco Pierre White.'

'Can you spell it?'

Then they moved on to Nic. 'What's your name?'

'Nicolas Munier.'

'Can you spell it?'

They looked seriously fed up when another passenger emerged from the car and said he was called Eduardo.

Then something weird happened. As I was being questioned, I noticed that a man – absolutely stark naked – was standing in the window of a house, observing us with a pair of binoculars. I said to the copper in front of me, 'You're not going to believe this but behind you there's a naked man with a pair of binoculars.' The cop was gruff and grumpy and then he turned and we all stood there in silence and watched the window, and the nude who'd been watching us very slowly stepped backwards into the darkness of the room so that eventually he had vanished.

Cut it short, we went off fishing but a couple of months later Nic was in court and earned some points on his licence and a fine. Let's hope there'll be no such hurdles when we come to do *Hell's Kitchen*, but there are bound to be other surprises. My agent, Peter Burrell, represents the retired boxer Barry McGuigan, so I said to Peter, 'Why don't you see if Barry would like to do *Hell's Kitchen* as one of the contestants?' Peter phoned Barry and put the idea to him, but the response was, 'Don't get me on the show. I'll end up punching that guy.'

When Peter explained that the programme would be hosted by me, Barry said, 'Oh, I thought Gordon Ramsay was still doing it.'

It'll be interesting to get back into the kitchen. I know I am not going to be as quick as I was, but mentally I am stronger now than I ever was and most probably more in control than I've ever been. I will try to structure it in a way that's pleasurable for everybody. I am not going there to belittle people. I am not going there to shout at people. I am going there to cook. I am not stepping into the ring to become a star. In fact, the person who has more to lose than anyone is me, and do you know something … maybe it's that little bit of danger which turns me on. That risk. Let's just roll that dice once more …

It's only a TV programme but I have to treat it as a restaurant opening, and I hope to inspire rather than impress. I've only ever seen snippets of *Hell's Kitchen*, but from what I've heard about the previous shows, there has been a distinct lack of romance, love, and understanding of food. It's been all about belittling people. I'll go back into the kitchen of one of my restaurants for a week, just to get the timings and coordination right.

My only concern is my back, and whether it will be able to survive a return to the kitchen. Years of being in a kitchen, bent over a table, working, dressing plates, working on meat, working on fish, presentation on plates, bent over a stove, bending down to an oven … it does in your back. The pain, when it comes, is precisely where the apron string used to cut into my spine. I'll go to the osteopath but there's nothing I can really do about it.

I would never have agreed to *Hell's Kitchen* if it weren't for this book. In a strange sort of way I look at this book as a snake shedding its skin. I've left a big part of me behind, moved on, left my anchor. I've developed as a person.

And then there's been New York.

As this book was published in the States, I had to fly out to New York for a promotional tour and it meant that I was reunited with Mario Batali, the much-awarded chef with whom I worked at the Six Bells, in Chelsea, in the mid eighties. He last saw me when I was chucking a pan of hot risotto over him. Mario met me at the Mercer Hotel, where I was staying, we had a bear cuddle and then he said he'd take me on a quick sightseeing tour on the way to lunch at one of his restaurants. We stepped out of the hotel and he handed me a motorbike helmet – no visor, no strap – and said, 'Put that on, let's go.' He then pointed at a parked Lambretta and I said, 'Mario, it's great to see you after all these years, but there's no way the two of us are going to fit on that thing.' He's a big man, and I'm not small. He said, 'Marco, put the helmet on.'

Somehow we managed to squeeze onto the saddle, and then we zoomed off. We did a lunch of pig's trotters (in breadcrumbs and with anchovy and olives and chorizo oil) at his Spanish restaurant, Casa Mono, and then squeezed ourselves onto the scooter and went to his two star Michelin restaurant, Del Posto. That night we were in the Spotted Pig, another Michelin-starred joint in which Mario has a stake. The following morning, I didn't like the look of the Mercer breakfast – weird combinations – so I decided to go for a stroll, a smoke and grab something to eat in a diner. I didn't really understand the menu – more strange combinations – but the one I understood was scrambled eggs with chorizo.

When it arrived it had barbecue sauce on it, and Mexican beans and the portion was so big I couldn't even look at it, let alone eat it. They very kindly did not charge me for the food because they reckoned 'you obviously didn't like it'. The manager came up to me and said, 'Do I know you?' I told him, 'I don't suppose you do as it's my first time in New York.' Then when I was leaving, the manager said, 'Chef White, it was good having you in the house.'

I had ten hours sleep over a three day period and somewhere along the way I managed to meet Anthony Bourdain, chef and author of the bestselling *Kitchen Confidential*. I'd met Anthony years ago in London, but this time I could have a proper chat with him and I realised that he's a very funny man, who's sharp and intelligent. Above all, he smokes Marlboro Red so he's one of the good guys.

I was in the hotel room one night, when there was a knock on the door and a man saying, 'Room service.' I replied that I hadn't ordered any room service, but the man said, 'I have three hookers for you, sir.'

I said, 'Pardon?'

'I've got three hookers for you, sir.' For a moment I wondered whether Mario was sending me an unusual gift, but when I opened the door the waiter was standing there with a plate, upon which were three ... cookies – complimentary biscuits to have with a bedtime drink. I tell you, I've got to do something about my hearing.

ONE

Blue skies over Leeds

THERE'S a picture I look at every day.

For years I have been studying this picture, giving it the time you'd give a masterpiece. It's a truly mesmerising picture; vivid, haunting, packed with colour, detail and movement. There have been nights when it has kept me awake, weeping. However, there have been many days when it has lifted me, inspired me, driven me on ... pushed me forward. If this picture had a title it would be *Death ... and Life*. It has a power that can change a life.

Its value to me is immeasurable, though I didn't pay a penny for it and I can't imagine anyone else would want to own it. It is a picture that is on display but which has only ever had an audience of one. It is a picture in my mind: one single, soulful memory of that moment when I last saw my mother. A lingering memory which has been there with me, from kitchen to kitchen, from poverty to wealth, from obscurity to fame. It was a recurring image, flashing in and out of my head when I worked my way up the ladder, sweating and toiling for those Michelin stars. And it was an image that was invisible to the press and my critics when they analysed my character and concluded that I was an angry young man, the rock-star chef. This image, this expressive impression on my mind, has been with me through marriages and at the birth of my four children.

It feeds the child that is wounded within me. It is the foundation of the man I am today. It is a snapshot in my head, a snapshot which was taken on Saturday, 17 February 1968, only a few days before my mother's death, when I was just a lad aged six ...

My mother with me and Clive; Auntie Luciana,
Nonna and Auntie Paolo are behind us during
our holiday in Italy in 1964.

... I am standing at a window sill in our council home, a two-bed semi on the outskirts of Leeds. My brother Clive, six years my senior, is at my side and we are looking through the glass, down onto the pavement below.

The ambulance is parked. And there is my mother, a blanket is wrapped around her, sitting in a wheelchair. She is being put into the ambulance. An ambulance man turns to my father and says, 'Bring the baby.' A baby needs a mother.

My father is standing there, dressed smartly in a grey suit. He is holding Craig, the youngest of the family. Ten days old.

Crisp, blue sky. Bright sunshine.

'Bring the baby,' the ambulance man repeats. 'He'll need feeding.' My father climbs in with Craig, who looks very snug and warm, wrapped up in a cosy white blanket.

Bang! Doors close, engine starts. The exhaust pipe pukes a dark cloud. The ambulance drives away, up the hill, out of sight. Gone ...

That was the last time I saw her. It was nearly forty years ago but I remember it better than I remember yesterday.

I remember holidays with my mother in Genoa. That's where her side of the family lived – her father was a grain exporter – and where she had lived before taking a trip to England and then another to Leeds and then on to the Griffin Hotel and into its bar, where she was chatted up by a chef called Frank White. I have happy memories of those holidays, recollections of picking fruit from the trees, fishing in the streams, making early morning walks to collect goat's milk from a nearby farm. And I remember sitting in the kitchen at home, watching her cook simple but delicious pasta dishes: throwing in the olive oil, sweating onions, adding tomato purée and creating the comforting scent of those combinations.

It is odd that my last memories of my mother coincide with my first recollections of my father. Though that is not to say that up until that February day my father had not always been there – he was not an absent dad or anything like that. It is just that my memory bank has done something weird so that it seems that on that February day Dad came into my life as my mother was leaving it. Hours before my mother's collapse he had taken me to have stitches removed (I had cut myself by my eye after running into the door handle at the newsagent's just down the road).

Dad and I had spent that morning in St James's Hospital, the place where my mother would find herself in the afternoon. I had been with Dad in the front room earlier on when Mum came in, complaining that she felt unwell.

Of course, she didn't know it at the time but she was suffering a brain haemorrhage – what would turn out to be the fatal after-effects of recently giving birth to her fourth son, baby Craig. She left in the ambulance and our neighbours looked after us for the rest of that day.

———

Every night for the next few nights Dad would give us our dinner before heading off to the hospital to see Mum. After the visit he'd return quite late, bringing bags of sweets for his boys and telling us, 'These are from Mum.' If he knew then she was going to die he never let on.

On 20 February, the Tuesday after she had been taken to the hospital, the doctors turned off the life support machine. That night Dad came home, woke us all up and told us to climb out of bed and go downstairs. He could not wait until the morning to break the terrible news. He had to deal with it straightaway, which I think was the right thing to do. He probably wanted company as well because he was obviously in pieces. His boys were his only reassurance in this dreadful episode of his life.

We gathered in the front room, where a few days earlier Mum had said she hadn't felt right, and Dad sat in his chair. I stared at his face and the tears on his cheeks. Then he told us, 'Your mother died tonight.' His words come thundering back to me, an unwelcome echo. Our mother had gone. Maria Rosa White – my father called her Maro – the woman who gave me so much more than my Italian name, was only thirty-eight years old.

The car that took us to the funeral at Lawnswood Crematorium was massive and luxurious. It wasn't a Rolls Royce, it couldn't have been because we couldn't have afforded it, but to me it seemed just as grand. On the two rows of seats in the back sat Dad, Graham, Clive and me. I must have thought I was going to the fair, or something equally exciting and adventurous, because I wasn't showing the usual signs of heartbreak. Clive snapped at me because I wasn't crying. Dad said, 'Leave him alone, Clive. He doesn't understand.'

He was right. I couldn't accept that I was not going to see my mother again. I was only six. Graham was thirteen years old and Clive was a year younger than him. They were both considerably older than me, old enough to know exactly what was happening. They would find their own ways of dealing with it but, in truth, we were all badly scarred, as you would expect. You never get over it but you find ways to accept it.

After the funeral I don't think I went home to play or be with my family. Instead I was dropped off at school and stayed in the playground with my friends. I had a toy car, a gift from someone or other, and my classmates were enthralled by it. It wasn't a Matchbox car but something quite substantial and to me it was like a trophy. I think I was in the playground for about ten minutes before being collected by I don't-know-who and taken to a strange house where I stayed for two, maybe three days. I still don't know where I went. It was a strange house with strange people who were obviously helping out Dad and who had kids the same age as me. It was as if I had been taken from my world into another.

I retreated into myself where I could be with my best friends, my thoughts, and that is where I stayed, pretty much, for the next ten years of my life, until I became a kitchen apprentice. The emotional part of my mind closed down, emotion was snatched from me. In a situation like that your instinct to survive takes over, that's the way I see it. Pain had penetrated my heart and frozen my emotions.

One day I'd felt secure, the security I'd experienced since 11 December 1961, when my mother gave birth to me at St James's Hospital in Leeds. One day I'd had that security, that contentment and sense of well-being, and the next day it was gone.

———

Her death removed the female influence that could have helped shape me. How different would my life have been had she lived? I would have to wait until I was thirty-one years old, around about the time that I met Mati, the woman who would become my third wife, before I could start to analyse the tremendous impact of my mother's life, and death, upon mine.

That snapshot in my mind takes me back to a time when softness was stripped from my life. I would take up a career in which I would be bullied, knocked, pushed and worked, worked, worked. And when things got too hard I would say to myself, 'I saw my mother taken away when I was six years old and she never came back. What could be worse?' Nothing.

I was the second youngest son in a tough, male-dominated household. Soon, however, I would become the youngest, because Fate, you see, had not yet finished messing with Craig's young life.

My mother enjoying life in Bardolino on Lake Garda in 1952, before packing her bags for a life in Leeds.

⌈ TWO ⌉

The champion bedwetter

DAD WAS a chef and the son of a chef. Dad was a gambler, too. He did the dogs, the horses and the pools. Clearly, he never won a fortune but that didn't stop him bringing out the bottle of Scotch and the Shirley Bassey albums at night time and sipping along to 'Hey Big Spender'.

The gambling, as well as a pint or two, provided escapism for Dad and he had a good deal from which to escape. The bitterness of my mother's death remained with him but it was by no means his first encounter with hardship. When he was a kid his parents had separated and divided up their four children. This meant that Dad was raised by his father, so like me he'd missed out on female influence in his life. He rarely spoke of my mother's death, he just got on with things, trying to cope with his damaged brood and apparently ignoring his own pain. Somewhere along the way I learned that he had made a promise to my mother to raise her sons, rather than putting us in a children's home. If he had put us in a home it would have been acceptable, even expected, in the late sixties. For Dad it was totally unacceptable. He'd have hated finger-pointing people saying, 'Poor Mr White, lost his wife and had to give away his children.'

He was a disciplinarian, born in the twentieth century but raised with Victorian principles and values. He was a stickler for standards, but while we were Catholics I think Dad had lost his faith in God and outings to Church didn't feature on Sundays. He may not have been a religious man but he programmed me and my two brothers religiously. Off he'd go to work, wearing a smart suit, a trilby, shoes that were polished with military precision and, if he was feeling unwell, he would still head off for the bus stop saying, 'Never call in sick.'

He was punctual as hell. Each morning he would wake the family at 6.45 and we would get up, dress and have breakfast in time for his departure bang on 7.30 to catch the 7.40 bus that took him into Leeds city centre. Sunday lunch was always a roast and was on the table at 2 p.m. On weekday evenings we had dinner at five sharp, and had to make sure our knees, hands and faces were washed before sitting down at the table. I have a vivid memory of running home one evening, petrified because it was 4.40 and I knew I was in for a beating if I was late for the meal. On Fridays Dad had a steak while Clive, Graham and I were given pork chops. We were not allowed to leave the table until we had finished every morsel of food on the plate – and Dad served massive portions. Perhaps there was something about his life of routine that I didn't approve of because, by comparison, I grew up to be spontaneous and cavalier.

Essentially, Dad believed he was destined never to achieve his dreams, whatever they may have been. My mother's death had reinforced his opinion of himself: that he was an extremely unlucky man. That's what he thought deep down. But if you met him you got a working-class Northerner with a dry wit who talked of betting non-stop. He was hooked on the adrenaline that comes with gambling.

Inevitably, his love of the horses and the dogs also became a major part of my life. On one occasion Dad had some leave planned and he sent me off to school with a letter for my teacher. He had written something like, 'My annual holiday is coming up and I would very much like to take Marco away for a week.' I was excused from Fir Tree Primary and when I returned after the break my teacher asked if I'd had a nice holiday.

I said, 'Very nice, thank you very much, Miss.'

'Where did you go, Marco?'

'York Races for a week, Miss.'

When he couldn't get his fix from a place in the grandstand he would resort to the telly in the front room at 22 Lingfield Mount. His favourite programme was *The ITV Seven*, which, on Saturday afternoons, broadcast seven horse races from around Britain. If you were a betting man in the seventies then you had to watch it. Dad performed a ritual as he watched. At the beginning of each race he would sit in his armchair but as the horses reached the halfway point he would quickly roll up his copy of *Sporting Life*, transforming the paper into a riding crop, and then, as the beasts galloped towards the finishing post, he would launch himself from his chair onto the floor, ending up in a crouching position inches away from the screen. He had become the mounted jockey, flicking his arse with the rolled-up paper as if he was administering a crack of the whip on an invisible horse. 'Go on m' son,' he would shout at the box and the little jockey within it, 'Go on m' son.' On Saturday evenings I would sometimes hear him on the phone, telling a mate that he couldn't meet up. 'Done m' bollocks,' he would say to the caller. 'I've really done m' bollocks.'

Like many gamblers, superstition played a major role in his life. One Saturday at *ITV Seven* time, I wandered into the front room just as the horses were racing for the finish. Dad was there, crouched and whipping himself with *Sporting Life*. His horse was in third place and looked sure to lose, but as I stepped into the room the horses that were in first and second suddenly fell at the final fence, enabling Dad's nag to plod past the finishing line and win the race.

In his mind there was no question that this stroke of good fortune was entirely due to me walking into the room. So for the next three Saturdays I became his lucky mascot and had to sit in the front room when *The ITV Seven* was on. Dad was satisfied that my presence alone would ensure he won his bets. My powers were limited, though, and by the fourth Saturday he was still not a millionaire and I wasn't asked to join him again.

An early morning sighting of a robin redbreast would, he was convinced, bring him good luck for the rest of the day. On Saturday mornings our semi was filled with the wonderful smell of sizzling bacon. Dad wasn't doing a fry-up for his sons, though; he cooked the meat to entice the robins. The fried bacon went onto a plate and into the back garden, then Dad would gaze out of the window, hoping for a hungry robin to fly by 22 Lingfield Mount and swoop down for the meat. The size of his bets depended on a sighting.

Our back garden was not only a canteen for robins but also a home to Dad's cherished trio of greyhounds which he raced on nearby tracks. Greyhounds were his true passion and each of the three dogs had a kennel in the garden. Two nights a week Dad's mate Stan Roberts would pull up in his Morris Minor (Dad didn't drive) and we'd head off to the racetrack. There'd be four of us in the car: Dad and Stan sat in the front while I'd share the back seat with a greyhound.

At the track I would hover outside the bar while Dad enjoyed a drink inside with his friends. The door would open and a bottle of pop and packet of crisps would be passed out to me. I'd sneak a glance into the brightly lit room (dimmer switches had yet to come along), a haze of smoke lingering like a white cloud above the gamblers' heads. Coming home at 11 p.m. I'd fall asleep on the back seat, a greyhound as my pillow.

Dad was out one day when there was a knock on the door. A bloke was standing there and he asked me, 'Do you sell greyhounds?'

We didn't but I told him, 'Yes.' I took him through the house and into the back garden to inspect the dogs.

'How much is that one?' he said, pointing at one of the animals.

'Fifty pence.' It was my first business deal – I've done better ones since then, I hasten to add.

The bloke handed over the money and left with the dog. I treated a mate, David Johnson, to goodies from the sweetshop and we headed off to play in the woods. My brother Clive, who must have been in the house and overheard the dog deal, came looking for me. 'Dad's gonna kill ya when he finds out you've sold one of his greyhounds,' said Clive. I was saved a slaughtering and was sent off to bed instead.

For Dad, greyhound racing was all about rigging the price and there were various tricks that he used. From time to time I assisted in this dastardly business. If you've got a dog that has won a couple of races in a row then the odds of it winning again are going to be short. So with a dog that was, let's say, black with a white patch on its paw, Dad would paint out the mark and enter it in the race as a new dog, thereby achieving a good price at the bookies.

Another devious trick went like this: the day before the greyhound was due to race it wasn't fed, but then last thing at night it was given a bone to chew on to keep it awake. The next morning I would take the dog for a brisk four-mile walk and later on, when it came to race, it would look pristine and might be a favourite but would be too knackered to win. The next time it raced it would get long odds because of previous form, but this time it would be in tip-top shape. I think I'm right in saying that one of Dad's dogs, The Governor, set track records at Halifax, Keighley and Doncaster.

I can't tell you much about the old man's abilities as a chef because I never saw him cook in a professional kitchen. He would have had a good apprenticeship at the Griffin Hotel in Leeds, where he met my mother in the fifties. He had also worked at The Queen's Hotel, the four-star landmark beside Leeds railway station. He would tell me stories of a brilliant French chef, Paul La Barbe, who worked in that kitchen but had trained in the grand restaurants of Paris. According to my father, Paul was a gifted chef who worked with great speed and an incredible lightness of touch. I don't remember specific tales of Paul's abilities, but I was left with the feeling that cooking could produce passion. Other fathers might have told their kids impressive stories about American superheroes, but I learned about a French supercook, and I didn't care one bit.

As far as I am concerned, cooking is an extension of the person. The old man was organised and keen on routine, so on that basis I'd say that in his day he was probably a highly competent, disciplined cook. He would not have been creative because creativity wasn't a requirement in those days. Chefs rarely moved away from buffet work.

In every professional kitchen there was a small book – *Le Répertoire de La Cuisine* – which was tiny but contained 6,000 brief, concisely written recipes from hors d'oeuvres to pastries. There are no pictures in *Le Répertoire* to help the cook know how to serve a dish, but it was still invaluable. Inspired by the great French chef, Auguste Escoffier, *Le Répertoire* told you, for instance, dozens of ways to serve potatoes, from à l'Algérienne (sweet potato croquettes, usually accompanied by small tomatoes braised in oil) right through to Pommes de Terre Voisin (baked layers of sliced potato, clarified butter and grated cheese). Chefs did not stray from the recipes and were rarely adventurous. In Dad's time most restaurants served the same food, *Répertoire*-type dishes such as lamb cutlets and kidneys with mustard.

After The Queen's he'd become the canteen manager at Jonas Woodheads in Leeds, and sometimes I would go to meet him there with my brother Clive. Dad's staff were quiet and worked away to feed hundreds of people every day. The dining room was always spotless and clean, the tables lined up beautifully and not a single chair out of place. It was regimented and perhaps, in this respect, he was a perfectionist. Maybe his way of taking his mind off the past was to focus on the minute details of day-to-day life.

I'd say I was a bit of a loner. I would play by myself in the woods or down by the river, rediscovering the side of nature I had been introduced to during those holidays with my mother in Italy. Academically, I was doomed. I was not only damaged by the death of my mother but also suffered from dyslexia. In those days word blindness was considered a sign of stupidity rather than a condition requiring a special needs teacher. One or two teachers were sympathetic but others humiliated me.

A few years back my friend Andrew Regan, the entrepreneur and businessman, and I took our kids off for a day at the seaside in Llanelli. Andrew is also dyslexic and we were all walking past the boats when I saw a sign that read: 'Mackerel Fishing, £7, No Nemesis.' I stopped and stared at the sign and said to Andrew, 'What does that mean? No Nemesis.' Andrew studied the sign and read the words aloud: 'Mackerel Fishing, £7, No Nemesis.' Andrew is a very clever individual but he agreed that he did not have a clue what 'no nemesis' meant. We were both absolutely baffled until one of the kids announced, 'It says, "On Nemesis". Nemesis is the name of the boat.'

I can laugh about dyslexia now but at school I assumed I was an idiot. What's more, I felt like a freak. Every pupil except me had a mother, and every other pupil, except me and a lad called Quentin whose parents had divorced, was the product of an apparently happy home environment.

To cap it all I had this strange name, Marco (my middle name, Pierre, remained a well-kept secret until I was in my twenties). I could only dream of what life might have been like had I been a John, Peter, Paul or Timothy. I just wanted to be like everyone else.

The housing estate where I lived in Moor Allerton – about five miles outside Leeds – was predominately Jewish and working class. It had a warm community spirit, one of those places where the women would stand outside the shops chatting about the latest developments in *Coronation Street*. Hundreds of small houses lined the roads that were mostly named Lingfield something or other. Years later, when I met Jamie (the Marquess of) Blandford he told me about his childhood, growing up on the Blenheim estate. 'When you think about it, Jamie,' I said, 'We both grew up on estates. It's just that yours had fewer houses on it.'

If I came out of my house and turned left it took me across Moor Allerton golf course and into the woods of the Harewood estate. If I came out of my home, turned right and strolled down the hill to the bottom of the road there was the parade of shops on Lingfield Drive. There was the newsagent's which was run by two women who had lost their husbands in the War. There was the Jewish baker's and Tom Atkins, the veg man. There was the fish man and the butcher, whose afternoon custom was to sweep up the sawdust, wash the floor and then, and only then, give his dog a bone to chew on the pavement outside. The off-licence was run by Harry Baker, and like other kids on the estate, I would sneak to the back of his shop, pinch the empties from their crates and then go in through the front door to reclaim the deposit. The parade is shabby today, but then it was the hub of our community.

———

There was little affection at home. At bedtime I would kiss my father goodnight and say, 'God bless.' But I would climb under the sheets numbed by the loss of my mother and fearful that I would awake the next morning to discover I had wet the bed. Urinating on the sheets would mean a slap from Dad. Getting a smack didn't really frighten me. What bothered me, what I found very hard to deal with, was a feeling that I had let my father down. Wetting the bed and thereby disappointing Dad, I concluded, was a failing within me as a human being. It must have been the trauma of my mother's death that turned me into an habitual bedwetter, but there weren't too many child psychologists around to explain that to my father.

Craig, the baby of the family, presented Dad with a more serious problem than sodden sheets, however. Craig was just thirteen days old when our mother died, and for Dad the prospect of leaving work to look after the family must have seemed an impossible one. Perhaps he was advised by friends; maybe he made the decision while sitting alone searching for inspiration from Shirley Bassey's lyrics. Whatever the case, he concluded within weeks of my mother's death that he could not bring up Craig as well as Graham, Clive and me.

It took a couple of months for Craig's adoption papers to be arranged and during that time he lived with temporary foster parents in York Road, not far from us.

I remember him coming home to 22 Lingfield Mount for a short spell. Then for the second time in three months, another member of my family was taken away, only this time round I can't remember the departure.

Craig did not disappear for ever, though. He was not going to become one of those poor souls who spends a decade of his adult life trying to trace his birth parents. Craig was adopted by my mother's

My parents on their wedding day in 1954.

brother, my Uncle Gianfranco and his wife Paola. Aunt Paola had previously been told that she would never conceive, so my mother's death provided the couple with a child. It was like a blessing from God. My father's loss was their gain. Craig was collected by Uncle Gianfranco and off he went to live with the couple in Genoa.

He underwent two name changes: White had to go, understandably, to make way for Gallina; and his first name was too much of a mouthful for his new countrymen. His middle name was Simon and so Craig became Simon, as in *See*mon. My Dad had handed him over and I don't think he ever saw him again.

There was little contact with the Italian in-laws. They would send us Christmas presents and then Graham, Clive and I would be instructed by Dad to sit at the dining-room table and write thank-you letters. My father did not have many kind words to say about that side of the family and I think they were equally unimpressed by him. He did not poison our minds by saying nasty things about them but I don't think he felt comfortable with the idea of Craig White becoming Simon Gallina. In later life, Dad told me that not one of my mother's Italian relatives had attended her funeral, which had obviously upset him.

When I was ten years old I visited my uncle and aunt for the last time. I flew from Manchester to Milan and there I was, for a couple of weeks or so, enjoying the Italian countryside to which my mother had introduced me. Simon, now four years old, didn't understand a word I was saying and I could not understand him.

There we were, two brothers living under the same roof but divided, quite bizarrely, by a language barrier. He did not know that I was his brother, and his adoptive parents did not tell him about his English roots and his mother's death until a few years later.

It is not my baby brother who initially springs to mind when I think back to that holiday. Instead, I immediately remember my bedwetting and the awful fear it instilled in me. I arrived in Italy weighed down by both my rucksack and the dread that I would soak the sheets in my uncle and aunt's house. News of my habit had obviously reached them and, on the first night at their house, as I climbed into the bed I could feel the unmistakable, uncomfortable hardness of a plastic sheet beneath the cotton one. As it turned out, I did not wet the bed, probably because I was at long last away from home and the memories that haunted it. Meanwhile my Italian relatives found me too difficult, partly because I didn't speak the language and partly because I didn't eat their food – their healthy fish seemed repulsive compared with the battered cod I was used to at home. A few days before my fortnight-long holiday was due to end, my bags were packed and I was driven to the airport and put on a plane home. My uncle and aunt had had enough of me.

The next time I saw Simon it was around about 1990, when I had Harveys, my restaurant by Wandsworth Common. During a phone conversation with Uncle Gianfranco, he mentioned that Simon – by now a man in his early twenties – was in a rut. 'Send him over here,' I told my uncle. 'He can come and work for me.' I went to Gatwick Airport and waited at the barrier to greet the brother I had not seen for almost two decades. It was a Sunday afternoon and very quiet in Arrivals. The first person to come through was a giant, a monster of a man, and I just thought, Christ, he's a big bloke. He was followed by the other passengers on the flight and when the place emptied the giant was still standing there. He must have been six foot eight, some five inches taller than me. He had to have been the tallest man in Italy.

We were brothers but hadn't recognised each other. We shook hands – perhaps we hugged each other, I can't recall – but apart from that we couldn't really communicate. I didn't speak Italian and his English wasn't fantastic. After he'd said hello he looked down at me and asked, 'Do you know a shop called High and Mighty?' Nearly twenty years and that was it: take me to High and Mighty. We swaggered out of the airport like a walking freak show: Italy's tallest man accompanied by his lanky, gaunt, hollow-cheeked older brother. At Harveys I put him to work on the pastry section, but it didn't work out and after a week or so he returned home. Just like my earlier visit to Italy, his trip to Britain was cut short. At the time Simon aspired to be not a cook but a policeman and that's what he went on to become. He told one of my Italian-speaking chefs that once he had got into the force he would return to Harveys and arrest me for the way I treated my staff.

Of my two older brothers, Graham and Clive, my recollections are minimal. I had more of a bond with Graham, who was often fishing, shooting pigeons, hunting rabbits and ferreting. In fact, on the day of my mother's death, his love of fishing had spared him the sight of her being taken away in the ambulance because he had been sitting on the banks of Adel Beck.

Clive, on the other hand, preferred motorbikes. For a while I shared a bedroom with my brothers, but they most likely didn't want to spend too much time with a little nipper like me and I never felt a great sense of camaraderie. When Graham was fifteen years old, and I was seven or eight, he left school and home, and went to work in the kitchens of the Griffin Hotel, where my Dad had started out. A couple of years later, Clive followed a similar path. He finished school and became a chef at the Metropole Hotel.

Both brothers were still living at home one Sunday when I returned from playing in the fields caked in mud. Dad went ballistic when he saw the state of me. He stripped me down to my underpants, swooped me up and carried me into the kitchen. He plonked me in the sink and called out for Graham and Clive to come and watch him dish out the punishment. As my brothers looked on, Dad channelled his aggression through a scrubbing brush, scratching the dirt from my skinny body. It hurt. He was a harsh teacher at times but I learned the lesson and never again returned home caked in mud.

The thing about Dad is that he was a one-dimensional man and, like most one-dimensional men, he believed in correctness. On those occasions when I could neither conform nor live up to his high standards, he could not contain his impatience and was overtaken by frustration, anger and abusive tendencies. His bitterness and resentment did not have time to subside. I would live in fear of the moments when his anger surfaced.

'Put on these clothes,' I remember him saying once as I looked at a pile of garments that were my Sunday best. I changed into them, then he packed me a suitcase, took me to the front room, pointed at the sofa and said, 'Sit there and wait.'

I asked, 'Why, Dad?'

'The taxi is coming to take you to the children's home,' he replied.

Terrified, I sat waiting and thinking, am I going to be the next one to be taken away? But there was no taxi. It was simply Dad's method of punishment. I must have done something naughty, though I can't remember what. The old man's failings were outweighed by his inherent goodness and decency, but it would take me a long time to realise that.

If he was looking for confirmation that he was the world's unluckiest man it came in 1972. 'Your father is going to be late home from work tonight,' my teacher told me. 'You are to wait in the playground for him to collect you.' I sat in the playground, a ten-year-old loner, waiting for Dad to arrive, and eventually he pulled up outside. He was with a work colleague, David Hince, in Mr Hince's Hillman. We drove the half mile back to the house and once inside Dad sat in his armchair. He had some dreadful news.

'I've been to see the doctor today,' he said. His delivery was emotionless and to the point. 'The doctor told me that I have lung cancer.' For a second or two I tried to absorb the statement. What did this mean? What would this mean? And then the sledgehammer statement, 'He has given me five months. The doctor says I've got five months to live.'

I already had a fear of wetting the bed and now I had an even more potent, crushing fear that preoccupied me at night as I lay in bed. It was a fear that come morning I would wake up and discover my father had died. I didn't sleep well. Once insomnia had got me I couldn't shake it off. From then on I had to learn to live on little sleep.

Weeks after Dad had broken the terrible news I saw him in the bathroom one morning, coughing up blood into the sink. The doctor was right, I reckoned. Dad was definitely on his way out.

THREE

Off my trolley

THE CHEESE trolley was just on its way out when I spotted it. We're in the mid-nineties now, and one evening shortly before service I was standing at the passe – the counter where the plates are collected by the waiters – in my kitchen at The Restaurant at the Hyde Park Hotel in London. The trolley was on its way out to the restaurant and six or eight cheeses were on it. There was nothing wrong with any of them – they were all beautifully ripe, plump and oozing – but I had a rule in the kitchen and as the trolley was being wheeled past me I noticed the rule had been broken.

The rule was simple: the cheese had to be the right size. In the afternoon, after lunch service, we would take a look at the cheese on the trolley and a decision was taken as to whether it needed replacing. If a particular cheese was substantial, the size of a dinner plate perhaps, and half of it had gone during lunch then the remaining half would still be large enough to merit staying on the trolley, and before opening for dinner it would be trimmed up, ready for serving.

However, if a cheese was small to begin with, the size of a saucer, say, and half of it had been eaten at lunch, then the rule dictated that it would be taken off the trolley. So we would always have back-up cheese which we would take out of the fridge to ripen up between lunch and dinner. As cheese is traditionally the responsibility of front of house, it was the maître d'hotel's task to replace the ones that had been hit hard over lunch.

The point was that I wanted to present a generous cheese trolley. If the presentation is not correct then it looks mean and should not go out into the restaurant. It must be grand and generous rather than a mess of lots of little cheeses.

But on this particular night when I was at the passe I saw the trolley going out carrying a cheese that was too small. My easy-to-obey rule had been broken by the maître d' Nicolas Munier. There was a cheese on that trolley that was two thirds eaten. That is when I flipped. What followed remains a subject of gossip in the restaurant industry, told as a story to illustrate my lunacy, but it's worth looking at the bigger picture.

I stopped Nicolas in his tracks and pointed at the trolley. 'Where are you going with that?' I asked.

He knew something nasty was coming. I could see it in his eyes. 'I'm taking it through, Marco.'

'No, Nicolas. No, no, no, no, no, no. Fuck, no.'

'Sorry, Marco.'

'Not right, Nicolas. Not correct, not right. The fucking cheese is not fucking right.'

'Sorry, Marco.'

I picked up the first cheese. 'Not right!' With all my might I threw it against the wall. It stuck to the tiles. I picked up the second cheese. 'Not right!' I chucked it at the wall. Like the first, it was so wonderfully ripe that it splattered onto the tiles and remained glued to them. Then I hurled the remaining cheeses, one after another at that wall. Splat after splat after splat; six or maybe eight times. The trolley was now empty, except for a cheese knife.

Most of the chefs looked down, carrying on with their work as if nothing had happened. Nicolas and a couple of cooks raced over to the wall, ready to prise off the cheeses and clear up the smelly mess. I shouted, 'Leave them there. Leave them there. Leave them fucking there all night. No one is allowed to touch them.' The cheeses had to stay on that wall all night so that whenever Nicolas came into the kitchen he would see them glued there. And he would never, ever make the mistake again.

It was extreme behaviour, I accept that, but I was driving home a point, and if it's OK with you I would like to put the incident into context. My restaurant at the Hyde Park Hotel was probably the most expensive restaurant in Britain. If you had the *foie gras surprise* followed by the *lobster aux truffes* and then a pudding, you were looking at £85 for a three-course dinner. If you wanted the *sea bass caviar* you would have to pay a £50 supplement. How serious is that? That was back in the nineties and I still can't think of a restaurant that charges prices like that today.

I had spent twenty years of my life building my reputation and people – the customers, in other words – were paying for my knowledge. By then I had won three Michelin stars, and was the only British chef to have them, and my great belief was consistency. When you are a three-star restaurant you have to get things right otherwise there's no point in doing them at all. How often have you been for dinner and had a great starter, a great pudding but a weak main course?

I could not allow you to endure any weakness at the Hyde Park Hotel. Whatever it was, from the bread to the amuse-gueules, the starters to the fish course, the main course to the puddings, the coffee to the petits fours, the chocolates to the cheese, it all had to be of a consistently three-star standard.

Everything's got to be right. If you're not consistent you'll never go from one to two stars or two to three. You've got more chance of losing a star. Even down to checking the taste and temperature of the soup, it had to be correct. It had to be hot, which might sound like an obvious point, but how many of us have ordered a soup that comes out tepid? I'm not happy with that and I don't think you would be. I could not allow that to happen at the Hyde Park Hotel.

To achieve and retain three stars is extreme, and that is why I was extreme. I could not say, 'Come on boys, let's try to get it right.' That just wouldn't have worked.

The cheese on the wall sent out a message to everyone working that night, from the youngest boy in the kitchen carrying food and serving bread to the maître d' bringing in an order. Every single member of the kitchen staff had to look at it because when they came to the passe the cheese was there, glued to the wall by its ripeness. An 18-year-old commis walks into the kitchen to collect a tray, he walks past it, he sees it and it's imprinted in his memory for ever. You have to deliver the message that they must never take a short cut. And if you are not extreme then people will take short cuts because they don't fear you.

Though he was a chef, my father did not inspire my passion for food. I did however pick up other crucial things from him that I would need in later life if I wanted to get to the top. He instilled discipline in me, and an ability to work long and hard on little sleep.

That extremeness stemmed from my childhood, as well. I never really felt I was acknowledged and those feelings transformed themselves into a chronic fear of failure and a fear that I was always under-achieving. I had something to prove to myself. As a child I felt I didn't achieve what I was capable of, and if you don't deliver what you are capable of then you are letting yourself down. We all know we can do better.

Could do better was how I saw myself, as a child and as a three-star chef.

And that was how I saw that cheese trolley – could do better. Nicolas, incidentally, did not quit. He was still working for me years later and is one of the best maître d's in the business.

FOUR

I delivered (the milk)

THERE'S SOMETHING to be said for requesting a second opinion. Dad's doctor may have been right to diagnose lung cancer, but he was way out when he predicted my father, then aged forty-five, would be dead in five months. Five months later the old man was still there. Five *years* later he was still there. He would live through his fifties, into his sixties and wouldn't reach the finishing post until he was in his seventies. He'd be around to see his children grow up and his grandchildren be born. Having survived so long without an operation my dad deserves a place in *The Guinness Book of Records*.

But he lived in fear that death was just around the corner and he set about programming me to work hard and bring in some cash. 'I might not always be there to protect you,' he'd say. They were frightening words but he wanted me to be able to cope in the big wide world. I wasn't sent off to work at the age of ten, though, I'd have to wait a couple of years first.

Meanwhile, family life continued in the belief that he would soon be dead. There was no point at which we said, 'Hang on a moment, what about the original diagnosis?' Dad jacked in his job on the grounds that he was terminally ill and we discovered quickly that his greyhounds could not be expected to bring in an income. He dabbled in 'antique dealing', and though we had never been wealthy we now plummeted into poverty, which brought new fears that my existence was simply an extra cost for my father. I prayed that Dad wouldn't notice my shoes had holes in the soles because I reckoned he couldn't afford to buy me a new pair.

He lost weight quickly, dropping from fifteen stones to about eight. On doctor's orders he stopped smoking and kicked the bottle, then he re-evaluated the situation with his gambler's mind and concluded that, as he was at death's door, he had absolutely nothing to lose by returning to the fags and booze, so that's what he did. He went on a health kick, of sorts, growing tomatoes and mushrooms in the garden, but we had always eaten well, and even before his illness Dad would never have tinned food in the house. We continued to have a weekly roast lunch and there was often a good steak and kidney pie or a hearty shepherd's pie.

Sure enough, he regained the weight he had previously shed, but he would never be 100 per cent and just climbing the stairs left him breathless.

Although he was apparently at death's door it did little to mellow his mood. One day I was four doors down at my friend Barry Wells's house, play-wrestling in his garden. It got out of hand when Barry hit me and I hit him back. Barry's hefty father must have spotted the scrap from the house and suddenly came bounding into the garden, picked me up by the ears and started swinging me around in the air. I felt like I was preparing for take-off.

'I'll tell me Dad,' I screamed, my ears burning with pain.

'Tell 'im,' shouted Mr Wells. 'And tell 'im if he wants some to come round here and I'll chin 'im.'

I scampered home, in through the door and into the front room where my Dad was sitting. 'Dad,' I screamed, 'Barry Wells's dad just hit me and he said he's gonna chin you as well.' I'd hardly finished the sentence when Dad leapt from his chair and set off, sprinting down the road faster than one of his treasured greyhounds. When he returned a few minutes later he looked victorious. 'We won't hear any more from him,' said Dad, and we didn't.

The old man must have reached a stage where he acknowledged the cancer was dormant but still he worried how I would fend for myself if he died. So when I was about twelve or thirteen years old I took on a few jobs. In fact, I became obsessed with work and did quite nicely out of it too. In the mornings before school I had a milk round, delivering the pints with a milkman called Stephen Sharpe, who was also kind enough to take me rabbiting. I loved doing the round, even though in the winter months my fingers would freeze and stick to the bottles as I picked them up. Stephen would stop the float and then we would race against each other to see who would be the first to pick up the empties and get them back to the float. It made me terribly competitive. Sometimes Stephen would take me to school in time for my first class. You've heard of rich kids being dropped off by the chauffeur in a Rolls: I was delivered by Stephen on a milk float.

After school I did a newspaper round which brought in thirty bob a week. On Saturdays I was a caddy at Moor Allerton golf course or at Alwoodley, charging golfers £1.50 a round. My skill at finding golf balls which had been lost on the course earned me a tenner per hundred as well as the nickname Hawk Eye. The great Leeds United FC manager, Don Revie, was one of my 'clients'. When I first caddied for him he hit a ball which disappeared into the trees. 'Don't worry, Mr Revie, I'll find it,' I said and went scurrying off to retrieve the ball. I did indeed find it, but when I picked it up I noticed it had the words 'Don Revie' imprinted on its dimples. Class act that he was, Don had personalised golf balls. I put the ball into my pocket and ran back to tell him it was lost, then I sold the ball for a pound at school, a marked improvement on the fifty pence I'd charged for Dad's greyhound. I handed most of my income to my father, supposedly for safe-keeping. 'I'll give it back to you, Marco, when we go on holiday,' he'd say, though when we trundled off to Bridlington I don't recall receiving the cash in its entirety.

When I wasn't working, I used my spare time to enjoy the countryside. I was happiest when I was outdoors with my whippet, Pip. I fell in love with fishing, hunting, shooting and poaching. When there was a teachers' strike in the seventies, we finished school at midday and my brother Graham took me fishing for the first time. He sat me down by the side of a bridge and cast for me while he and his

My fishing skills are recognised in 1977.

mates went and fished the best spots. I caught a trout of about a pound – the first fish I ever caught – and from that day on I was hooked, so to speak.

Graham also introduced me to poaching. My early poaching days involved chucking logs at the pheasants when they were roosting. The birds would fly down from the trees, land on the ground, and then I'd have to run after them and catch them by hand. I remember Graham taking me to Eccup, part of the Harewood Estate, to shoot for the first time, but he was mean about sharing the air rifle. Graham shot four heavy hares and made me carry them across the ploughed fields, rain pouring down on us. I was his chief gofer.

I have a vivid memory of sneaking into Graham's room when he wasn't around and rummaging around for two-two pellets. Suddenly I heard his footsteps and quickly dived under his bed to hide. Graham came into the room, undid his belt, dropped his trousers and then lay on the mattress, while I waited underneath quietly. His masturbation was interrupted by the sound of my dad coming up the stairs shouting for me. As Graham struggled to pull up his trousers my dad came into the room. 'Have you seen Marco?' he asked.

Graham, flustered, replied, 'No, Dad, I've not.'

If I could find the time, my mate Briggsy and I would take the bus to Otley to fish a trout stretch. We would roll up our trousers and walk into the river with a maggot bag containing a loaf of bread for bait. We used to catch sixty or seventy trout in one day; we'd keep a lot of them, kill them, and on the way back to the bus we would knock on doors and sell them for ten pence each. This was my first experience of being paid for pleasure.

There were moments that were not so pleasurable, though, like the day Briggsy and I went pike fishing at Eccup Reservoir. We'd catch perch, half kill them, then cast them on the surface of the water to lure the pike, but as I tried to cross a stream I got caught in quicksand and Briggsy saved my life by pulling me out.

In between my jobs and the life of a young adventurer outdoors, I managed to find time for school. Life at Allerton High followed a similar pattern to my stint at Fir Tree Primary, in that I distinguished myself as perfectly unacademic. In my first week at Allerton I upset the PE teacher who was known (though not to his face) either as Smooth Head because of his baldness or Toby because, I imagine, he was as handsome as a Toby jug.

During our first lesson I was mucking around and Toby told me to lean over a bench. He then hit me very hard, several times, on the arse with a plimsoll. It was a deeply disturbing experience. Dad had given me a slap in the past, but I had never had a beating like the one administered by Toby.

After the thrashing, I was sent off with the rest of the class on a cross country race and as we were running I kept pulling down my shorts and asking my mate Mark Taylor to examine my swollen flesh. 'Christ, Marco,' he kept saying as he studied the skin while trampling over the mud, 'it's bloody terrible.'

The minute I got home I found a mirror and examined my backside. The skin was mostly maroon, purple in places. I showed my bottom to my brother Clive and then, during dinner, Dad noticed that I was distressed. 'What's wrong?' he asked.

Before I could respond Clive chipped in, 'He got whacked at school. You should see his ...' Dad made me pull down my trousers and was horrified by the sight of my maroon arse. The next day a prefect came into the classroom and said that I had to go to the deputy head's office. I knocked on the door, entered, and there was Mr Richardson with another man who had his back to me. I saw the trilby on the table. It was my dad. 'Show Mr Richardson your backside,' he said. Once again I had to suffer the indignity of pulling my trousers down. Mr Richardson was horrified. For the next three years Toby didn't lay a finger on me.

As it turned out, I excelled at cross country, but not because I was desperate to win. The thing is, I was determined to be the first person back to the changing rooms because I was terrified my hairy classmates would see that I didn't have any pubic hair. I was a late developer – the trauma of a parent's death can have that effect on a child. I set cross-country records purely so that I would be showered, dried and back in my school uniform long before the rest of the breathless bunch had finished the run.

I didn't sit CSEs or O levels. In those days you were allowed to leave school without taking your exams and so that's what I did. I left Allerton High on Friday, 17 March 1978, and as the other pupils went off to see *Star Wars* and enjoy the Easter holidays I was gearing up for my first job. My final lesson on my last day was Games with Toby. Everyone else changed into their shorts and T-shirts but I was having none of it. The teacher said, 'Where's your kit, White?'

I turned surly. 'I didn't bring it. I don't want to do Games.'

He went into his office and re-emerged with a spare kit, which I promptly told him I would not wear. My intention was to remind him that he could not intimidate me. Dad had always said to me, 'Never forget what people do *for* you or *to* you.'

Toby gave me some paper and told me to copy out of a text book while the Games class continued, but when they returned from the field I hadn't written down a single word. Minutes later I would be out of school, never to return. 'White,' he couldn't stop himself saying through gritted teeth, 'you'll be nothing, lad.'

I left school with the memory of Toby's bullying but also with the memory of a particularly sweet girl whose name was Jayne MacDonald. She was a bit older than me and went out with a mate of mine, Steve Gardener. Jayne was kind to me and she had beautiful brown eyes and mousy hair. She left school before me and went to work in a shop. A few months after she'd gone I went into school assembly and the headmaster walked onto the stage. He always wore a black gown and hat and every morning, because of his fancy dress clothes, the pupils would hum the Batman theme tune as he stepped onto the stage. On this occasion, as the giggling subsided and we hushed to listen, the headmaster announced to his young audience that Jayne was dead.

It was not natural causes or a car crash, Jayne had been murdered. It was the most brutal slaying you can imagine. Her murderer, it would later transpire, was the Yorkshire Ripper, Peter Sutcliffe. The lunatic had set out to kill prostitutes and mistakenly – what a tragic mistake – thought that Jayne was a hooker, which she most certainly was not. I'll spare you the details of the butchery. It was said that Jayne's father, Wilf, died of a broken heart. Sometimes when I'm fishing, my mind wanders and I think of Jayne MacDonald and how her life was ended.

––––––

Dad was not fussed about me leaving school before sitting my exams. Getting out there and finding a job fitted in nicely with his programming and, after all, Graham and Clive had done the same before me. 'Become a chef,' Dad had told me, 'People will always need feeding.'

He instructed me to go and search for work in Harrogate because it was less than ten miles away and crammed with hotels. The final stage of the programming was drawing near. One morning he made me sandwiches, gave me the bus fare and sent me off. I arrived in Harrogate, went to the Hotel St George and knocked on the kitchen door.

'I'm looking for a job as a kitchen apprentice,' I said to the head chef, just as my dad had told me to say. That was it. He gave me a start date – Monday, 20 March 1978, the week leading up to Easter – and I took the bus home to deliver the good news to Dad. I didn't have any interest in food at this stage. Cheffing was not my dream, it was just a job, or at least that's how it started.

In order to work at the George, I would have to give up all my other jobs. And on the day before I began my cheffing career I caddied for Mr Bradley, a nice old boy who would always drop me home in his Bentley. We were walking up the eighteenth fairway when he said, 'You've caddied for me for three years. You've been good to me; never let me down. Today is the last day you'll caddy for me. What are you going to do with your life, Marco?'

What was I going to do with my life? I was too embarrassed to tell him that come the following morning I would be a chef. I didn't think he would approve. So I replied, 'I don't know.'

'Do you want some advice from an older man?'

'Please tell me, Mr Bradley.'

He stopped walking and turned to look at me soberly. 'You're not a bad-looking lad,' said Mr Bradley. 'Go to Miami, Marco, and be a gigolo.'

FIVE

The George

'YOU little cunt,' yelled Stephan Wilkinson, the head chef who could have been a drill sergeant had he been tall enough to get into the army. Welcome to the world of gastronomy. I had been in the job for a week and I had cocked up something or other. Burned some toast, maybe. Or had I over-scrambled the eggs?

There was a ferocious glare from this dwarf of a man in his tall white hat and apron that touched his shoes and then another boom came out of his vulgar mouth. It was a drill sergeant scream that rose above the bubbling of sauces, the sizzle of frying meat, the clatter of copper pans against iron stove, the sharpening of knives: 'What are you, White? What – are – *you!*'

This tornado of furious abuse engulfed me. 'A little cunt, Chef,' I replied. 'I'm a little cunt.' Forgive the language, please, but in the kitchens I've worked in the most popular four-letter words have got to be cunt and salt. To the outside world cunt is considered highly offensive, but in the heat of professional kitchens cooks frequently call one another cunt. You just need to work out whether it is being said in a nasty way – 'Do that again cunt and you won't have a job tomorrow' – or a friendly way – 'See you tomorrow, cunt'. Sometimes it's an adjective: 'Who nicked my cunting knife?'. Sometimes it's an adverb: 'Stop cunting talking and get on with the job.' When Stephan called me 'a little cunt' it was the word 'little' that seemed odd, since I was the one looking down on him.

And so I took my first step along the long, bully-laden, work-obsessed, sleep-deprived, nicotine and caffeine-fuelled, passionate, hot and winding road that would end with three Michelin stars.

It's a bit shabby today, but in the spring of 1978 the Hotel St George was still an imposing Edwardian building on Ripon Road in the heart of the delightful Yorkshire spa town of Harrogate. Today the St George is a different entity. It is the Swallow St George Hotel, part of the Swallow chain. Swallow St George doesn't have the same ring, does it? But in the late seventies it was an independent hotel which had yet to be bought out. Back then the St George was a three-star hotel, privately owned by a man called Mr John Bernard Kent Abel and the food reflected the grandness of this exceptionally busy hotel.

My life may well have been very different if I had started out two or three years later, but as it was I stepped into the dying days of the golden age of gastronomy. I saw standards and style which, like so many other hotel kitchens, had been inspired by the French chef Escoffier, a man whose philosophy was 'good food is the basis of true happiness'.

I don't think the St George was where I discovered a passion for food but the romance of that golden age did not pass me by. For instance, boiled ham at the George wasn't just boiled ham. The meat was cooked and then coated in a chaud-froid sauce – a béchamel or velouté sauce made with clarified butter and flour, turned into a roux and then moistened with milk, cream or onion stock, with gelatine (originally calf's foot jelly) added to it. The sauce was then layered onto the ham. The first layer would be allowed to set before another layer was added, and then another layer, and so on until the ham was totally white. The ham was then meticulously studded with chopped truffles to form a picture, then that was covered in an aspic jelly and the finished product was placed on a huge silver platter and carved in the dining room. It was a magnificent sight and one that we are unlikely to see again because the restaurant business now is governed by percentages and portion control.

I started to see that food could be beautiful. And I would discover that I could express myself through food because I certainly couldn't express myself through words, though this discovery would take a bit of time. There were probably fourteen staff in the kitchen, serving the hotel's two restaurants, The French Room and the more informal Lamplighter, and we were busy but I didn't mind. My father's programming was paying off. Hard work was a necessity of life and it did not cross my mind to pack it in and find another career. I was the son of a chef and the grandson of a chef, my brothers were chefs. Cheffing was in my blood.

I'd do breakfasts twice a week and when Sacha Distel stayed at the hotel he became the first famous person I cooked for. I made him bacon and eggs. It was carried up to his room and then I sneaked away from the kitchen and up to his door, bent down and peered through the keyhole. There he was, Sacha Distel, eating my English breakfast.

In the mornings I'd work in the larder, doing the Lamplighter buffet, and one of my duties was to do the salads – waldorf, bagatelle (with mushrooms), à la grecque, niçoise and coleslaw. I found that I could be a little bit creative with the salads and no one made a fuss, and eventually I found that I could experiment with artistic presentation on whatever I liked. So if I was given a sirloin of beef I might slice it very thinly and then arrange it around the joint in a fan shape. I wasn't doing anything new – there were cookery books which had pictures to inspire – but I could create my own pictures. We might do a honey-glazed ham which I'd decorate with cloves, studding them so they made the shape of a harlequin. Or I would do a chaud-froid of ham, using the studs of truffle to create a vase of flowers, perhaps.

The back door would open and wonderful ingredients would be carried into the kitchen. Each season brought different ingredients and the menu would change accordingly. Strawberries, asparagus, game. I stood in awe, watching as wild salmon – there was no such thing as farmed salmon – arrived to be poached, left to cool and then covered in scales of thinly sliced cucumber. Whole lambs would be brought in and chopped up in the kitchen. Again, there was no such thing as portion control. Meat did not arrive pre-cut into equal-sized portions, ready for the pan. The beef was brought in as sirloin and rump attached in one enormous joint. The leg of veal came as a rump, the whole loin attached to it. Milk would arrive in giant churns, rather than in plastic bottles or cartons. This was yesterday's world, when fish and chip shops served food wrapped up in newspaper.

Standards at the George were high. If you made sandwiches you had to trim the edges of the bread to perfection and serve them on a silver platter. Customers dined on dishes like beef stroganoff and steak Diane. Nothing went to waste. If boiled ham was served hot the remaining meat would be used later for sandwiches. Roast lamb might be served with petit pois à la française and pommes dauphinoise and the left-over lamb would be served cold in the following day's buffet. Once in a while we'd serve a spectacular baron of beef, which is the two sirloins and the ribs – so big it's the best part of a cow. The baron was too big for the ordinary kitchen ovens so it would be hung in the bakers' oven and roasted pink. Once it was cooked it was put on a sort of stretcher and two chefs would carry it into the dining room for carving.

Perhaps I had inherited my father's desire for high standards because I admired everything I saw. On top of that I pushed myself with the hours I worked, I think because the old man had instilled a work, work, work ethic inside me. Some days I would do fifteen or sixteen hours, bumping up my basic wage of £15 a week to £60 with all the overtime I did. As an apprentice I received a salary rise of a pound a week on my birthday, but along with the golden age, my job description was on the way out, and today it's rare to come across a kitchen apprentice.

I did a bit of everything. Time with the kitchen's butcher, hours working on the larder section and sometimes I'd help the pastry chef by making lemon syllabubs or piping cream onto the trifles – very good trifles which didn't have jelly. When I turned seventeen on 11 December 1978 I had a day off, but I still went into work. Was I already hooked on the security of the kitchen? I had seen on the menu that they were doing Châteaubriand sauce béarnaise for a private party and I wanted to learn how to make béarnaise, a derivative of hollandaise, so I asked if I could come in to watch it being made.

My days at the George would teach me speed and organisation – two crucial things if you want to be a good chef. You see, in a large hotel you don't learn much about cooking but you are forced to learn the discipline of being organised. You have to. There are not only a couple of restaurants to cater for, there are also functions, as well as bar food and room service. At the George we might have a party for 350 people and I'd have to do pommes de terre château, where the potato is 'turned' so that it is perfectly olive-shaped. With five little potatoes for each plate, that's 1,750 pieces of potato. Compare that with a restaurant, where you might do six portions of pommes de terre château in one night and in one evening at a hotel I had accomplished what it would have taken me nearly sixty nights to achieve in a restaurant. So I picked up the disciplines of speed, organisation and one other thing – how to discipline my hands, almost programme them, so I became really fast with a knife.

It didn't matter how hard I worked, bollockings were still part of the job. Bollockings from Chef. Bollockings from the older chefs. I was the apprentice, the whipping boy, but several things stood me in good stead. To start with, I could take the bollockings because I had been toughened up by my childhood. It was as easy as stepping from one male-dominated, bullying world into another. I had also developed my own survival mechanism so that when the screaming started I would tell myself, 'After my mother's death, what can be worse? Nothing.' The memories of her death – ten years and one month before I joined the George – would help turn me into a man.

Being bollocked was no big deal. Most of the time I found it rather entertaining and enjoyable. I savoured Stephan's rage.

But there was something else which would make my life a little easier at the George. Stephan, like my dad, enjoyed a bet, and something happened which helped to mellow him a little. A few weeks after I joined the brigade Stephan let off one of his drill sergeant yells, 'Marco! Your dad's on the office phone.'

I went into the office and took the call. The excitement in his voice said it all. 'Marco,' he started, 'I've just had Johnny Seagrove on the phone and he says there's a horse racing in the three ten at Ripon. It's a good one. Do a pound each way.' He told me the horse's name, I repeated it and then said goodbye. Stephan, who had been within earshot, was curious. 'What was that all about?' he asked.

'That was my dad. He's mates with lots of trainers and jockeys and he's had a tip.' Stephan's eyes widened with delight, his jaw dropped. He was more than a little impressed, he was agog. Now he saw me in a different light. This teenage lad standing in front of him, young Marco White, had connections.

News of my connections spread rapidly through the hotel. Within days my popularity had soared. Chefs and waiters, barmen and chambermaids would track me down to say sweetly, 'Hello, Marco. Spoken to your dad?' If I nodded they'd put a pound or two in my hand and ask me to back the horse for them. 'Off you go,' Stephan would say, pointing towards the door, and I would sprint to the bookies in my chef's whites to place the bets. I wonder now whether I spent more time in the bookies than in the kitchen.

Through this I devised an ingenious way of getting them back for bullying me. I used to announce to the brigade, 'My dad's calling with a tip tomorrow,' and the hotel's staff would rush towards me, handing over their cash. Then I'd go to the betting shop and put all their money on a horse of my choice. If it won I took the profit and then gave them their money back saying, 'There was no tip from Dad.' If the horse lost I'd give them their betting slips to show I'd put the money on. It meant that on a good week I was earning more than Stephan. I felt like an entrepreneur.

The George also taught me that chefs and waiters hate each other. There's a variety of reasons but usually it boils down to nationality. At the George, the chefs were British while the waiters were mostly French or Italian. The George's restaurants must have had a charming ambience, but in the kitchen there were battles between the front-of-house regiment and the back-of-house brigade. Usually it was just bickering, but I remember a scuffle between drill sergeant Stephan and Giovanni, the restaurant manager.

Giovanni was in the kitchen when Stephan started taunting him and it could have got quite nasty, but Giovanni was carrying two buckets of ice which he dropped onto the floor. As the two men attempted to hit one another the ice beneath them formed a mini ice rink and in the end they fell to the ground, arms wrapped around each other Laurel and Hardy-style.

Despite all this I liked Giovanni, and because of our Italian roots we bonded. He was the staff playboy and drove a 1000cc Harley Davidson. He was the coolest man in the hotel. In fact, he was the coolest man in Harrogate, and must have been the only one with a Harley. He had the best room in the hotel and would spend his days off lying in bed with his girlfriend, Joanna. Sometimes I'd chat to Giovanni and he would go all Marlon Brando on me, saying, 'One day I will leave the hotel, Marco, and when I do I will leave you two things: my room and my girlfriend.'

Eventually that day came. Giovanni climbed onto his Harley, Gary Cooper mounting his horse, and rode off into the Yorkshire sunset. I did indeed end up with his luxurious room, which meant I could move out of home. However, Joanna was heartbroken at losing her lover and I didn't have the courage to tell her Giovanni had promised her to me. Incidentally, a few years ago I was at a party and a little man came up to me, saying, 'Remember me?' I looked down at him and studied his face. 'I'm terribly sorry, but I don't,' I said. It was Giovanni, whose coolness had significantly evaporated with time.

I was not good with the opposite sex. There was a posh university undergraduate whose name I forget and who had taken a holiday job as a chambermaid at the George. She seemed quite interested in me and I mustered up the courage to invite her to dinner in Harrogate. It was my first date and I took her to Vanni's, an Italian restaurant in Parliament Drive, but the evening did not go well. As I was trying to make her laugh with a funny story, I waved an arm and accidentally knocked a glass of red wine onto her white blouse. A waiter sprang into action, trying to wipe away the wine with a napkin, and I sat there dying. She said, 'Don't worry,' and I paid the bill and we went back to my hotel room, the room where Giovanni had been so lucky in love. She removed her sodden blouse and I gazed at her black bra before she put on one of my white shirts. Then she removed her trousers, revealing black knickers, and lay on the bed.

Uncomfortably, I lay next to her and stroked her bristly thighs. Christ, her legs are hairier than mine, I thought. Who's the man on this bed?

I wanted to explore, to experiment, but she said, 'You're too nice, Marco, you're too young. I can't do this to you.' Some years later, around about 1985, she got in touch and I took her out for dinner in London's King's Road. There was unfinished business, but by then I no longer fancied her and had to make my excuses, as they say.

The kitchen porter at the George disliked me intensely. He was a big slob of a man, six foot four, with horrible greasy hair. When he walked past me in the kitchen a reflex action compelled him to give me a sharp poke me in the kidneys with his thumb. Probably I deserved the pokes but I'd have to get my own back.

'Chef, can I clean the walk-in fridge?' I asked.

Chef looked over at me. 'Of course you can.'

The walk-in fridge was enormous. I removed hundreds of bowls and containers, one by one, and put the food into clean containers. It was a laborious job for me, but it meant that the porter was left with a mountain of bowls and containers to wash up and in those days everything was washed by hand. My regular fridge-clearing exercise would drive him mad. 'It's your turn for a beating,' he'd say, his hands like prunes, and then we'd go in circles around the stove as he tried to get me.

I made friends with another chef Michael Truelove and together we would think up ways to annoy the porter. I would phone the kitchen pretending to be Mr Abel, the hotel's owner, and Michael would answer the phone. He'd then tell the lackey, 'Mr Abel's on the phone. He wants to speak to you.' When the porter came on the line I would do my owner's impression and say to him, 'There are some boxes in my office for the chef. Can you come and get them, please?' Big and scruffy, he would waddle into Mr Abel's office saying, 'I've come for the boxes,' and an irritated Mr Abel would ask, 'What on earth do you mean? What are you talking about, man?' Then the penny would drop and he'd return to the kitchen raging, 'You're in for a beating.'

Michael and I were the kitchen's practical jokers. One night he helped me climb into the chest freezer and when Mary, a waitress, came into the kitchen and asked Michael where to put the unused table butter he said, 'In the freezer, love.' She opened the door, saw a chilled body inside, threw the butters into the air and bolted out of the kitchen. A few minutes later the hotel manager, Barry Sterling, came into the kitchen. 'There's a body in your freezer,' he told Stephan. Chef went through the freezer, chucking out the frozen vegetables while shaking his head and saying, 'There's no body in here.'

One of my chores was to mince the scraps of meat which would then be used for staff meals like moussaka, lasagne and cannelloni. One day I was mincing when the meat got stuck, so I attempted to push the meat through with a metal spoon. The next thing I knew the machine was juddering as it minced the metal spoon, and within seconds the spoon was stuck in the mincer. Horrified by what I'd done, I went to Michael, my ally.

'Michael,' I said, 'I don't know what to do. I've minced the mincer.'

'What do you mean, you've minced the mincer?'

I explained what I'd done and Michael told me I would have to tell Stephan. A minute later I was standing in front of Stephan's desk. I said, 'Chef, I've minced the mincer.'

He said, 'Come again.'

'I've minced the mincer, Chef.'

'What do you mean, Marco, you've minced the mincer?' I

explained the problem and then Stephan tried to mince the spoon through the mincer, unsuccessfully, of course. Smoke poured out of the back of the machine.

I had to go and see Mr Abel and it looked like I'd be charged for the cost of a new machine. Fifty-two quid. However, Len, the hotel's handyman, said, 'Don't worry. I broke a glass door and Mr Abel never charged me so you'll be fine.'

Standing in front of Mr Abel's desk, I listened as he said, 'It was a terribly stupid thing you did and it's going to cost fifty-two pounds to replace it. The chef and I think it only fair that we deduct a pound from your wages for the next fifty-two weeks.'

I don't know what possessed me, but I found myself saying, 'I think that's a terrible injustice. Len told me that when he broke a glass door you didn't charge him. So I think it's unfair for you to charge me on my small wage when you didn't charge him on his big wage.' Mr Abel promised to rethink the situation. Hours later handyman Len was on the warpath. He'd been told that he would have to pay for the glass door.

In the afternoons I used to go and see Bill and Ken, the hotel's porters. I'd have a cup of tea with them and help polish the guests' shoes. One day I walked into their room and, in order to sit on my favourite chair, had to remove a book that was on the seat. I glanced at it as I picked it up. It was the Lucas-sponsored *Egon Ronay 1976 Guide to Restaurants and Hotels*. I sat down and started flicking through the pages and realised for the first time in my life that there were restaurants out there that were awarded stars.

I stopped on a page which mentioned a restaurant called the Box Tree. The guide said it was the best restaurant in Britain. I was fascinated and later asked around in the kitchen to see if anyone had heard of it. They had, but said it was impossible to get a job there; Box Tree staff were apparently blissfully content and rarely left so there was hardly any chance of vacancies arising.

At some point in 1979 I picked up the phone and called the Box Tree to see if there were any jobs going. Luck was on my side.

Someone had just handed in their notice and I was invited for an interview with Malcolm Reid and Colin Long, highly regarded as a success story in the industry but also figures of fun because of their campness. Their sexuality provided an opportunity for ridicule in the macho world of cooking, and when I told people I had been invited for an interview they joked that I would be going for 'a Long Reid in bed'.

I went shopping for an interview outfit and bought myself a smart jacket, a shirt and tie. The only shoes I could find to match the clothes were half a size too small but I got them anyway. I took the bus to Ilkley, arrived early and sat on a park bench at the top of Church Street. My feet were killing me, so I took off my new shoes to let the blood flow. When I tried to put the shoes back on, though, my feet had swollen. I managed to squeeze myself into them but only with extreme discomfort. I minced across the road to the Box Tree, walking like a man in women's stilettos. I'm sure I got the job the minute they saw my camp walk.

Messrs Reid and Long kept me there for two and a half hours and showed me the food. The pain in my feet subsided as I gazed at a magnificent duck terrine. I was looking at perfection. When they offered me the job I accepted immediately and hobbled back to the George to hand in my notice. I was about to discover my passion for cooking. My world was turning from black and white into colour.

———

By now my father had gone from my life. I had lost touch. It was my silly fault, really. During my first few weeks at the George I had lived at home. And after moving into the hotel I had made weekly trips back to 22 Lingfield Mount to join him for Sunday lunch.

Then one day, shortly after I had taken the job at the George, he got married. Dad had met a woman called Hazel – he might have known her years – and very quietly they tied the knot at a register office. I have to be honest, I couldn't deal with it. Of course he was right to remarry – after all, my mother had died ten years earlier – and Hazel wasn't a bad woman and she stayed with him until the end. And Christ, who am I to judge?

But back then, as a teenager, I was too immature to appreciate that the show must go on, the world keeps moving, and life continues. I don't recall talking to Dad about the marriage, but one Sunday I didn't go home for lunch. The following Sunday I missed lunch again. Then perhaps after missing five or six lunches, that was it. A week turned into two weeks, which turned into eight weeks, which turned into thirteen years. I never dealt with it because I didn't have the courage. I bottled it every time.

The bond was broken. He would write to me but I wouldn't write back, and eventually, he didn't know where I was, which kitchen I was working in, or where I was living.

The bottom line was I had grown up with many fears, but the greatest of all was my fear of my father. I think I used Dad's marriage to Hazel as an excuse to break away from him. Added to that was my selfishness of wanting to fly the nest and do something for myself for once. For years I had lived by his rules – he controlled me – but now I had discovered freedom. Years would pass before I picked up the phone, called him and re-established a relationship with the man who had raised me.

SIX

Black and white into colour

MY FIRST great love affair was not with a blousy Yorkshire lass but with a restaurant that sat on a dog leg of the A65 in the sleepy village of Ilkley, somewhere between Leeds and Bolton Abbey. Stepping into the Box Tree was like stepping into a massive jewellery box. All the emotions that come with romance were fired up within me. I was seventeen years old and for the first time I felt acknowledged, an important part of a great team.

It was more than that, though. Messed up teenager that I was, the staff and owners virtually adopted me. They became my new family, and for the next eighteen months of my life I was given responsibility, and with that came confidence, kitchen confidence. This is where I discovered my passion for food and formed my food philosophies. I arrived happy and excited, but eighteen months later I would leave by the same door, feeling traumatised and destroyed. It would all end in heartache. Love affairs often do, don't they? Yet the Box Tree remains in my memory as the most special restaurant I have ever walked into, let alone worked in.

The Box Tree was the creation of the two men who had interviewed me, Malcolm Reid and Colin Long. We called them 'The Boys', though they were both in their forties. Malcolm was the serious one, seemingly pushing the business forward, while Colin was the joker. Colin would see me whisking a hollandaise sauce and say something camp like, 'Oh, that's lovely wrist action you've got there. Fancy coming into the larder with me and earning yourself five woodbines?'

There was a great story behind the success of the Box Tree. At some point in the fifties The Boys had bought Box Tree House – originally an eighteenth-century farmhouse which had box trees in its front garden – and opened it as an antiques shop and tea room. Tourists heading to and from the Yorkshire Dales would stop off for scones and jam. Trade was good. So Malcolm and Colin expanded the business by serving lunches. That worked, too, so they opened up for dinner. They were doing so well they decided to rethink the whole set-up. In 1962 they did away with cream teas and lunch and simply opened for dinner. And what a dinner it was.

The Boys were exceptionally clever. In fact, they were the greatest restaurateurs I have ever met. Every now and again they would head off to Paris on a Saturday night and return on the following Tuesday morning, having dined out every day from midday to midnight in the French capital. Their mission in France was to eat the finest food, cooked by the greatest chefs, and then replicate it for their customers back in little old Ilkley. Malcolm and Colin would return to the Box Tree, sit down with their head chef, Michael Lawson, and recount the dishes they had eaten.

With meticulous detail, they would go through each dish, describing the presentation, the flavours, the tastes. 'And then we went to this place and that place and we had this and we had that ...' Michael would listen intently, nodding along as he absorbed the information. He'd see the pictures on the plate and recreate the dish in his head. 'And that evening we went to Bon Auberge where Malcolm had this and on Friday we had dinner at La Sel where Colin had that ...'

Then it was Michael's job to copy each mouth-watering dish for the restaurant menu. Sometimes he'd be able to reproduce it within a day or two. Other times it might take him a couple of weeks to perfect the recipe, as he made one attempt after another to get it right. Malcolm and Colin would come into the kitchen to taste and see if he was close to success. Finally it would be, 'That's it, Michael. You've got it.' And onto the menu it went, alongside Michael's own clever dishes.

No one in Yorkshire had ever seen food like this. They didn't know such food existed. There weren't the beautifully illustrated cookery books we have today, or the food magazines and cookery programmes on telly. The world back then was a much smaller place.

Aside from serving classical French cuisine, the Box Tree also had the feel of a good restaurant that you might stumble across in a village in France, kitted out with beautiful antiques and great paintings. There was an extensive list of French wines and the restaurant had those classic qualities then associated with the French: style, finesse and attention to detail. The menu was written in French with English thrown in, or was it written in English but with French thrown in? So there was Roast Partridge, Pommes Garnished. When I later went on to own restaurants, I'd write my menus in the same English–French way.

By 1976 the Box Tree had won its first Michelin star. In 1977, a couple of years before I arrived, it was awarded its second star. The only two-star restaurants at the time were The Connaught in London, Albert Roux's Le Gavroche in London, his brother Michel Roux's Waterside Inn in Bray – all with their powerhouse kitchens – and little old Box Tree in the middle of nowhere with just six kitchen staff.

I started on hors d'oeuvres, though my other duties included watering the flowers at the front of the restaurant, polishing the brass and washing the Cadillac that belonged to The Boys. From the outset I was fascinated and enchanted by the extraordinary system that operated within the restaurant. It had only fifty covers, but there were two sittings, one at 7.30 p.m. and the next one at 9.30 p.m., so we did 100 covers but only needed a staff large enough to serve fifty. One coffee waitress could look after all of them.

Then there was the price of the meal. A three-course dinner might have been twenty quid, making it possibly England's most expensive restaurant in the late seventies. And it was packed. Crammed with rich Yorkshire mill owners, the guys who had made money out of textiles in the fifties and sixties. Bentleys lined the streets outside.

Michael had his sous chef and I was one of four or five assistants. There were bollockings, sure, but not with the ferocity of those I'd received at the George. Box Tree had a friendly environment and Michael Lawson was gifted. I watched as he prepared, for instance, his game pie. He got a big breast of new-season grouse, a piece of fillet steak, put them into the pie dish, topped it with shortcrust pastry and cooked it so the meat was pink. This was classy. This was not the stuff of *Répertoire*.

Along the way there were philosophies to be picked up. Words of wisdom that would stay with me for ever. I remember Malcolm starting up a conversation by saying, 'You know what I think?'

'No, Mr Reid,' I replied. 'What do you think?'

'It doesn't matter what you spend as long as you get the desired effect.'

I think that's inspiring. It's the sort of thing that made me realise the Box Tree bunch were passionate. Money, what the hell? If we're going to do this, let's do it properly. And he wasn't just referring to the dishes when he talked about desired effect. Malcolm and Colin would spend, spend, spend in their quest to create the desired effect in the dining room. Malcolm might nip out to buy a newspaper and return with a £500 painting. As a lad from Lingfield Mount, I had never seen such extravagance, but this sort of spending taught me that creating a good restaurant requires thinking just as much about what goes on the wall as what goes on the plate.

They never did a stock take and they never did percentages which would really alarm today's chefs, who have a knife in one hand and a calculator in the other. Malcolm and Colin would just say, 'Three courses with English turbot. That'll be twenty quid.' Costings were never taken into consideration.

After hors d'oeuvres I was put onto veg for about three months. Then Michael got me to help doing meat and fish main courses, so that Michael and his number two, Stephen Walker, were the front line and I was the back-up. I already had the speed, thanks to my spell at the George.

It was while I was at the Box Tree that I discovered a truly inspirational book, written by the great French chef Fernand Point. It was not so much the recipes but the stories about the man and his philosophy that 'perfection is lots of little things done well'. These eight words did more than simply stick in my mind; they became my philosophy, and without it I might never have gone on to win three Michelin stars.

Michael put me in charge of Pastry and I was given a week to learn the craft. A lot of the best chefs have done Pastry. Michel Roux of the Waterside Inn is one of them. Why is Pastry so important? Because it is all about science, and the knowledge of culinary science is vital. A precise measurement of that ingredient mixed with a certain amount of that ingredient produces this result. It's chemistry.

I beavered away, practising dishes like Sorbet Poire Genet, a delicious ball of pear sorbet decorated with a little slice of fanned poached pear, a mint leaf and drizzle of pear liqueur. It was served in a pear-shaped glass bowl, the top of which was removed by the customer to reveal the sorbet inside. The pink grapefruit sorbet was another beauty. If you make pink grapefruit sorbet it will turn white, so we added a touch of grenadine to give it that pink tinge. The Box Tree menu would change every day and I would build the pudding menu out of about thirty dishes.

If I wanted to introduce something it would have to be tasted by The Boys when they had their dinner at 6.30 in the snug. Now that I had my own section I really began to excel. I could express myself and create dishes … I took a tuile biscuit and added rosé ice cream, glazed strawberries in their own coulis and put a sugar cage over the top of it. Very simple but with a raspberry sauce. 'Excellent,' said Messrs Reid and Long. 'We'll call it Timbale de Fraises Pompadour.' It became a speciality of the Box Tree and years after my departure it was still on the menu.

I was beginning to realise that the kitchen was the best place in the world. At the George I had discovered that cooking enabled me to express myself and at Box Tree I was acknowledged. There was 'well done' and 'that's good'. For the first time in my life I was being recognised. One night Ken Lamb, the head waiter, confided in me that he had heard The Boys discussing me. Mr Reid had said to Mr Long, 'Marco's the best pastry chef Box Tree's ever had.' That sort of comment was a welcome confidence booster for an eighteen-year-old chef.

A recipe is one thing but method is another. It's about understanding and questioning what you are trying to do. I've always done that. I can't help it, it's in my nature. For example, a pastry chef making Tarte au Citron – a lemon tart – might trim the edges of the pastry around the dish before putting it in the oven, but then the pastry would shrink slightly. I would roll out my pastry, drop it into the bowl and push it into the edges, but I'd leave it flat and then bake it blind.

Then I would add my custardy lemon tart mixture, cook it, and once that was done I would cut the pastry. I also discovered that Tarte au Citron was best cooked late in the afternoon, rather than early afternoon, because when the customers came to eat it, it would still retain a bit of warmth and the perfume of the lemon.

At the Box Tree they used to make ice cream using a crème anglaise with milk and then add cream. But I felt this wasn't maximising the flavour of the crème anglaise, so I started to make a crème anglaise with half milk and half cream so the ice cream didn't crystallise.

Michael Lawson took me under his wing. Like me, he was another damaged soul. Damaged by death. As a young man he had arrived at the Box Tree and worked his way up to become head chef. Somewhere in the distant past he'd met a girl and asked her to marry him. She accepted his proposal and the wedding was organised, but shortly before the big day she was killed in a car accident, so the rumour went, when she was on her way to collect her wedding dress. Michael, poor man, had never recovered from the loss or found another woman. He had never wanted to. Instead, all his love and emotion had gone into the Box Tree. On our days off he would take me for a drink at the pub and I would sit there listening to him talk about food, the menus he had devised and Box Tree kitchen stories.

It was while at the Box Tree that my romantic life, up until now barren and bleak, perked up. On Sundays I would work at a nearby pub, the Cow and Calf, where I met a part-time waitress called Fiona. She was a year or two younger than me and I was thrilled when she accepted my invitation to take her out for dinner. I took us by taxi from Ilkley to Harrogate, where we had dinner at a very posh restaurant, Olivers, before getting another cab back. I lost my virginity to Fiona in bed at Mr and Mrs Fox's house where I lodged during my time at the Box Tree. I was 18 years old. For a few months, maybe six, we existed on a relationship called sex.

Sadly, Fiona left me for the restaurant manager at the Cow and Calf and they went on to have children together. Being ditched did nothing for my confidence, but I convinced myself that Fiona was simply turned on by power and that is why she had deserted me for him.

For many men, the loss of virginity is a great confidence builder, but that was not so in my case. Away from the kitchen I was socially inept, vulnerable and quite shy. When I got into a relationship, as you shall discover, it made me more insecure because it had the effect of exposing me to emotions. Relationships were a distraction and I would come to realise that much of the time I could only manage brief flings. I suppose most teenage lads would have mapped out their lives around the days and nights when they saw their girlfriends. My girlfriends, meanwhile, would be fitted in around my days and nights in the kitchen. This may seem terribly disrespectful but none of the girlfriends meant anything to me because my childhood and formative years had ensured I didn't have the knowledge or experience to invest my emotions. It seemed almost impossible for me to embark on a relationship. I got more turned on by food. If I met a girl I'd go round to her house when her parents weren't in, we'd have a quick shag and that was it. Bonds were broken long before the word love could be mentioned.

I remember meeting one young girl at a club and taking her home. As we stood by her gate I was just moving in to kiss her when we were lit up by the headlights of an oncoming car. It was The Boys in their Cadillac. The car stopped and Colin jumped out. 'In, Marco,' he ordered me. As I sat in the back seat being driven home by my bosses, Colin explained, 'We had to get you away from that girl. You don't know what you might have caught.'

My days at Box Tree started to come to an end when Steve Walker, Michael Lawson's sous chef, handed in his notice and Malcolm and Colin asked if I knew of anyone who could replace him. I was too inexperienced for the job, they had quite rightly thought. The only person I could suggest was Michael Truelove, the chef who first taught me how to use a knife when I worked in the kitchen at the Hotel St George. He had been good to me, at times protecting me from the head chef Stephan's bullying, and I liked him. 'Michael is a very good cook,' I told Malcolm and Colin. 'About five years older than me and a hard worker.'

Michael Truelove was offered the job and he accepted. But his arrival would ultimately lead to my departure. Once he'd arrived and settled in he encouraged me to look for another job. 'You don't want to stay in the sticks, Marco,' he'd say. 'You want to spread your wings.'

Ridiculously immature, I decided to hand in my notice without having a job to go to. I thought I'd be asked to work a six-week notice

period and during that time I'd find another job. Michael Lawson
turned pale when I told him I was off. 'I'm not telling the bosses,' he
said. The prospect of relaying bad news frightened him. 'You'll have
to tell them yourself, Marco.'

I mustered up the courage and broke the news to The Boys.

'Let's talk about this in the Chinese Room,' said Malcolm and we
went upstairs, where the three of us sat at a table. They offered to
increase my salary, which then was about £30 a week.

'It's not about the money,' I said. 'I've made up my mind and you
can't persuade me to stay.'

It was wrong of me to assume they'd want me to work out my
notice, staying on for a month or even six weeks. They were so badly
hurt by my announcement that they came back with a blow that
broke my heart.

'Go now,' said Malcolm.

'There's no point in staying,' added Colin. 'It's best if you get your
things together and leave now.'

I was numbed by what I saw as brutality. What's more, they
wouldn't give me a reference. Looking back, I can understand their
reaction. I don't blame them. I had rejected them so they were
rejecting me. But to have happiness snatched from me in a matter of
seconds seemed cruel. Malcolm and Colin had been like my adopted
family.

I had never imagined that I would leave on bad terms. If only I
had been able to work my notice and leave on a high ... I was
traumatised; my world had been shattered. I walked out of the Box
Tree there and then, burdened by the sense of loss that comes at the
end of a great love affair and full of regret that I had made the wrong
decision. Somewhere within me I still feel that regret.

About twelve years later I was at the stove at Harveys, my
restaurant in south west London, by then the winner of two Michelin
stars, when the kitchen phone rang. 'Hello, Marco. It's Michael ...
Michael Lawson.' It was lovely to hear his voice and I told him so. He
said, 'Would you mind if I came to dinner?' I told him to come

whenever he wanted, at which point he revealed that he was phoning from the public phone box outside the restaurant. Poor Michael had felt nervous about walking into the restaurant. Stage fright or something like that. I ran through the restaurant and greeted my mentor at the door. I sat him at table nine and gave him a grand meal with wine. When service had slowed down I went out to have a chat with him. 'The meal you fed me tonight', said Michael, 'was better than anything we ever did at the Box Tree.' It was a compliment that went some way towards repairing my tarnished memories of that wonderful little restaurant in the middle of nowhere.

SEVEN

It was meant to be

I MISSED a train, which in turn meant I was too late to catch the right coach home. At the time it seemed like a double dose of misfortune, but now I often wonder where I would be today had I not missed that train and coach.

It was the summer of 1981 and I was a nineteen-year-old in a rut, back in Leeds. After my abrupt departure from the Box Tree I'd been drifting. I took a chef's job at Froggies, the restaurant of a Leeds casino called the Continental, where the head chef Jacques Castell served good old-fashioned food. There I worked alongside a lad called Simon Gueller, who would become a dear friend of mine and, years later, in a bizarre twist of fate went on to become the Michelin-starred chef and proprietor of a little restaurant in Ilkley ... the Box Tree.

I had to escape Leeds. Having escaped once, albeit only the short distance to Harrogate and then Ilkley, it seemed odd to return to a place that didn't have a lot to offer. I had gone back to Leeds because I knew it, but now I was there I saw the city in a different light. I didn't like it any longer. As a child I'd often felt I didn't fit in there; now I fitted in even less. I had caught a glimpse of life outside the city.

———

At the Box Tree I had witnessed luxury, attention to detail, passion. None of these were to be found at Froggies or any other restaurant in Leeds.

There was an added complication. I was a lodger in Moor Allerton, in a house owned by a Spanish woman called Esperanza. This put me in the peculiar and uncomfortable position of living just around the corner from Dad and the house where I had grown up. As Dad and I hadn't spoken for a few years, and I could not bring myself to resume relations, I found myself having to hide from him.

Sometimes I would spot him walking down the road and would have to turn away so he didn't catch sight of me, or scurry away in the opposite direction. I don't think he ever saw me – I don't remember cries of, 'Hey, Marco, what the hell are you doing here?' He had no idea that we were living within a few hundred yards of one another. I feel very sad about it now. It was a ridiculous situation.

I had to move on. In an effort to escape Leeds for good I applied for two jobs. The job I really wanted was at Le Gavroche, the two-star Michelin restaurant in the heart of London. Box Tree staff had talked romantically about this fine establishment in the capital. Albert Roux, Gavroche's chef patron, was hailed as an excellent cook. The press, the critics and customers loved his classical French food. It is fair to say that Albert Roux and his brother Michel – who ran the Michelin-starred Waterside Inn – were the most talked about chefs at the time. Or they were in Yorkshire, at least.

So I set my sights on Gavroche and phoned to ask for an application form. Around about the same time, however, I heard of a pastry chef vacancy at Chewton Glen, a country house hotel that sits on the edge of the New Forest in New Milton, Hampshire (today it is considered one of England's finest small hotels).

When a letter arrived from Le Gavroche I opened it excitedly, knowing it would be the application form. I was distressed by what I saw. Every single question was written in French and I imagined that the responses were expected to be in the same language. I think it was the Roux way of saying that they would take chefs of any nationality, as long as they were French. I didn't speak a word of French so I concluded, alas, that I would have to rule out Le

Gavroche. I chucked the application form into the bin. I pinned my hopes on Chewton Glen and was delighted when the head chef, Christian Delteuil, invited me to the South Coast for a job interview.

On Thursday, 18 June 1981, I took the coach from Leeds to Victoria coach station in London, travelled across the capital to Waterloo and from there I caught the train to New Milton. There was nothing particularly memorable about the interview. I liked the head pastry chef, a nice old boy, but I don't recall having a great deal of respect for the head chef and, having worked for Michael Lawson at the Box Tree, respect for the boss was a necessity. The chef's parting words were, 'Give me a call next week and I'll let you know if you've got the job.'

I would have called him, of course, but the extraordinary events of the next twenty-four hours ensured I never needed to pick up the phone. It therefore remains a mystery to me whether or not I landed the pastry chef's job.

Beginning my journey home from Chewton Glen to Leeds, I arrived at New Milton station and discovered, annoyingly, that I had missed my train. By the time I got to Waterloo I found a British Rail ticket collector and asked how I could get to Victoria. 'I'm not from British Rail, I'm with Royal Mail,' he replied, but he happened to be going to Victoria so he offered me a lift in the back of his van, and I made the journey perched on sacks of post.

At Victoria coach station I was told, 'You've missed it, mate ... the next coach back to Leeds isn't until the morning.' Bed and breakfast was not a consideration; firstly I was a nineteen-year-old lad and nineteen-year-old lads don't do B&B when they've missed the coach; secondly I was skint. So I took a stroll. This was my first time in the capital and I was going to make the most of it.

I didn't know where I was heading, but I ended up wandering along a brightly lit street and then I stopped dead in my tracks.

There I was, quite by chance, standing outside Le Gavroche in Lower Sloane Street. I stood on the pavement, mesmerised. The lights were still on in this exquisite restaurant, a two-star heaven, and

I pressed my nose up against the window. Inside there were a few customers, happy and well fed, finishing off their meals with midnight cups of coffee. It seemed elegant, stylish and grand, with the warm golden glow of dim lights and candlelight.

I couldn't stand there all night, though, I'd have been arrested. So I headed back to the coach station where I met a German lad who was about my age and equally forlorn, and together we embarked on a sight-seeing tour, walking to Buckingham Palace and Parliament Square. We went to Trafalgar Square to look at Nelson's Column, before my companion, who had more cash than me, bought me a cup of tea and a cheese sandwich.

When morning came and the Leeds-bound coach pulled out of Victoria I was not on board.

Instead I returned to Le Gavroche, knocking on the back door and asking to see the head chef. A pastry chef called Baloo (as in *The Jungle Book*) told me the restaurant was closed for lunch and that no one else was around. I was about to walk away, perhaps back to Victoria, when he added, 'You could always go to Roux brothers' head office. It's not far.' I walked down Lower Sloane Street, crossed the Thames at Chelsea Bridge, went straight up the Queenstown Road and took a left onto Wandsworth Road, and there, a few hundred yards along, was Roux HQ.

God knows what I looked like when I walked through the door. Actually I know what I looked like. I looked like shit. It was about ten in the morning and I hadn't slept for more than twenty-four hours. Albert, a dapper little Frenchman, was sitting there and I recognised him instantly. He was kind enough to make no comment about my shabby appearance.

'Mr Roux, I'm hoping to get a job in one of your restaurants.'

He said, 'Where have you worked?'

I showed him my references and mentioned that I had worked at the Box Tree. 'You were at the Box Tree, were you? How long were you there?'

'About eighteen months, Mr Roux.'

The magic name Box Tree worked well. 'Go back to Leeds,' he said, before adding, 'Get your belongings and then come back down on Monday. Report here on Tuesday.' And that was that.

Someone once said that all journeys have secret destinations of which the traveller is unaware. Wise words. After missing the train, and then the coach, I cannot argue with that belief because I was taken to a destination that remained secret until I arrived. My efforts to make the return journey to Leeds several days earlier – one hitch after another – had not only left me in a different place geographically but also in a different place in my career and life. Albert would be my boss, my mentor and eventually my close friend. Before our friendship ended, he would be the best man at my wedding and a fishing companion.

My painful rejection from the Box Tree had done me serious emotional damage and I still feel a jolt of sadness when I think about that episode in my life, even though I know I am wrong to feel hard done by. There's no doubt, however, that the fact that I wasn't at New Milton station on time meant that my journey enabled my heart to find a secure – I hesitate to use the word *happy* – destination, a destination with a sense of purpose.

———

I obeyed Albert's orders, and the following Monday when I returned to London the company put me up in a little bedsit in Clapham, just around the corner from Roux HQ. On Tuesday, 23 June 1981, I became a Roux robot – what rivals in the industry called the mechanical chefs who worked for brothers Albert and Michel.

I did not start off in the kitchen at Le Gavroche but at Le Gamin, the Roux-owned City restaurant beside the Old Bailey. I did a couple of weeks there, under head chef Dennis Lobrey, who cooked good, proper food. What I saw for the first time in my life was a high standard of food served in a couple of hours to 130 people. The only desserts made on site were ice creams and sorbets; the other pastries – things like Charlotte aux Poires or Truffes au Chocolat – came from

Roux head office. It was a smoothly run operation.

Then there was a bit of upheaval in the expanding Roux empire. Gavroche moved to Upper Brook Street, where it remains to this day, and the now vacant Lower Sloane Street site became Gavvers, which served Gavroche's classical dishes as watered-down versions. We'd make things like Sablé à Pêche, which was a Gavroche speciality, but rather than having two layers, you'd have one layer because it was cheaper.

Dennis's second chef, Alban, was put in charge at Gavvers and took me with him, and from there I would end up at Gavroche. I made friends with Mark Bougère who, as the chef tourner of the company, would go from one Roux restaurant to another, standing in for chefs who were ill. He was, in effect, Albert's right-hand man. Mark was a very fine chef, an elegant cook with a great touch, and he took a real liking to me and taught me a lot.

He taught me, for instance, how to make great sorbets with a concentrated flavour and wonderful sauces. He also started me off on the process of questioning what I was cooking. He was one of the most knowledgeable chefs I've ever come across and I still have an image of him making a mousseline of fish beautifully. It was clear to me why he was the most trusted of Albert's staff.

When Peter Chandler, one of the top chefs in the company, broke his collarbone I was sent over to replace him at one of the banks in the city which paid Roux to cook lunch every weekday for the bank's directors. Naïve soul that I was, it took me a while to realise that all the waiters were gay, and when they kept asking me if I wanted a gin and tonic at nine o'clock in the morning I would politely decline the offer.

I am indebted to Baloo, the Gavroche pastry chef, and not just because he was the man who directed me to Roux HQ, but because he offered me a place to stay in his flat in Queenstown Road. One night I was walking home when I spotted Baloo talking to someone outside our flat. It was Nico Ladenis, the Michelin-starred chef who owned Chez Nico in Queenstown Road.

Nico asked if I would like to do a bit of work for him. At this stage Gavroche did not open for lunch so I had that part of the day available. I took the job. When Gavroche moved to Upper Brook Street it started opening at lunchtime, but up until then I would work in the mornings from Tuesday to Saturday for Nico in his tiny kitchen, picking up fifty quid a week on top of the £67 I was paid by Albert.

Gavroche's kitchen was a powerhouse while Nico's was tiny. I'd prepare the meat and fish while the sous chef did the starters and puddings like Prune Armagnac Parfait, sorbets, Caramel Parfait. The sous chef was camp, very precious and had a good sense of humour. He would take a bollocking from Nico and then duck down under the counter so his boss couldn't see and pretend to suck him off.

Nico, meanwhile, had established a reputation for being a perfectionist. He did not like customers to ask for well-done meat and he wouldn't allow salt and pepper on the table. He thought his palate was perfect, which I don't think is right – you have to accept that everyone's palate is different. Nico's may well have been perfect, but someone else might like a little more salt, it's as simple as that.

One morning I was in the kitchen and an electrician walked into the restaurant asking to speak to Chas. We all stood there, scratching our heads. 'Chas? There's no one here called Chas.' The electrician was insistent. 'Chas Nico,' he said.

I only did a short stint with Nico, but we became good friends and both won three Michelin stars on the same day in January 1995. The last time I met him for lunch, Nico said, 'What shall we talk about?' I replied, 'What do you want to talk about?' And he responded, 'Let's talk about all the cunts in the industry.'

One day I was on my way to Gavvers, walking down Queenstown Road towards Chelsea Bridge, when a Mini Metro pulled up beside me and a voice shouted, 'Jump in.' It was Albert.

All talk in the Roux empire was about whether or not Albert would collect three stars in *The Michelin Guide*, which was due to be published the following January, and as I was in the company of the man himself I thought I would raise the subject. 'Albert,' I said, 'do you think you will get your three stars?'

Eyes firmly on the road and deadly serious he said, 'If I don't get my three stars I will throw myself in the Thames.'

I went silent, pondering the words of a determined man. I had never heard a chef threaten to take his life if he didn't achieve such status in a guide. Do actors say a similar thing in the run up to the Oscars? Do athletes feel the same way about Olympic medals? How apt, I thought, that he should mention throwing himself into the Thames when the river was just beneath us. When January came Albert was spared a watery grave. *The Michelin Guide* awarded Le Gavroche three stars – Albert had reached the top.

I started to see the set-up of the finest restaurants as something akin to the Mafia (without the violence and corruption, needless to say). On this basis, I decided that Albert was definitely the Godfather, the boss of bosses. He was Marlon Brando … in an apron. He was a father figure with a very dominant presence and could philosophise in that Godfather style. While you worked for him you felt you had his protection. You knew you were with the don.

The way I saw it, there were five families in this mafia of Michelin winners: Albert Roux, head of the Roux family; Pierre 'The Bear' Koffmann, was head of the Koffmann family; Nico 'Nic the Greek' Ladenis, head of the Ladenis family; Michel Bourdin, head of the Bourdin family; and Raymond Blanc who, with all his craziness, could only be Al Mascarpone.

EIGHT

Albert, the boss of bosses

STRANGE though it may seem, there are many chefs who suffer a fear of the stove. You will find them in the finest kitchens in Britain. They might be great cooks, with heads crammed full of culinary knowledge, but the minute they are thrown into a busy kitchen they wobble, lose it and need baling out. Until they conquer that fear they are destined never to rise through the ranks and find a place in the kitchen hierarchy.

You need confidence to shrug off your insecurities, push your way past the other chefs and take control of the stove. Step into a powerhouse kitchen like Gavroche and you won't hear 'excuse me' or 'would you mind'. Each man has his own dishes to create, his own job to do, and he has to have the required strength of character to barge his way past the others in order to cook.

When I finally made it into the three Michelin-starred kitchen at Gavroche, Albert Roux was keen to let me know that I should never be frightened to push in with my pot or pan. One night at Gavroche, shortly after I had joined the brigade as an assistant on the meat section, Albert called me into his office – something akin to a large glass bowl – for a chat. He gave me a Benson & Hedges, which was his way of saying 'At Ease'. 'Don't be scared of the stove,' he said to me and then waved a hand towards the kitchen. 'You can cook as well as any of those people. You have nothing to worry about.' He had got me wrong: I wasn't scared of the stove, what I didn't want to do was push out of my position.

Yet I understood precisely what Albert meant about fear of the stove. I had seen it before, just a couple of months earlier when I'd worked at Gavvers. There had been a chef there who was about my age and I remember him being extraordinarily precise in what he did, but in my view he was also a bit slow. He had been trained in one of those big kitchens in France, where there's such a massive infrastructure that chefs have the luxury of being able to take their time.

When this young lad arrived at Gavvers he was put on Meat and I was on Fish, which is a tough section because it doesn't allow for error. We were doing more than a hundred covers a night and to feed that number of people you have to be really quick at the stove, but he found it hard to deal with. It doesn't matter how much knowledge you have as a cook, you can't run a section if you appear slow. So he moved from Gavvers and went to work at Le Gamin, where I think he helped Dennis Lobrey on the passe, shouting out the orders.

Perhaps I might never have seen that young man again were it not for the fact that he was Albert's son, Michel Roux Junior. Michel would go on to run Le Gavroche, taking over from his father in the nineties, and he runs it very well.

Albert may not have wanted any of his team to suffer from a fear of the stove but the Gavroche brigade was driven by fear nonetheless. We were driven by a fear of failing, a fear of fucking up, a fear of upsetting the boss.

The hierarchy there kept everyone in their place. Gavroche had a traditional kitchen hierarchy like that found in the finest restaurants in Paris. At the top was Albert, the chef-patron or chef-proprietor. Beneath him was the head chef, René, who stood at the passe shouting out the orders and making sure the dishes were perfect before being sent to the table. The head chef is the composer. Under René was the sous chef, the head chef's right-hand man or deputy. Then there were the chefs de partie, the ones heading up the different sections. Those sections were Meat – sometimes referred to as Sauce – Fish, Pastry (making all desserts rather than just ones with pastry) and Larder. Some kitchens have a section for Cold

Albert Roux and I savour a very
private lunch at Harveys in 1989.

Starters and another for Hot Starters. Within each section the hierarchy continues: each chef de partie has a premier commis chef, or assistant, which is where I started at Gavroche. And the premier commis is in charge of a couple of commis chefs, also called assistants. Then there's the kitchen porter, who does the washing up.

Out of service, Albert was the chef-patron – the general – who would sit in his office composing menus, dealing with paperwork and suppliers. Occasionally he would come into the kitchen to carry out inspections. He would open a fridge and peer inside, and if something was not right – an over-ripe piece of fruit, perhaps, or a sauce which had spilled and not been cleaned up to his satisfaction – he would scream for the head chef, René, and the bollocking would start. 'This is fucking filthy? What is going on?' René would always get it first from Albert, and the bollocking would then be passed down the hierarchy. René would bollock the chef de partie. The chef de partie would bollock the premier commis. The premier commis would bollock the commis. During these inspections it was rare for Albert to bollock the commis in the first place: hierarchy had to be respected.

In service Albert stopped being chef-patron and became head chef, barking the orders from the passe and making sure everything came together. Now he was the sergeant major, seeing out the food, shouting, bollocking anyone in his path, and no one dared disobey him. When he was at the passe nothing bad got past him. He saw everything that went out and if he didn't touch the dishes with his hands – rearranging the ingredients on the plate to perfect the picture – then he touched the dishes with his eyes, and that is really important.

Young chefs would do a year at Gavroche, just to have it on their CV, and then move on. From day one they would be mentally preparing their letters of resignation, but because of Albert's awesome presence staff were scared to hand in their notice. It was easy to gauge the terror – when chefs arrived at the restaurant they raced to change into their whites; no time to stop and have a cup of coffee in a café while you contemplated the day ahead. Every morning I found myself hurrying into work, petrified by the thought of arriving late. Once, when I committed the sin of turning up five minutes late, I dashed in to be greeted by Albert, scowling. Would I be marched to the wall and shot?

'There's always an excuse for being an hour late,' he said. 'But there's no excuse for being five minutes late.' After that I would virtually run off the bus to work. Even though I was in early and worked through my breaks, conscientious soul that I was, that sort of diligence was never acknowledged in Gavroche.

Head chef René initially took a dislike to me and gave me one bollocking after another. I think he dreamed of having a kitchen full of French and Italian cooks. He had the French and the Italians – his favourites – but I was just another Englishman who annoyed him. René amused himself by telling me to go and get something from the main fridges which were at the front of the restaurant. I would sprint from the kitchen, run round the side of the building to the fridges at the front, collect the ingredients and then dash back. I'd have a second or two to gather my breath and then René would shout, 'Cream from the fridge' and whoosh, off I'd go again. Run forward, run back, run forward, run back. That was my existence in the early days at Gavroche. René, or maybe Albert, gave me the nickname 'Horse' because even before service I had run the equivalent of Aintree.

René's sous chef, Danny Crow, was half-Italian, and when he discovered that I also had Italian blood he became my friend and helped René see me in a different light.

There were fifteen or sixteen of us in the Gavroche kitchen and there was no chit-chat. If anyone spoke it was only to talk about the menu or the food. Overall, there were hours of silence, punctuated by orders from René and barks of, 'Yes, Chef.' We all beavered away, sticking to the recipes and being precise and methodical. I could certainly see why the troops commanded by Albert and Michel were known, outside of the organisation, as the Roux robots. Later on, when I went on to run my own kitchens, I too would insist on silence. At Gavroche I discovered that there is something beautiful about the sounds – chopping, clattering, sizzling – of a working kitchen.

My chef de partie on the Meat/Sauce section was a Belgian called Claude. He was the Roux robot prototype. Organised, consistent and perfect for Gavroche, Claude did not play around with the recipes that came from Albert's office; he stuck to the original and never veered. There was another lad, Stephen Yare, who was about my age and, like me, was an assistant, and a few years later we would work together under Raymond Blanc at Le Manoir aux Quat' Saisons. There were also a couple of Japanese guys who were also good, mechanical Roux robots.

We were doing big numbers – eighty covers – in a fast and hard, aggressive service, so it was essential that we all had three attributes: knowledge, touch and organisation. I thrived on the pressure and stress of the workload. If I wasn't already an adrenaline addict I was fast turning into one. I found gears within myself that enabled me to step up a level as the kitchen pressure increased. You cannot let the pressure get to you, though very few chefs can do big volumes and maintain a consistently high standard.

There was one guy who really stood out, and not only because of his distinctive white clogs. Roland Lahore had knowledge, speed and a sensational flair. Roland moved quickly, worked quickly and cooked elegantly. I can still see him now, doing a scallop of salmon, cooking the fish beautifully and adding a handful of sorrel to the sauce. Roland would make terrines which, when sliced, were like glorious mosaics on the plate: he had visualised the finished terrine before assembling the ingredients. I watched him finish off a sauce by throwing in a segment of pink grapefruit and breaking it up with the whisk so the fruit infused the sauce with a perfect balance of acidity: always finish a fish sauce with citrus or vinegar.

But Roland was a soloist, a Maradona. He was playing his own game and his wild streak must have rubbed off on me. If you're working in a big kitchen team you have to be synchronised. Imagine you have two chefs, one is on Meat and the other is on Fish, and they are cooking dishes for the same order. If the chefs are good they will work together, so the four dishes make it to the passe at the same time. One of the chefs will shout out, 'Ready in three minutes,' and the other chef will work to that.

But Roland lived in his own world, and inevitably that meant he wasn't synchronised. He was in charge of the Fish section but he might be behind or ahead of the man on Meat. So if there was a table of six – three meat, three fish – the fish would be on the passe but the meat wouldn't be ready, or vice versa. Roland tended to forget about the rest of the kitchen. He worked only with his unit of two assistants, who were whipped along and kept in line by him.

He had done his time at Troisgros in France and then worked for Michel Bourdin at The Connaught in London. He left the latter because they couldn't control him, and at The Waterside Inn Roland was deemed equally unmanageable. But though others may have found him difficult, I had the utmost respect for him, and Roland liked me, too. Maybe he related to me on a mental level, perhaps he could spot the similarities. Who knows? I was not yet a soloist but it wouldn't take long. Like me, Roland worked through his breaks – if he didn't he knew he'd be in trouble during service – and he never once sent a bad plate to the passe.

Though I would go on to become good friends with Albert, our relationship at Gavroche was strictly business. If you had finished your job he would find you another. If it was 6.30 in the evening and the first customer wasn't due in until seven, giving you half an hour to kill, Albert would fill the gap by finding you something else to do. He was that disciplined. One night Albert gave me a severe bollocking, though I can't remember what it was about. An hour or so afterwards he called me into his office and produced the Benson & Hedges signifying I should be at ease. I was convinced that I was about to get the sack but I was wrong. 'I'm sorry,' he said. 'I over-reacted.'

It struck me at the time that while it was good of him to apologise, it was wrong of him to do so in private. If he wanted to bollock me in front of everybody that was fine, but if he wanted to be correct about it he should have apologised in public, too. When I eventually came to run my own kitchens I promised myself that if an apology was due I would make it in front of the rest of the staff.

Despite instilling fear Albert also instilled confidence. In one of those B&H moments in his office he told me that I did the work of two or three men. And he said, 'I know which plates are yours on the passe, even when you don't deliver them. I can tell they are yours just by the way you dress them. I know it's your hands that have dressed those plates, no one does it like you. You have more natural talent than anyone else in this kitchen.' What had I done to earn such compliments? I can't remember. But I had seen talent in other chefs – it's just the touch, the way the food falls, the way the sauce pours, the way the garnish is put on the plate. If you watch a great chef he moves elegantly as he cooks. Someone can tell you how to do a picture. They can give you a paintbrush and paper and then give you instructions – paint a circle, paint a square, put a brushstroke here and another there. But the paintbrush is in your hand, so it's all down to your artistic talent. Can you paint the perfect circle? Can you paint the perfect square? Are the brushstrokes too heavy or too light? Are the colours right?

———

The King's Road was a honey pot. Young people swarmed there; punk was born here. The place was magical. The stretch of road running from Sloane Square to Parsons Green was one long, crowded parade of ultra-trendy clothes shops, cafés, bars and pubs. If you were skint it didn't matter because you could still enjoy yourself by strolling and watching, observing the confident young rebels on show. On days off, I would walk down Queenstown Road over Chelsea Bridge and up the King's Road. It was the early eighties but there were still a few die-hard punks around, with their nostrils pierced, swastika tattoos on their foreheads, spiky hair dyed pink, purple and lime green – and those were just the girls.

I would go to Pucci's, then the coolest café in the world, to sit and drink coffee and smoke. Queues of people would hover outside waiting for a table and Pucci himself was nicely grumpy. If the queue was too long he'd dash over to the people at the end of it, yelling, 'Go away! Go Away!' Customers who annoyed him got a blast of his pidgin English, 'Shard up!'

I must have gone to Pucci's so many times that eventually I became a familiar face. I struck up conversation with other regulars, an assortment of New Romantics and youthful aristocrats. I was a lowly cook, but was welcomed into the Chelsea set; it was a slow process because confidence was a requisite factor for membership, and I didn't have much of that. I positioned myself close to the whirlpool, though, and slowly I was sucked in.

A day in the life of the Chelsea set member would go like this: coffee outside Dino's, then off to Oriel at Sloane Square to sit outside and bird watch, back up to Pucci's for a drink in the evening and then on to Crazy Larry's. In between there were clothes to be bought: dressing up was a big thing. In their colourful waistcoats and frilly pirate shirts, people looked like something out of Adam and the Ants. One of my favourite garments was a black T-shirt with the words Bobo Kaminsky stamped on it. I bought it from a cool shop called Jones and paid a fortune for it. Don't ask me who Bobo was.

Just as Gavroche had a hierarchy, so did the Chelsea set. At the top was Robert Pereno who I think I'm right in saying was the man behind the one-night clubs that eventually became raves. To me, Robert was the king of the King's Road, the role of Queen being played by his girlfriend, Lowri-Ann Richards, a singer and actress. Then there was James Holdsworth – Little James – who helped Robert instigate the one-night clubs. And there were others on the scene and doing clubs: Rusty Egan, who was in Visage, and Steve Strange. They might hire Crazy Larry's for the night and when I finished work I'd head off there. I was fascinated by these people, their creativity and their energy. I'd sit there making a single beer last me the whole night. I had Pils because it was all part of the image, but I didn't like the taste of beer and lager, and in the eyes of my new friends it would have looked odd to order a glass of wine.

The Chelsea Set also included some wild young aristocrats and children of upper-class parents. The kids tended to have been at Eton before bailing out of education and life as we know it. They wanted to lose themselves in the mayhem of the King's Road. Chelsea was a magnet for junkies, be that drug-takers or adrenaline-addict chefs. Nowadays, young aristos want to have good careers rather than spend their days on the King's Road, but there was a period of a few years – a window in time, I suppose – when rich kids managed to escape responsibility and parental pressures, and the King's Road was where they went. I'd grown up thinking aristos were snobs who looked down their noses at the working classes, but the ones I met then didn't give a damn that I was a cook with a state-school education who earned in a year what they got in weekly hand-outs from their folks.

Often they spent their money on drugs, heroin being the drug du jour. There was dear Charlie Tennant, the son of Lord Glenconner, who was polite and gentle natured but also heavily into smack. His parents tried to help him by booking him into the Lister Hospital, just off the King's Road. They could have picked a different location. Charlie would break out of the Lister and only had to walk a few hundred yards to get a fix. Chronically afflicted by the effects of the drug, he used to bounce up and down. The last time I saw him was in Fulham Broadway, where he had a house. He invited me in for a coffee and did one of those obsessive-compulsive shuffles a hundred times before putting his key in the front door. Sadly, Charlie has since died, and inevitably there were one or two others who had drug-related deaths, though I'm pleased to say there were many members of the set who managed to avoid the temptation of drugs.

Among the girls there was Victoria Lockwood, who went on to marry Princess Diana's brother Charles Spencer, as well as Sophie

Ward, daughter of the actor Simon Ward, who became a well-known actress and then left her husband for a lesbian lover. Then there was Willy Harcourt-Cooze, a Pucci's regular. He'd sit at one of end of the bar while I sat at the other, and for months we didn't introduce ourselves, but when we finally got chatting Willy told me how his father had died when he was a child and I told him about my mother's death. A bond was formed and, years later when I opened Harveys, Willy became a regular customer who remains to this day one of my closest friends. One of Willy's girlfriends, by the way, and another Pucci's regular was a young Rachel Weisz, who went on to become a great actress and win an Oscar (for her role in *The Constant Gardener*).

I talked to my new friends about food with such passion that they all thought I'd lost the plot. They were amused by my obsession. In terms of their usual topics of conversation, eating came after drinking, clubbing, hair and clothes. At times it seemed as if I was the only one with a job. When they were getting up I was already into my sixth hour in the kitchen.

My Yorkshire accent disappeared and I started to sound a little posh. If you're in your late teens or early twenties and go off to the States or Oz, there's a good chance you'll start sounding like an American or Australian. My journey from Leeds to London was not that far, but I can understand why as a young, impressionable lad I ditched the accent in an attempt to fit in. I thought, I'm just a boy from a Leeds council estate, but I've been accepted by all these toffs. Three years earlier I'd used my spare time to fish or poach, now I was in this melting pot of rock 'n' roll people. The contrast seemed extreme. They did what they wanted, when they wanted and that attitude was infectious.

At the end of that decade I was being described by the press as a rock-star chef, which has got me thinking ... I was something of an empty vessel before arriving in London, and empty vessels need contents. In the kitchen I absorbed the knowledge that made me a chef, while on the King's Road I absorbed a confident attitude, passion for life, wildness and pace. If a rock-star chef was born, then it must have been there on the King's Road.

It was also on the King's Road that I met the man who would become my publicist, the rock star's PR, if you like. Alan Crompton-Batt was the manager of a brasserie called Kennedy's, and when I was in there one day, sitting at the bar having a coffee, he started up a conversation. He had been an Egon Ronay inspector, he said. 'You must know the Box Tree,' I said. And he did. He had eaten in its dining room when I had worked in its kitchen.

I became a regular at Kennedy's and Alan was always kind enough to give me free drinks. We would talk food and restaurants and one day he said to me, 'You're going to be the first British chef to win three Michelin stars.' I don't know what prompted him to make this prediction, but not only was it flattering, it also came true.

On Saturday mornings I would go to Kennedy's for breakfast and sit at the same table as another regular, the actor Tom Baker who played Dr Who. With wild hair and big frames, Tom and I looked alike. People would come up to the table to ask for his autograph and then point at me and ask, 'Are you Tom's son?'

NINE

Pierre 'the Bear': head of
the Koffmann family

MY DAYS at Gavroche came to a hasty, unexpected end in September 1982, when Albert picked up a soup ladle and started waving it in front of my face in the middle of his three-star kitchen.

I hadn't started that day in the best of moods and was feeling grouchy. For a week or so I'd been suffering from a stomach problem – the beginning of my ulcer, maybe – but I still turned up at the kitchen every day, working late into the night. I was a sleep-deprived, mop-haired wreck with a stabbing pain in my belly, and when head chef René rounded on me with a thunderous verbal assault I answered back. I can't even remember what started him off; I have no recollection of what I was supposed to have done wrong. But Roux robots were not supposed to answer back – it showed a fault in the programming – and my attempts to defend myself only increased the volume of René's rant.

The sound of the commotion must have penetrated the glass walls of Albert's office and he emerged at a galloping pace, swooping up a ladle from a kitchen surface. He was the knight embracing his lance, and he was heading towards me. Was he going to dispose of me with a long-handled, copper kitchen implement? Was I about to be ladled? Adrenaline pumped through my twenty-year-old body but what with my stomach ache and exhaustion, I didn't have the patience to stand there and take a bollocking from the boss. Albert stopped his charge when he was a foot in front of me and raised the up-ended ladle into the air, moving it in a pecking motion in front of my face.

The spoon part of the ladle came towards the bridge of my nose and then, before it could touch me, it was swiftly retracted. Forward, back, forward, back in pendulum fashion, though metal and skin never connected. Albert stared at me and, swinging his ladle he uttered the words, 'Now [peck] ... you [peck] ... listen [peck] ... to [peck] ... me [peck] ... my [peck] ... little [peck] ... bunny [peck].'

'My little bunny' – now that was patronising. By all means give me a bollocking and shout at me, I thought, but please don't patronise me. I grabbed the spoon. 'That's it,' I said to him, as the rest of the robots carried on mechanically with their chores. 'I don't like being patronised. I don't need this shit.' Then I marched. I marched out of the kitchen, changed out of my whites and buggered off. I don't think Albert tried to stop me leaving and, anyway, I scarpered pronto. The magic chef's little bunny vanished.

I would meet Albert a couple of months later, but in the meantime I had to find another job. I found work at a small restaurant on the other side of the river, in Battersea Park Road. We only did about thirty covers a night, but boy did those customers eat well because I was cooking them Gavroche-style food at a fraction of the price. The kitchen was run by a man called Alan Bennett – no, not the playwright. We got on well and I would later work for him at the restaurant he owned, Lampwick's, in nearby Queenstown Road. When I look back on it now, I can see that Alan was a very gentle man, soft and kind, and perhaps I needed reminding that the world was full of such people.

It was in December that I bumped into Albert, and he was extremely apologetic about the way it had all ended at Gavroche. 'Why don't you come back?' he asked, and I didn't need much time to think about it. In the interim period of a couple of months I had reflected on the soup-ladle incident, and now I could appreciate the comedy behind my departure. My decision to leave had been irrational, I told myself, so I accepted Albert's offer and pitched up to start my second stretch at Gavroche.

It didn't last long. The magic wasn't there anymore. In that short period of time, from September to December, my friends Roland Lahore, Danny Crow and Stephen Yare had gone, moved on. I saw the restaurant in a different light. What had previously seemed grand, exquisite and stylish no longer had the same effect upon me. I wasn't blinded by the silver any more. At some point early in 1983 I left Gavroche once again, this time on the most amicable terms. I left the restaurant but I didn't leave the company. I took a job at the Roux brothers' spectacularly upmarket butcher's shop, Boucher La Martin, in Ebury Street.

Based on the Parisian shop of the same name, Boucher La Martin was run by Mark Bougère, the highly gifted chef who had been Albert's right-hand man when I had joined the company nearly two years earlier. We not only supplied Albert's restaurants, we also provided fine meat and poultry to the well-heeled shoppers of Chelsea and Knightsbridge. Being a butcher, or rather a Roux butcher, has to be one of the toughest jobs I have ever done.

The working day started at 5.30 in the morning. My first duty was to prepare the ducks. Entering the bird's back cavity, let me tell you, requires the utmost skill. A lot of people are too heavy handed, and when they're finished you could drive a bus up the back cavity. At Le Boucher I had to master the skill of opening up the cavity so that it was just large enough to get my fingers in and carefully scoop out the insides without staining the bird with its blood. The liver and heart were brought out whole, as well as the lungs, which had to be removed because if cooked they add a bitterness to the final flavours. Each morning I would prepare about twenty ducks, their sharp bones stabbing my fingers. To ease the soreness I would have to wash with cold water and a bit of bleach.

The duck process took me about four hours and then I would tend to the customers in the shop. This was not the sort of butcher's where you'd walk in and simply buy a chicken. Everything was prepared to order. If a customer wanted a poulet de Bresse for a fricassée then I would chop it up accordingly; if it was a chicken for roasting then the bird would be beautifully tied and trussed. I had to be disciplined with my knife and hands and I had to work quickly. In the end it shut down, but Boucher La Martin has to have been one of Britain's finest butcher shops and is another credit to the legendary Albert.

Although money had never played an important role in my life, I spotted an opportunity to earn a fortune and that is what seduced me away from the butcher's shop and the Roux brothers' empire. There was a pub called The Six Bells serving the punters who shopped in the hustle and bustle of the King's Road and I learned that the landlord was looking for a head chef. When I turned up to see him he seemed quite impressed by my experience and offered me the job. However, he was adamant about the money. 'I'll give you a staff budget of five hundred pounds a week,' he said. 'That's your budget. Spend it how you like.' Maybe he thought I'd have to take on a staff of five and a washer-up, but I had devised a way of earning a staggering amount of money. I paid myself £400 per week, which was a fortune for a chef then, and even by today's standards would be good money for a pub chef. That left me with £100 from the budget, so I hired a sous chef who was about my age, an American lad called Mario Batali. There was no cash left for a washer-up, so Mario and I agreed to share the chore. I was quite proud of the deal – signs of my business brain were evident even back then.

Pony-tailed, sturdy Mario was an interesting guy, but not half as interesting as he would later become. After getting a degree in Seattle, he came to London to train at Le Cordon Bleu, but he got bored with the course and chucked it in – Cordon Bleu's loss was my gain. He found it very difficult to get out of bed in the morning, but while he obviously liked his sleep he also loved his food. He was passionate about cooking. What he needed was a bit of discipline, so I found myself treating him as harshly as I had been treated by my former head chefs. I used to murder Mario every day, physically, mentally and emotionally. If he cocked up a dish then it went in the bin. I would push him along – 'Move it, Mario, faster, faster' – and after service he would head home to his bed, nodding off to his favourite band, Joy Division, and their hit song 'Love Will Tear Us Apart'.

From the tiny kitchen of that pub I would eventually go on to win three Michelin stars while Mario returned to the States where he's today hailed as the king of New York's restaurants and his places include Babbo and Lupa. He's won a heap of awards and plaudits including 'Man of the Year' from *GQ* magazine. Although we only worked together for a matter of months, he regards me as a mentor, which is nice, and in interviews he often mentions me in affectionate terms. In July 2004 he said, '[Marco] was a genius, and an evil one at that. Last time we spoke he had launched a hot pan of risotto at my chest in service.'

———

There were only three Michelin starred restaurants in London in the summer of 1983 – Chez Nico, Gavroche and Tante Claire. I had worked in the first two, and you'd be forgiven for thinking that such a pedigree would secure me a job in the third. Not so. I jacked in the job at The Six Bells because I missed working in fine kitchens. The pub wage, while amazing, was outweighed by an overwhelming desire to cook in the best restaurants. I needed to acquire knowledge and experience, so thought I'd try my luck at Tante Claire.

It was a small restaurant in Royal Hospital Road, Chelsea, and while it had neither the magic of the Box Tree or the grandness of Gavroche, it was run by one of the finest chefs of his time. French-born Pierre Koffmann, who years earlier had worked with the Roux brothers, had picked up his second Michelin star in 1980. Known as Pierre the Bear, he was a big, bearded man somewhere in his forties and he served big, hearty food such as pavé de boeuf, pig's trotters and turbot à la grande moutarde. He also had a reputation for being hard but straight – no bullshit – and it was said that he employed only French chefs.

English and proud of it, I turned up and knocked on the door, just as I had done five years earlier at the Hotel St George and then later at Le Gavroche. I told Pierre that I had worked at the Box Tree, but it didn't matter, there was no room at the inn, so to speak. 'I'm sorry,' said Pierre. 'I have no vacancies, simple as that.' Then he added, 'Why don't you go and ask at Le Gavroche? They might have something going.'

It sounds silly now, but I didn't want to tell him I had already worked at Gavroche. Perhaps I was just reluctant to get into that conversation because when I thought of Gavroche the first image that came into my mind was of a soup ladle pecking my nose and Pierre had better things to do than stand there and listen to that story. 'But it's here that I want to work,' I insisted. 'Not at Gavroche. I really want to work here at Tante Claire.'

Again he came back with, 'But I haven't got any vacancies.'

I had no choice. 'I'll tell you what I'll do,' I said, 'I'll work for nothing.' Pierre wasn't going to turn down a freebie and he swiftly ushered me into the kitchen so I could start my new job, or should I call it a pastime, because for the first month of working in his small kitchen I wasn't paid a bean.

I think that even Pierre, who was seriously passionate about food, was slightly taken aback by my enthusiasm. I worked hard through my breaks and didn't even stop for lunch. I often felt his gaze upon me as I whipped up sauces and speedily prepared dishes, absorbing the pressure of his Michelin-starred restaurant. When he asked me to do some specialities I produced dishes mastered at Gavroche, and that's when the penny dropped. Clearly confused as he watched me rustle up dishes being served by Albert Roux's team, Pierre said, 'Marco, where did you learn those things?'

I turned to my perplexed boss; it was time to come clean. 'I used to work at Gavroche,' I told him and then carried on whipping and speedily preparing.

Although I was thrilled to be working at Tante Claire, I saw many other chefs come and go. In fact, I've never seen staff turnover like the one in Pierre's kitchen. Every week, the brigade went from ten chefs on a Monday to four by Friday, and this is why: at the beginning of the week a batch of six chefs would arrive from France, despatched by one of Pierre's Parisian contacts. They would start off jolly, thrilled and privileged because they were working for the great Monsieur Koffmann. But they soon cracked.

To begin with they couldn't take Pierre's bollockings, his insistence on perfection. Most of the time, Pierre had a big palette knife in his right hand, and chefs who fell behind would get a whack on the arse. 'Is he always like this?' the French lads would whisper to me. Their lives were made even more wretched by the claustrophobic conditions. The kitchen was cramped and our work surface was a big table in the middle. Like sardines in a tin we had to fight for space. As the week went on they would drop out. By Tuesday, we might be one man down, then another would fail to show up on Wednesday; the remaining Frenchmen would invariably break on Thursday. Come the following Monday morning a new batch of chefs would arrive from France, like troops going over the top.

Then came Pierre's day of reckoning– his new recruits failed to make the Channel crossing, I imagine – so he made me an official member of staff. Don't ask me how much he paid, but it was probably pitiful and I was glad of my savings from The Six Bells. French recruits aside, there were now four regulars working at that table in the kitchen: Pierre and his assistant Bruno and then the English contingent, i.e., me and the kitchen porter, Big Barry, whom Pierre adored.

Pierre was a workaholic who got through the day by having three ritualistic tea breaks. Each break lasted precisely five minutes and took place at a specific time – the first was at noon; the second at six forty-five, just before evening service; and the third at the end of evening service at ten thirty. The tea was always made by Big Barry who, as a reward for serving it, was allowed a cuppa himself. No one else in that kitchen was entitled to a tea break. It was a rule that distinguished the boss from his minions.

Pierre 'the Bear' Koffmann
joins me and my fags in 1989.

However, one morning just before midday, I heard the kettle go on and saw Barry reaching for the tea bags when Pierre shocked me by asking, 'Would you like a cup of tea?' It is probably the most common question asked in tea-loving Britain but here, in Koffmann's kitchen, it was a question I had never heard. It was symbolic, a turning point: I felt acknowledged. Positively flattered, I joined Pierre and Barry for a noon cuppa and then, at six forty-five, my self-esteem was boosted once more when Pierre asked those special words, 'Would you like a cup of tea, Marco?' Again, at ten thirty, I was handed a steaming mug of Tetley. I had made it into the inner circle. Tante Claire's elite club had just increased its membership by a third. The duo had become a trio.

Pierre had finally recognised my talents and devotion to the job and what's more, his lovely wife Annie – who ran the show, front of house – took a shining to me and I came to realise that if Annie liked you then her husband would think twice about getting rid of you. However, it was not as easy to endear myself to the other members of the French staff who worked front of house. Traditionally, Pierre's wife had looked after the restaurant, but when I was there she had just had a baby, I think, and so she only came in for a couple of hours each day. This meant the maître d' was running the show. He looked a bit like Dracula and I don't recall him being very friendly to me. I convinced myself that he saw me as the English boy, the one he and the waiters didn't like.

Every day there was a staff lunch before service and everyone would eat the meal in the restaurant, but because I always worked through my breaks, sweeping the back yard or preparing some scallops, I had never gone for lunch. One day, however, Pierre said, 'Leave your work, Marco, and come through for some lunch.' I couldn't say no to the boss so I helped myself to some food from the kitchen and went through to the restaurant to join the rest of the team. The chefs and waiters were all sitting together at a big table but there was no room for me and I was reluctant to ask someone to move up. I started to walk back through to the kitchen – I would have my lunch in there – when I noticed that a smaller table had been laid. One little table with one chair, one napkin, one knife and one fork. It had been laid for me, but there was no way I was going to sit there alone. I'm not having that, I thought, I'm not going to be treated like an idiot. Pierre spotted the problem. 'Everyone move up,' he yelled at the staff. 'Marco, come and sit next to me.' It was the only time I had been in Tante Claire's dining room and it would be a few more years before I could walk in there again, as a paying customer.

After service Pierre would sometimes offer to give me a lift somewhere and I'd ask him to drop me in the King's Road. I might go to the Up All Night, where you could, surprisingly, sit up all night drinking coffee. I met girls and they seemed to find me amusing, but relationships rarely progressed further. My success rate at pulling wasn't great because I didn't have a huge amount of courage when it came to making the first move. I was in the Up All Night with Eddie Davenport, the young clubbing entrepreneur, when he introduced me to a posh girl who I shall call Suzie. She was a beautiful girl, but for weeks nothing happened between us. Sometimes I would stay at Suzie's flat in Chelsea, sleeping on the floor while she was in her bed. Then one night she just came and cuddled up with me and after that we started going out with each other.

I was in the kitchen one lunchtime when Pierre the Bear said, 'Your old boss Albert is here.' I glanced around, expecting to see my former mentor clutching a soup ladle. 'No, he's in the restaurant,' said Pierre. 'He's come for a meal. You can make it for him.' Albert ordered the Gelée de Lapin aux Champignons Sauvages, which, I must say, I went to a lot of trouble to make. I took care to ensure it was pretty and arty, then I placed the dish on the passe for Pierre's approval, but he didn't compliment me on the presentation. Instead, he raised a hand above the plate and brought it crashing down onto the food. Then, as if he was playing a piano concerto with one hand tied behind his back, he used his large fingers to mess up the dish. Rabbit terrine and mushrooms that had once looked glorious became a pile of roughed-up rubbish. He had duffed up my dish.

Without saying a single word, Pierre had told me precisely what he thought of Albert. After his lunch, Albert came into the kitchen. 'What are you doing here?' he said to me. Word had not reached him that I was working with Pierre and he must have thought I had messed up the presentation of his dish, maybe as revenge for the soup-ladle drama.

┌ TEN ┐

Raymond Blanc: the Oxford don

ALBERT ROUX and Pierre Koffmann may have had little time for one another, but they would have both agreed on one thing: discipline was the way to run a kitchen. The prospect of receiving a loud bollocking from either chef forced me to discipline myself: arrive on time, keep surfaces tidy, absorb the pressure and cook well. But there is a major flaw in severe discipline: it suppresses flair, imagination and talent. At Gavroche, remember, Albert was the one who came up with the menus and his brigade of Roux robots didn't dare alter the recipes.

'Do this,' was the command.

'Yes, Chef,' was the response.

I had never really paused to question the screaming and shouting. It seemed natural to me and I had come to accept it. 'Must be prepared to take bollockings,' was part of the job description. But when I was twenty-three years old, after I had done time with Roux and Koffmann, I found myself working for a chef who was soft and inquisitive. He was a man who actually asked for my opinions and who wanted to know about my passion for food. In fact, Raymond Blanc was so enthusiastic and encouraging that I discovered a sense of freedom, and that is when my confidence started to grow. It seemed as if I had done painting by numbers and now I was being given a blank canvas. Or even a Blanc canvas. If I had never worked with Raymond I would never have gone on to achieve my three-star dream.

———

It was Nico Ladenis who, in the winter of 1984, told me about a job going at Le Manoir aux Quat'Saisons, Raymond's country house hotel in Great Milton, some eight miles from Oxford. Nico had called to say that one of Raymond's chefs, Nigel Marriage, had handed in his notice, thereby creating a vacancy. Although Le Manoir had then been open only for about six months, it was doing very well and was destined to win awards and become a huge success. In fact, the hotel's restaurant already had two Michelin stars to its name, as Raymond had been allowed to transfer them from his restaurant Les Quat'Saisons in Oxford.

'You've got to ring Raymond,' insisted Nico, so I made the call and arranged an interview date. Before our meeting, however, I landed the job with Pierre Koffmann at Tante Claire. I was quite happy working with Pierre, but I felt obliged to keep my appointment with Raymond, even though it might lead to my departure from my London job.

My former employer Alan Bennett, who was also now my landlord as I was lodging at his house in Battersea, offered to drive me to the interview. We arrived at Le Manoir, originally Great Milton's manor house, and my first impressions of Raymond were, 'Christ, he's small.' The look on his face said he was thinking, 'Wow, he's big.' I did not get the job there and then. Raymond asked me to fix a date when I could do a two-day trial period in his kitchen.

Although the interview is a blur, I have a vivid, treasured memory of the meal that followed our chat.

———

My chauffeur Alan had been kicking his heels for about an hour while I was being grilled, so to speak, and had developed an appetite. When I said I was ready to leave Alan declared that he had absolutely no intention of driving home until he had lunched in the restaurant. He invited me to be his guest and I accepted.

It was probably the finest meal I had ever eaten and certainly the most expensive. The bill for the pair of us came to £134 (and I wasn't even a drinker in those days). I can see each dish now as if it were on the table in front of me. I started with Terrine of Foie Gras with Leeks, Truffle and Wild Mushrooms; then I had Salad of Offal, which was made up of calf's sweetbreads and calf's brains; as a main course I had Pigeon en Croûte de Sel with a Sauce Périgueux – a Madeira-based sauce with veal jus and chopped truffles; and I ended the feast with a fantastic Soufflé de Pommes.

It wasn't necessarily the ingredients that made the meal so magnificent. As I moved from one course to another, I studied each plate, and then it eventually dawned on me that these were the sort of dishes the big chefs in France were serving. Raymond was clearly more in touch with the development of cuisine in Paris than either Albert or Pierre. He was doing something new and exciting.

Magazines and books had kept me up to date with how the great chefs in Paris were refining the classical dishes, so while Albert was giving his customers classical cuisine – often masculine, hearty dishes like Daube de boeuf – braised cheeks of beef in a robust sauce – Raymond's food was more feminine. The foundations of his food were classically French, but the concept was lighter. There were no full-bodied sauces. Raymond knew that Mother Nature was the real artist.

To illustrate the point let's compare the veal dishes served by Messrs Roux and Blanc:

At Gavroche we did Veau à l'Ananas, which was 140 grams of veal fillet cut into small medallions; put into the pan briefly and then out; a touch of chicken stock into the same pan; a bit of curry sauce and hollandaise in there – you had to work it so it didn't scramble – back in with the veal and then in with the big batons of pineapple; toasted almonds on top and served in a dish with rice on the side.

In contrast, Le Manoir served an Assiette de Veau, which was veal fillet with the spinal cord on top of it, but on the same plate were three slices of brain and three slices of sweetbread. The visual impact was improved because on top of each slice of brain was a mixture of capers, lemon and parsley cooked in butter. And then another touch to the picture: on top of each slice of sweetbread there was a mixture of flaked almonds and pine kernels, which had been ground in butter. Very light.

Raymond not only used more ingredients than his rival Albert Roux, he also invested more energy in the presentation. At Le Manoir six or seven pans were used for one dish, which meant that three main courses could involve twenty pans. The Gavroche's Veau à l'Ananas was all done in one old-fashioned flambé pan.

'What did you think?' asked Alan as we headed down the M40.

'It was visual,' I said. 'There was freshness and lightness but it was so visual.' What I was really saying was, 'I like his style. I want that job.'

A few weeks later I was back at Le Manoir for my trial period. On the first day I worked with Nigel Marriage who, fingers crossed, I would replace. I was also reunited with Stephen Yare, my old friend from Gavroche, who now worked in Raymond's kitchen. On day two Raymond came into the kitchen and said to me, 'I would like you to cook me a meat dish for lunch.' I sensed it was make-or-break time. What would I give him? Or rather, what would I *need* to give him to get the job?

A few weeks earlier I had seen a cookery book that contained dishes by a Michelin-starred French chef called Jacques Maximum. One of the dishes was a tienne of lamb that was sliced and presented on the plate in a circular fan shape. What he had done looked as interesting as pink meat on a plate can look, yet it was clearly enough to inspire me. I thought I would cook the lamb for Raymond's lunch, but I would try to improve on Maximum's idea.

I pan fried the fillet of lamb and cut it into rondelles, just as Maximum had done, arranging it so that in the centre of the plate there was a single circular piece of lamb, with the other pieces fanning out around it. On the outside of the fan I created another circle: a tiny turned potato sat next to a stuffed courgette which was next to an aubergine, then another potato and so on until the circle was complete. I put tomato fondant on the aubergine and maybe on the courgette.

Then I added a couple of black olives to the dish. The plate was now the round border of a symmetrical picture of Provençal-style ingredients. I suppose it was circles within circles. Over the lamb I poured the roasting juices, juices which had been enhanced by rosemary at the end of the cooking to retain the freshness and then, once on the plate, I split the juices with a dash of olive oil.

The plate went out to the restaurant where Raymond was sitting. It came back clean, closely followed by the man who had eaten from it. 'Delicious,' said Raymond, who looked slightly shocked, I think because he had expected me to do a Gavroche-style dish. I was pleased, obviously, that he didn't mention Jacques Maximum and assumed that he thought the whole thing had come out of my head.

But I had tapped into Raymond. When you think about it, the ingredients I had given him were always going to work because we all know that lamb, rosemary and Provençal vegetables go well together. What was significant was what I had done with the ingredients. I had given him a dish that was fresh, light and above all visual. It had everything that he responded to in food. Surely Raymond realised then that I was on the same wavelength as him.

However, he set me another challenge, asking me to cook him a fish dish for his dinner. I could only work with the ingredients that were in the fridges and ended up doing Panaché of Red Mullet and Sea Scallops with a Bouillabaisse Sauce. I can't recall either how I cooked it or how I presented it but I don't remember a complaint from Raymond.

I completed the trial, left on the Saturday, and on the Sunday I got a call from Stephen Yare. He told me that Raymond had served his customers my tienne of lamb as a speciality. I was flattered and then came the offer of the job.

If I was looking to feed my work addiction then I had certainly achieved that at Le Manoir. I would start off on the Sauce and Meat section and signed the standard Manoir staff contract, which meant working a six-day week from January to the end of the year. There were no summer holidays for staff and no Easter breaks. Staff were only allowed to take holiday in the following January, when Le Manoir shut its doors to the public for a fortnight or so.

It was January 1985 and my days of virtual solitude were about to change. Five of us, including Stephen and his brother Desmond – who worked on Pastry – decided to move in together, and we went to inspect The Bridge Inn in nearby Wheatley. Set beside the river, it seemed nice enough. We did a deal with the owner, took the rooms for a year and I nabbed the only one that had an en-suite bathroom. 'We have a nightclub here on Fridays and Saturdays,' said the owner as he was handing us the keys, 'and there's an admission charge. But as you're living here you won't need to pay. You can get in for nothing.' We beamed with glee. It was as if we had just been awarded lifetime membership of an exclusive club in Mayfair.

After our first night we compared notes and all agreed that the place was overrun with mice. From then on we referred to our new home as either the Mouse House or, inspired by our place of work, Maison Mouse.

After our first Friday at work we returned late at night, pretty shattered. Deafening music blared from Maison Mouse. It was Fingles, the nightclub to which we got free entry. The club was directly beneath my bedroom and the ear-splitting amplifiers rattled everything in the room, including me. I talked to the other lads and together we decided to take advantage of the free admission.

Fingles was the roughest nightclub in history. The blokes were rough, the girls were rough and the doormen were rough. They were all out to get pissed, get shagged and have a fight. Fingles was a rat-hole in the Mouse House. It took ten minutes to get from the table to the bar, not because there was a sea of people to push through but because the floor was littered with so much chewing gum you had to stop every three paces to peel the goo from your heels otherwise you'd be glued to the carpet. Young, drunk lunatics pogoed along to Duran Duran's 'Wild Boys', and there were cheers as the DJ played Madonna – little did I know that years later she would be a dear friend. Every now and again a punch-up would erupt and the 'dancers' would form a ring around the brawlers.

To think that just days earlier we had gratefully clutched the hand of the owner as he awarded us VIP status. Now we wanted to throttle him. On Friday and Saturday nights, I would sit in Fingles with my Coca-Cola, observing the show. The thud of the music meant that Stephen and I became expert lip readers. And I never scored. I was still far too inept at chatting up birds and anyway, none of the Fingles girls ever walked over to my table; perhaps the chewing-gummed floor prevented them making the journey. In Chelsea I'd seen a bit of posh, but the Fingles mob reminded me of the Leeds I'd been happy to leave behind. It seemed strange that I had done time in the King's Road, the buzziest place in Britain, and was now enduring a rather dull social life of which the highlight was a darts match in the local pub. There was one positive. During my days in Oxford I met Piers Adam one night in Brown's, a burgers-and-steaks restaurant that's still in business. Piers was standing at the bar, surrounded by beautiful girls, and introduced himself. He went on to become a highly successful nightclub impresario and we are still friends to this day and have been business partners. The fact is, I had no real desire to socialise. If I could have been in the kitchen at two in the morning, that is where I would have been.

Somewhere along the way, it seemed, I had developed a reputation for being oblivious to bollockings. Stephen told me how

Raymond had announced my arrival during his Christmas speech, 'We have a new boy starting next month. His name is Marco White and he has worked for Albert Roux, Pierre Koffmann and Nico Ladenis. None of them could break him.'

Raymond was certainly not going to be the one to break me. Though gifted in many ways, he desperately lacked the authority of his Michelin-starred rivals. He was like the headmaster who was too kind to discipline the wayward miscreants in his 17-strong brigade.

Stephen and I, as well as the other Roux robots who had washed up at Le Manoir, took advantage of Chef's gentle nature. We were never foolish enough to be ill-prepared for service, but when the opportunity arose we were like kids who had been let loose in the playground. Stuck in the middle of nowhere, we craved light relief, practical jokes and fun. I would answer the kitchen phone by pretending to be an answer phone. 'Please leave a message after the tone,' I'd say, before letting out a high-pitched shriek to give the caller a migraine.

It was that sort of immature humour, sometimes cruel and merciless. A catering college student arrived one day to do a bit of work experience and the all-male brigade decided – in a typically childish way – that she was the size of a bear. The poor girl was given the chore of shelling peas for a day, and as she got on with this menial task the boys, one by one, ambled past her putting stickers on her back. After a couple of hours her back was plastered with ridiculous messages: 'Do not feed the bear', 'I love Raymond', that sort of thing. Raymond wandered into the kitchen and was horrified when he saw the sticker-covered student but he didn't give us a bollocking. Gentleman that he is, he positioned himself next to the lass, saying something like, 'Continue ... I just want to see how you're getting on,' while he removed the stickers, one by one, so she would never know of our wickedness. It just wouldn't have happened at Gavroche.

Raymond's wife Jenny, who ran the business with him, objected to the tribe's boisterousness. She would come into the kitchen and raise her nose at us. 'You lot behave like farmyard animals,' she'd say, and we'd answer with a 'Moooooo!' and 'Oink! Oink!' and 'Baa! Baa!'

Raymond tolerated our wildness, but looking back I can see that it was not what he needed at the time. His marriage to Jenny was not flourishing like the couple's business and they would later divorce. He must have been burdened by the preoccupations of his personal life, although it was a subject he never discussed with the staff.

There were weekly rows between Raymond, Jenny and the maître d'. Invariably, every Sunday the three of them would have an argument in front of the passe and the boys would bend down under the kitchen table and start banging the pans, egging Raymond to have a punch-up with the maître d'. 'Chin him, Chef. Chin him,' we'd shout. 'Hit him. Don't take any shit.'

Raymond, it might surprise you to know, was rarely in the kitchen. Unlike my former bosses, he did not stand at the passe barking out the orders during service. He preferred instead to stay front of house, schmoozing his guests. Charming and charismatic, he was the perfect host. When he did enter the kitchen he tended to alternate between being a genius and an unintentional comedian.

When he was at his best he was the finest cook I have ever worked with. Note that I didn't say finest *chef* but finest *cook*, and there's a big difference. Albert Roux was a chef who could manage a kitchen and its staff. Albert could drive his troops forward, while Raymond lacked that quality. He was a three-star chef who never got his three stars.

When he wasn't being a genius cook, he was a comedy act; a funny, accident-prone figure – like Peter Sellers as Inspector Clouseau. He would often clumsily bang and crash into people and things before cursing at himself in his native tongue. When he came through the doors from the restaurant into the kitchen his team could expect another instalment of slapstick.

I remember him rushing into the kitchen and crashing head-first into a waiter carrying a tray laden with glasses, sending everything soaring into the air. He also once set the grill alight when he forgot

Me and the genius, Raymond Blanc. He's laughing so I must have been reflecting on what it was like to work in his kitchen.

he was toasting almonds. And on another occasion he swivelled around by the kitchen stove and smashed his skull against a hanging saucepan – he had to lie down in a dark room because he was seeing stars and didn't resurface until the following morning.

'Take a seat, boys,' Raymond instructed one morning and the brigade crammed onto the bench that lined one of the kitchen walls. He thought he would teach us how to make raspberry jam. The jam was already bubbling in a barrel-sized pan, which he had positioned on top of two wooden spoons so it didn't directly touch the surface of the stove. He was cooking on a very slow heat, in other words. For a moment it looked impressive, but then he started fiddling with the pan and suddenly it toppled onto the floor. We all sat there, transfixed by the sight of jam seeping across the kitchen floor like lava from a volcano. With the kitchen gradually flooding in jam, Raymond hopped kangaroo-style over the molten mass, crying out to the kitchen porter, 'Don't just stand there, get the mop.'

Most of the time, though, he avoided the hanging saucepans, molten jam and flying glass, and that's when I really learnt from him. He was masterful and magical. And what's even more remarkable is that Raymond never set out to be a chef. After leaving his home near the French–Swiss border in the early seventies he had started out as a waiter in Britain. He found himself in Oxford, cooking at a restaurant called Les Quat'Saisons, and not only cooking but cooking well enough to win two Michelin stars. He had been canny enough to buy Great Milton's fifteenth-century manor house and had impressive plans to enlarge it. When I was at Le Manoir it had a dozen bedrooms, but today it has thirty-two – and probably as many awards.

Although his creative influence was sporadic it was more often than not inspired. He would get an idea for something – a vision – and then he would throw on an apron and get to work. I would watch and absorb. He showed me how to question every little part of creating a dish and taught me how to question my palate. A typical Raymond lesson would go like this, 'Say you take two decilitres of chicken stock in two different pans. You reduce one down quickly, the other slowly. The taste of each stock is completely different because if you reduce something rapidly you retain the flavour. By reducing it slowly it stews and you lose freshness and sharpness.'

Or he might say, 'If you're making a stock, taste it every fifteen minutes and try to understand what's happening in that pan. Try to understand how the taste is developing. You'll get to a point where it's delicious and if you let it cook too long it will start to die.' When most people make a lamb stock they throw in carrots, celery, onions and in the end it doesn't taste of lamb. At Manoir we'd use lamb bones roasted with caramelised onions and simply cover those two ingredients with water and a generous dollop of veal jus; it allowed the flavour of the lamb to come through in the sauce.

Then there was the question of seasoning food. 'Don't just chuck in some salt and think that you've seasoned it,' he'd say. 'Taste it, taste it, taste it. Get inside the food.'

When people talk about seasoning they usually mean adding salt and pepper. Seasoning to me is adding salt. Salt enhances the flavour of the ingredients. Pepper changes the flavour. I very rarely season a sauce with pepper. I was taught to monter au beurre, where you use butter to emulsify the sauce at the end of cooking. The idea is to enrich it. But I stopped doing that because in my opinion butter has a very strong flavour of its own. By putting butter into a pigeon jus or a lamb jus, you're adding another flavour and detracting from the natural flavour of the juices. So if I ever used anything, I would use a little bit of cream to stabilise because cream is a neutral; it doesn't have a flavour.

Precision was the name of the game; a crucial factor in the creation of Blanc's Michelin-standard dishes. If Raymond made a jus de pigeon, it was twenty minutes exactly, rather than *about* twenty minutes. I could feel my confidence growing. 'Can you make me an asparagus mousse?' he asked me one day. I made the mousse and sent it through to his table in the dining room. I was smoking a Marlboro outside when Raymond suddenly came dashing through the kitchen's back doorway, full of excitement. 'The mousse,' he said to me, 'it's spectacular. How did you make it?'

'With chicken, Chef. I made it with asparagus and chicken.' He grabbed my arm and steered me back into the kitchen. 'Make it again,' he said and I had to re-produce the dish in front of Raymond, who studied every detail, nodding along as he made mental notes. The traditional ingredients of an asparagus mousse would be asparagus, eggs, a little bit of milk and then some cream to lighten it. I had a problem with this traditional recipe because there's no texture or body. What I had done for Raymond was use chicken to give it the two features I felt were missing. On top of that, the chicken would provide flavour. I put asparagus, raw chicken and egg white into a liquidiser, then sieved it and added a little cream before cooking. That mousse – *Chartreuse d'Asperges with Truffles* – became one of Le Manoir's specialities.

Raymond not only encouraged me to share my knowledge and thoughts about food, I could also get away with a little cheekiness, but there were limits. If I pushed it too far I could seriously wind him up. I remember a Saudi prince coming for lunch one day and requesting a green salad. Raymond insisted he would make it himself and scampered into the vegetable garden, returning laden with lettuces. He dressed the vegetables beautifully, but a minute or two after the plate was sent out it came back again. 'The lettuce is gritty,' explained the maître d'. Raymond had forgotten to wash it. I followed him around the kitchen, clutching the rejected plate and saying, 'Chef, they've sent the salad back. Chef, they've sent the salad back.'

Eventually Raymond had had enough of me. I had crossed the line. 'Yes,' he snapped and then glared. 'I know they've sent the fucking salad back.'

I crossed that line again when a film crew arrived at Le Manoir to make a programme called *Take Six Chefs*. Raymond thought he would treat them to a special late lunch in the restaurant when it had emptied of paying guests and he asked me to do the main course. I served plain lasagne – the staff lunch – to Raymond and his guests, but I served it on exquisite plates. 'Use the cloches,' I told the maître d'. The plates were carried out and I could see Raymond and his guests eyeing up the cloches and thinking, What are we getting? As the cloches were raised, jaws dropped when they saw the boring pasta dish. Raymond sprinted into the kitchen. 'What are you trying to do?' he screamed. 'Give me a fucking heart attack? I'm trying to impress them and look what you've given them, a staff meal.'

'You didn't tell us what you wanted, Chef,' I replied. 'You just said, "Feed us".'

Impressing the *Take Six* crew was one thing, but Raymond was never more excited than at the prospect of cooking for his rival Albert Roux. 'We have had a booking from a Monsieur Roux,' Raymond told the brigade late one afternoon. 'Albert is coming to Le Manoir tomorrow.' When we all arrived for work at 8.45 the following morning there was a mountain of mucky pots and pans rising from the sink to the ceiling and there was Raymond, manic and grimy, grafting away as he finished off dozens of canapés and petits fours. 'This is the day Albert comes,' he told us, as if we could have forgotten. I'm sorry to say that Raymond's efforts were in vain. The Roux who arrived for lunch that day was neither Albert nor a chef.

ELEVEN

White-balled

THE WHISTLE did not leave Raymond's mouth. He made up for his lack of control in the kitchen here on the village green as he refereed our staff football match. The chef was now Ref. He bit the whistle, sucked it and every ten seconds blew hard, piercing the blissful tranquillity of Great Milton with its high-pitched rattle. On one side were Le Manoir's French waiters, with the other team being made up of the restaurant's chefs, who were mostly Brits. Raymond, as you can imagine, was doing all he could to swing the game for his fellow countrymen.

It seemed like every time the kitchen brigade got the ball Raymond's cheeks would puff up and we'd hear the dreaded shriek of his whistle. It didn't matter whether or not we'd fouled, Raymond would stop play to award free kicks to the waiters and wave cards at the chefs with the agility of a croupier.

'This is crazy, Chef,' I shouted a few minutes into the second half. 'You're blowing the whistle every two seconds. You're nuts.'

He flipped. For a second or two he was speechless, perhaps pondering my impudence. Then, crimson-faced, he raised an arm and pointed towards the sidelines. I thought I was about to be sent off, but instead he yelled, 'You are sacked.' I was astonished. The huddle of villagers who had gathered to watch the game started muttering. Great Milton had never known such drama.

I repeated the word back to Raymond, 'Sacked?' It was all too comical for words, and when I started to snigger Raymond looked puzzled.

'Why are you laughing at me, Marco?'

'Because when I get back to London I'll tell Albert that I was sacked for playing football and he's going to think you're a lunatic.'

As I marched off the pitch I heard him bark, 'In my office at five thirty.' I got changed and contemplated my next step in catering. It would be unfair if I lost my job but I'd been around long enough to witness many bizarre and swift departures. I tried to reflect on the match rather than my future. Although it had been billed as the English versus the French it was something akin to Millwall (chefs) versus Chelsea (waiters). In the kitchen we'd come up with a motto, an adage that explained our tactics: 'The ball might go past but never the player'. The waiters had certainly sustained a few injuries and maybe Raymond was right to be so whistle-happy.

At 5.30 I went along to Raymond's office, which was next to the kitchen. It was not what the average person would describe as an office. Barely larger than a broom cupboard, it accommodated Raymond's tiny desk and chair, and he had to share the space with boxes of dried goods. 'Come in, Marco. Close the door.' Like a rebel in the head's office, I stood in front of Raymond's desk. I had to stand because the carton-sized room didn't allow space for a second chair. Would this be it? Was I to get my P45 for calling him crazy on the pitch? Raymond, however, was remorseful and drained of rage. 'Let's forget about what happened in the football game,' he said and we shook hands.

I'd got my job back. In service that evening and for a few days afterwards, the waiters were limping like walking wounded. Diners being greeted by black-eyed Frenchmen must have felt as though they'd stepped into A&E at Oxford General. The waiters never mentioned a re-match, though the staff at a rough hotel up the road were keen to take us on. They challenged us to a match on the village green and mistakenly assumed we were a bunch of fairies because we worked in a hotel with pink parasols in the garden. We faced each other on the pitch; they were all pristine in matching kit while our brigade was a shambles in bits and bobs, ragged T-shirts, putrid socks and shorts. We stuck to our motto – the ball might go past but never the player – and hammered them, 3-1.

Raymond and I quickly forgot the 'sacking' incident. In a way, it strengthened our relationship and we became good friends. He had given up trying to break me, if indeed he had ever really intended to. 'To break you,' he once told me, 'you need an iron bar across your back.' I became the only member of the brigade to socialise with him and we'd go into Oxford to chat over coffee. He was a natural wit, deep and philosophical, and he trusted me. Not all of the chefs in his brigade were given the freedom to come up with specialities, so the way in which he treated me was like a status symbol. I felt important. And even more so when Club des Cent, a group of one hundred gourmets, held a dinner at Le Manoir and Raymond put two of my specialities – my asparagus mousse and a pig's trotter dish – on the menu.

There were signs, too, that he depended on me. The kitchen phone rang one day and it was the police asking for me. In London seven months earlier I had witnessed a stabbing in a fishmonger's shop and now Fulham CID were saying I would have to be in court in two hours because I was the only witness. I said, 'That's impossible. I'm about to do my lunch service and I can't get there in time.' I was told that if I refused to go a police car would be sent to the restaurant and I would be arrested. I cupped the receiver as I told Raymond the problem.

He took the phone. 'Hello. I'm Raymond Blanc, proprietor of Le Manoir aux Quat'Saisons,' he began. 'It is impossible that Marco comes to court today because he is working. We are very busy and he is about to do his lunch service so he just can't get there.' He might have been able to pull strings with PC Plod in Great Milton but would the big boys at Fulham CID be so easily impressed? Raymond paused and I can't imagine what fearsome words he heard coming back at him, though his next remark was conveyed with utter politeness in a much gentler tone, 'Not a problem, sir. I shall arrange a car immediately and make sure he is there for two o'clock.'

Gather round for a quick lesson: which tastes more of a tomato, a cooked tomato or a raw tomato? Get a tomato, cut it up and put one half under the grill. Have a bite of the raw tomato, nice isn't it? Now taste the grilled tomato.

So which one tastes more of tomato? Answer: the cooked one because by cooking it you've removed the water content, and by removing the water you've removed the acidity and brought through the natural sweetness of the tomato. Cook an onion and you'll bring out more flavour for the same reason: because you're removing the acidity and water content. Whether you want to eat a raw tomato or a raw onion is irrelevant. What's got more flavour – a raisin or a grape? A raisin because it is condensed. All that sugar is condensed. A prune or a plum? Yes, a prune. Now you've got it …

At Le Manoir, Stephen Yare and I controlled the place, ruled the roost. Our bond, if you like, was that we had come from the same world. And at Le Manoir we were synchronised. If I did Fish, Stephen did Meat; if I did Meat then Stephen did Fish. That's all we ever did. We worked well together, were never disjointed and we respected each other.

There was a problem with Le Manoir's style of cooking. Up to thirty or forty covers and it was most probably the finest restaurant in Britain. But when we had eighty or ninety covers the system fell apart because the food was too complex. Each dish comprised so many components and different cooking techniques that it was extremely difficult to keep up. If you were doing a table of two it was OK, but if you were doing a table of eight then you could be stretchered.

You can afford to be frilly and artistic with cold food because it can be prepared before service, but when you're dealing with hot food it's a different story and there wasn't much chance of every component being cooked perfectly or presented in the way Raymond had intended. When we were doing big numbers the cracks were visible. Someone might forget to put an ingredient on the plate, or customers would end up waiting a long time for their food. It goes back to my point about consistency. At forty covers the food was consistently good but by eighty covers it had lost that consistency and consistency is the thing that might have taken Raymond from two stars to three.

To make matters worse, Raymond would occasionally come into the kitchen. For all his elements of genius and spontaneity, he had an annoying habit of changing things at the last minute – adding an ingredient, playing around with the picture on the plate – in the middle of service. 'I don't like the presentation,' he might say.

If Raymond asked if you were OK the response had to be, 'I'm fine, Chef.' I didn't want him joining in. I kept my surfaces clean and tidy and that way Raymond thought I was all right. If there was mess all over the place, he reckoned I was in need of assistance. I was on Meat once when I sensed his presence and heard that chilling question, 'Can I help you?'

'Can you do the duck please, Chef?'

'Where is it, Marco?'

'In the oven, Chef.'

Raymond bent down, removed the pan from the oven and placed it on the stove. Then he took the duck from the pan, chopped up the bird, turned around without the cloth and seized the scorching pan handle with his bare hands. His palm sizzled and Raymond crouched down in agony. He had welded himself to the blisteringly hot metal. Even the customers in the restaurant must have heard his torture-chamber screams of misery. The skin on his palm rapidly tightened and I zoomed in for an inspection of the claw. In the centre of his purple palm there was a white dot, left by the hole where the handle hung from a hook. I feel for him now, but at the time it was the sort of Raymond episode that made the brigade chortle.

Raymond came into the kitchen one day, shortly before lunch service on a Sunday, and headed towards Duncan Walker, who was on Hot Starters and just about to slice the Terrine de Poireaux et St Jacques. The terrine is straightforward enough in terms of preparation – mix it, mould it, steam it in between paper, add a bit of beurre blanc – but sliced too slowly or too quickly and the whole thing will collapse. You have to get it just right. Duncan started to slice, with Raymond watching from just a few inches away, when, predictably, the terrine started to cave in. Raymond must have been having a bad day and the sight of the sinking terrine was just too much. He wrapped his fingers around Duncan's ox-like neck and spat out the words, 'You massacred my terrine. You massacred my terrine.'

Duncan stood up to his full height of six foot and Raymond's fingers uncurled themselves, his grip loosening. 'Bollocks,' said Duncan, whipping off his apron, 'and bollocks to your job.' He chucked the apron at Raymond's chest and started to motor out of the kitchen. Raymond grabbed Duncan's arm to stop him leaving, but the beast was too powerful. The boss was dragged along the floor, almost as if he was waterskiing. Raymond, defeated, turned to me. 'That's not good, Chef,' I said.

Raymond, hair ruffled, said, 'What's not good?'

'We've got no one on Hot Starters and nearly a hundred are booked.' So Raymond had to do Hot Starters.

Apart from Stephen, I made another good friend while at Le Manoir. One morning in June I was the first in the kitchen and there was this lad, shelling peas, the sort of menial chore I had done in my first job at the Hotel St George in Harrogate. I was intrigued by him because it was a hot day but he was wearing a woolly jumper.

'Who are you?' I asked.

'Heston.'

'What are you doing?'

'I'm just here on work experience because I like cooking.'

'Take off your jumper, Heston,' I said. 'I'll give you an apron.' That's how I met Heston Blumenthal. He tells the story slightly differently. In his account, he was working in the kitchen with a French chef who was trying to pick a fight with him. Apparently I said to Heston, 'You don't want to work with the French. Come and join the English.' He stopped what he was doing and came to work with me on my section.

He spent about a week working alongside me in the kitchen and says that on the second day he saw me fighting with a waiter. Again, I don't remember it. According to Heston, the waiter was clinging onto the work surface and I was trying to drag him out of the kitchen, but he wouldn't loosen his grasp. Anyway, Heston seemed keen enough, but after his stint of work experience he decided cooking was not for him and went to work for his father's business.

It would be a few years before Heston re-assessed his ambitions and we were reunited when I gave him a job in the kitchen at The Canteen. And it would be a few more years before our memorable meeting when we talked about a restaurant he was going to buy (with the help of his Dad) and wondered what it should be called. 'Why not call it The Fat Duck?' I suggested, 'because then its address will be The Fat Duck, Bray-on-Thames, and everyone will think it's got a view of the river. When they arrive and see that it hasn't, they'll hardly turn round and go home.' He took my advice and has since won three Michelin stars for The Fat Duck as well as the accolade of being voted the best restaurant in Europe. Oh, and he's got an OBE.

During those summer months the rest of the world was talking about that global jukebox Live Aid, but at Le Manoir we were more excited about the cover coming off the swimming pool. If staff handed in their notice they were carried past Raymond's cherished vegetable garden, through the grounds, squealing and kicking, and chucked fully clothed into the pool. Inevitably, it went too far.

I can still see the look of horror on Jenny Blanc's face as she stood at the side of the pool trying to absorb the vision before her: chefs and waiters ducking each other in the water (the English versus the French again). 'What's going on?' she yelled. 'We haven't even finished serving the customers.'

Raymond, however, enjoyed the ritual and once led the pack towards the duck pond, suggesting it was a better place for a dunking. It was a wild scrap, with Chef pinning himself to the pond's surrounding wall so he didn't end up in the water. The soft headmaster had succumbed. There at the duck pond, Raymond Blanc was being as childish and silly as all his wild schoolboys. It would have made a lovely picture, with the fitting caption, 'If you can't beat 'em ... '

TWELVE

Coming home

RAYMOND kept a camera by the passe with which he would photograph the new dishes created so the brigade could copy the presentation from the pictures. Quite clever, really. Before leaving Le Manoir, Stephen and I thought we would use the camera to take some snaps of each other, little mementoes by which Raymond could remember us. When it was my turn to pose I got a pig's trotter, sat on the butcher's block, unzipped my flies and positioned the trotter so it was protruding from my crotch and resting on my thigh. In terms of maturity, Stephen and I had a long way to go.

We had reckoned on Raymond getting the film developed once we had left Le Manoir, but we realised our timing had been wrong when he stormed into the kitchen clutching a set of photographs. 'You two, my office,' he yelled, jabbing a finger towards us. I don't think I had ever seen him so angry. The three of us crammed into his miniature office and Stephen and I studied the floor while Raymond started, 'Fucking hell, boys. I took the film to the chemists. The lady there is very sweet and we had a nice chat. And then I go to pick up the pictures and she's laughing at me.'

At this point he lobbed the envelope of photographs that he'd been clutching, and as it landed on our side of the desk the snaps spilled out. I glanced down at them.

———

The trotter's resemblance to a gigantic human penis was astonishing. 'Sorry, Chef,' I said, and Stephen feigned regret as well.

'And you, Marco' said Raymond, his voice a little softer, more caring. 'Now I know why you can't get a girlfriend with something that size ...'

A year at Le Manoir was enough. Around about Christmas 1985, when my contract was coming to an end, I took stock of my life. The best chefs in Britain had trained me, but I suppose I had always been intrigued by the great chefs in France, men I had never met. When I looked at a cookery book that had been produced by one of these Paris-based Michelin-starred masters I was like a child engrossed in a fantastic fairy story. Paris was the magical kingdom. I should go there. Acquiring knowledge of cooking was far more important than staying in a job simply to rise through the ranks.

So I devised a plan which, on reflection, was not particularly well thought out. In twelve words the plan was: Go to Paris, knock on kitchen doors and ask for a job. After all, my knuckles had got me into this profession at The George, Gavroche and Tante Claire.

I phoned my Battersea-based friend Alan Bennett, who lived above his restaurant, Lampwick's, and asked whether he'd mind if I stayed at his place for a week before heading down to Dover for the cross-Channel ferry. My journey, however, contained a secret destination. What happened next has echoes of the way in which I got my job at Gavroche after missing the coach back to Leeds. If I hadn't stopped off to stay with Alan then I would never have ended up with Harveys, the restaurant that launched my career, changed my life and transformed me into the so-called rock-star chef.

It was a chilly January day in 1986 when I arrived in Battersea and, following Alan's instructions, I collected the keys from the blacksmith's beside Lampwick's. But once inside the flat I realised something was wrong: all the furniture had been removed except for a TV, a three-piece suite and a desk. When Alan returned home he made the tea, sat me down and told me the story. His marriage had collapsed, he said, and his wife had left him. She had taken the kids, along with most of the furniture. Emotionally, the man was on his knees.

Business wasn't good. Lampwick's was in Queenstown Road, about a mile from Chelsea Bridge, and in the same road there were two Michelin-starred restaurants: Nico Ladenis's Chez Nico; and L'Arlequin where the chef was Christian Delteuil, the same chef who had interviewed me for a job at Chewton Glen back in 1981.

At weekends Lampwick's snatched the punters who couldn't get a table at either of Alan's impressive neighbours, but on weeknights it was quiet.

In addition, Alan was drinking heavily – restaurateurs with sorrows to drown don't have to travel far for their next drink. I felt desperately sorry for him and when he started to say, 'I'm in the shit. If you fancy staying on …' I could see what was coming and jumped in with, 'Well, let's see. I mean, I can work for a bit to help out.'

I revised my plan. OK, I convinced myself that I had revised my plan: work for nothing at Lampwick's and do a bit of work in Nico's kitchen; then when Alan was on the mend, I would be on that ferry to Calais. Give it a few weeks. Six months later I was still at Lampwick's, and as I was refusing to take a wage from Alan, I had chewed my way through my savings from Le Manoir. I would have to wait more than a decade to see Paris.

I had come from Le Manoir's seventeen-strong brigade, but in the kitchen at Lampwick's there were just three chefs, which included an assistant chef called Sian and the head chef, young Martin Blunos. Highly talented, hard-working and keen to learn, Martin had worked under Alan when the latter was head chef at a restaurant in Covent Garden. Although Alan was a chef by profession he tended not to interfere in the kitchen at Lampwick's, remaining mostly front of house, drinking with the regulars.

Martin was cooking classical French food, and I brought in my experience and, in particular, the special Manoir touch. So I would do

Terrine of Leeks and Foie Gras for starters, maybe Pigeon en Vesie (pigeon cooked in a pig's bladder) as a main course and for dessert I might do Terrine of Fruits. Martin was sponge-like, absorbing every detail of each dish as I showed him how it was created. He has since said it was as if Roux, Koffmann and Blanc were there in his kitchen, giving him a lesson.

I taught him how to do Pigeon en Croûte de Sel, which I'd first had at Le Manoir on the day of my job interview. Done well it's a superb dish. The pigeon is gutted, trimmed, stuffed with thyme, then sealed and left to get cold. Then you make a salt pastry – salt, flour, egg whites – let it rest, roll it half an inch thick and mould it around the bird, carefully creating a pigeon shape. The excess pastry is used to make a little head with a small beak, with cloves for the pigeon's eyes. The whole thing is brushed with egg white, and sea salt is sprinkled on the breast part of the pastry, so that as the salt bakes it colours the egg. It ends up with a varnished oak appearance. At Le Manoir the dish was carved at the table. The pastry head was removed and put to the side of the plate like a garnish; then the pastry body was cut so that the herby aroma steamed out to whet the appetite.

'We haven't got the space to carve it and we haven't got the staff,' said Martin.

'We must,' I told him. 'That's the way they do it at Le Manoir.' And we did.

It's not surprising that Martin went on to become a two-star Michelin chef with his restaurant in Bath, Lettonie, and more recently he won a star for the Lygon Arms in Worcestershire. He was passionate about food at Lampwick's, but he was more fascinated by his assistant Sian. The couple went on to marry and have a family together. Martin says his memories of working with me include the times before service when we changed into our chefs' whites. Real chefs don't wear underpants because working in hot kitchens can leave you with a painful condition known in the profession as Chef's Arse, caused by over-sweating. Anyway, Martin remembers me showing him my testicles as we got changed, and that is what first springs to his mind when the name Marco Pierre White is mentioned.

Meanwhile, Suzie – the girl I met at Up All Night before going to Le Manoir – came back into my life. With some style, I might add. I woke up in the middle of the night and she was sitting on the end of my bed. I said, 'Suzie, what are you doing here?' She had put her hand through the letterbox and opened the door. She said, 'I want to go to Yorkshire with you.'

'When?' I asked rather than why.

'Now.'

She didn't seem quite right but I agreed to go with her. It seemed like an adventure, something spontaneous. We pulled into a petrol station near Selby on the A1 and she went into the shop. I opened up the glove compartment and all these drugs fell out. Cocaine, speed, God knows what the drugs were but they were drugs. So when she got back in I said, 'What the fuck is this?' She went ballistic and told me to hand them over. I refused. She got out of the car, so I followed and put her back in it, then we drove off. There was a nationwide police manhunt going on at the time and I think someone must have seen me pushing Suzie into the car and suspected I was a kidnapper. We were half a mile from the petrol station when police cars surrounded us. I had to stuff Suzie's haul down the front of my trousers and no arrests were made. Suzie soon disappeared from my life.

I found a new girlfriend. Lowri-Ann Richards was three or four years older than me and a card-carrying member of the Chelsea set. LA, as she was known, was also something of a starlet. As previously mentioned, I had met her a few years earlier, before I left for Le Manoir, when she was going out with Robert Pereno. LA and Robert had been in a band called Shock before setting up another group, Pleasure and the Beast – LA, in her revealing outfits, was the pleasure to Robert's beast.

They released a single called 'Dr Sex' but chances are you've never heard it. While they couldn't crack the charts, LA and Robert were revered in the King's Road as members of the hierarchy. Pleasure and the Beast were among the New Romantics who used to play at the highly trendy Blitz club, where, incidentally, a certain George O'Dowd worked as a cloakroom attendant before going on to become Boy George. Their stage performance was raunchy, bordering on outrageous, though they abandoned an Apache dance routine after Robert accidentally broke LA's arm while trying to impress the audience by throwing her about.

LA was a confident girl. She was also an actress, stage-work mostly but she had appeared (as Jane) in the 1980 movie *Breaking Glass*, which starred the singer Hazel O'Connor and was a cult classic, a sort of punk version of *A Star is Born*. Years later LA was a Welsh Teletubby, I think.

At the time, though, she was just what I needed. There had been a year of celibacy at Le Manoir and I was craving a bit of attention: it was a draining experience mothering poor Alan. Finances weren't great and I needed stability in my life. LA was a caring person and, behind the façade of Chelsea vixen, she was utterly polite and the type of girl who would charm your parents.

She brought fun into my life. Together we would go to parties, bars and clubs, with a mutual physical attraction holding the relationship together. When she was 'resting', as they say in the acting profession, she earned a living serving customers at Joe's Brasserie in Battersea, and I bumped into her at Joe's after a session in the Lampwick's kitchen. 'Didn't you used to go out with Robert Pereno?' I asked, and that's how it started. And when she landed a part I would be there in the audience. I went to see her in a show at the Players' Theatre and when she did panto in Swindon I had a seat in the stalls.

LA invited me to move in to her place, a three-bedroom flat, and I hastily packed my trunk and escaped Alan's sparsely furnished pad. We shared the flat with her sister, Morfudd, who was a maître d' in a West End restaurant, and our home was a five-minute stroll from Lampwick's, in the appropriately named Sisters Avenue.

It was a good time to live south of the river. The phrase Yuppie had yet to be coined, but nevertheless young upwardly mobile professionals were settling in up-and-coming areas like Clapham, Wandsworth and Battersea. They weren't just flash City blokes in chalky pinstripe suits; they were any young men and women making a bit of cash and living one big party. They worked hard and played harder, drinking and eating to excess, and then using their staff expense accounts to reclaim the cost of their exuberance. Their parents had lived the swinging sixties, but these kids were swinging even more than their parents. These young professionals liked Chelsea – many of them had grown up there – but the property there was too expensive, so they crossed over to the south side of the Thames where they could get more for their money. They flooded in, clutching their beloved copies of *The Sloane Ranger Handbook* and chuffed that they were still so close to Peter Jones and the bustling King's Road. All of a sudden SW11 was a cool place to live and its popularity sent property prices booming. I remember one friend buying a two-bed flat in Battersea for £25,000 and selling it eighteen months later for £80,000.

It was an exciting time in my life and my food was being noticed. Fay Maschler, the *Evening Standard*'s restaurant critic, came for dinner one night and gave me my first review. She was quite polite about the food but I have no recollection of what I must have done for her to describe me as 'the volatile but rather beautiful Marco, his intensity can glaze a crème brûlée from ten yards'.

Meanwhile, that black cloud finally showed signs of shifting from its seemingly fixed position above Alan's head. Two of Lampwick's regulars, a pair of property entrepreneurs, had asked Alan to go into business with them. Nigel Platts-Martin and Richard Carr had bought a wine bar called Harvey's, which served nothing more ambitious than well-cooked burgers to a hungover crowd that craved comfort food. Harvey's was in a good location, amid a pretty parade of Victorian shops on Bellevue Road, a couple of miles from Lampwick's, and it overlooked Wandsworth Common. Nigel and Richard intended to split the business three ways, the idea being that

Alan would be the head chef, or that they'd hire Martin to run the kitchen. Grasping for a chance to improve his wretched existence, Alan agreed to the deal. He closed Lampwick's in the summer of 1986, which of course meant that I had lost a job, though I was pleased for my friend. The new venture was going to bring him the fresh start he so badly needed.

I got a job at Leoni's Quo Vadis, an Italian restaurant in Soho, which paid me the extraordinarily high salary of £350 a week (though years later it would pay me considerably more than that when I co-owned it with the PR gurus Matthew Freud and Johnny Kennedy and the artist Damien Hirst).

The head chef at Quo Vadis was an old boy known only as Signor Zucchoni. He had been cooking the same sort of Italian trattoria-style dishes for forty years and cooking them very well. He was a traditionalist in a tall white hat and to begin with he viewed me as some sort of peculiar beast. There were moments when I used to catch him studying me with a look of horror in his eyes. He was thinking, 'Big man with long hair, not right.'

I endeared myself to Signor Zucchoni by working very hard. Then when he asked about my background – 'How come you godda name like Marco'– I explained that I was half Italian and he smiled warmly, the same sort of smile that had crossed Danny Crow's face at Gavroche when I had mentioned my Italian roots. There was another way in which I won admiration from the boss and his assistant, Pepe. They both enjoyed a drink, so each day I would ask the restaurant manager for two bottles of wine, explaining that I needed to use them for the speciality dishes. Back in the kitchen, I handed the vino to my two superiors. They used it to pick up their spirits, rather than perk up my dishes.

When Jimmy Lahoud, the owner of Quo Vadis, opened Café St Pierre on Clerkenwell Green, he asked me to be head chef and I took the job, but it didn't last long. My life was about to change dramatically and it all started with a phone call from Nigel Platts-Martin.

'Would you be interested in doing Harvey's with us?' said Nigel. I was confused. Surely Alan Bennett was going to be the chef. Not anymore, said Nigel.

He and Richard didn't think Alan was up to it; the pair of them must have known that Alan liked a drink, but they appeared to be the only two men in London who didn't realise just how much he relied on alcohol. Nevertheless, I felt there was something going on behind Alan's back; was I being approached without his knowledge?

'I can't step on Alan's toes,' I told Nigel. 'Sort out your problem with Alan. If he says he doesn't want to get involved in Harvey's, then sure, come back to me.'

He did come back to me, about a week later. Nigel said Alan was most certainly out of the picture. Martin Blunos had lost faith in Alan because of his boozing, so he'd gone off to work in Covent Garden. Then Nigel reiterated that he and Richard had also lost faith. 'But whatever we think of him as a person is irrelevant,' added Nigel. 'He hasn't been able to come up with the cash to buy his share in the business, so he can't be a partner. Simple as that. Do you want to be head chef?' asked Nigel.

'My problem,' I replied, 'is that I can't actually afford it, Nigel. I don't know where I'd get the money to invest ...'

It was only later that I realised Nigel and Richard were not, in fact, asking me to be a shareholder. The thought had never crossed their minds. I had wrongly assumed they wanted me to fill the position left vacant by Alan. But by now they were only after a head chef. When I told Nigel that I didn't know where I would find the cash to invest I had inadvertently put him and Richard in a vulnerable position. I had misinterpreted what they were offering, but now they were thinking, 'Christ, we're opening a restaurant in six weeks' time. We haven't got a head chef and we don't know any chefs. To keep him happy we'll have to make him a shareholder.'

In the end they arranged the finance for me. Richard acted as a guarantor for a bank loan of £60,000 and all I would have to do was establish an amazing restaurant that brought in enough money to pay off the loan, leaving me with some cash for rent. I was a businessman, at the age of twenty-four. I was a chef patron, a chef proprietor. Nigel would sort out the wine list and Richard would do the accounts.

It was October 1986, and I needed to find some staff. I phoned Michael Truelove at the Box Tree to see if he knew of anyone and he sent down a young chef called Simon Simpson, who I called (with affection) Simple Simon. I gave a job to Mark Williams, who had cheffed for Christian Delteuil at L'Arlequin. That made three of us in the kitchen. The search for a maître d' was not exhaustive. LA's sister Morfudd Richards, with whom I shared my home, agreed to do it. She was happy working in the West End, and today she reckons that had the job offer come from anyone else she would not have accepted it because she didn't really want to work south of the river. But she had come into Lampwick's with LA one night and seen me cook: Morfudd had faith in me.

The restaurant opened in January 1987. It had a friendly name, we all reckoned, but I didn't like the apostrophe – it was ugly – so it had to go. Harvey's became Harveys. Its days of selling fried beef patties in baps were finished.

THIRTEEN

Harveys: an amuse bouche

I DON'T recall her name but we met at Harveys, on the staircase that took customers from the restaurant to the toilets. She was a brunette, full-bodied and somewhere in her early forties, dolled up in a low-cut black dress, and she smiled at me as we passed each other on the steps. I interpreted her friendliness as willingness and so I asked, 'Would you like to see my office?'

'Where is it?'

'Up there.' I pointed towards the top floor, to the door marked 'Private', a door that led into the room where I would sit post-service, compiling menus and scribbling drawings of dishes while the rest of Wandsworth slept.

Together we walked up the stairs and into my office, where we fumbled and groped, unzipped and unbuttoned. The newspapers had described me as the Jagger of the Aga. It wasn't hard living up to the reputation.

Three storeys beneath was a busy restaurant, where customers were eating Michelin-starred food and enjoying good company, as you hope to do when you eat out. And amid them was a table for two where a man was sitting alone. He was alone because his companion had left the table to pop to the loo. The man filled in the first few minutes of solitude by observing his surroundings. Perhaps he had gawped at the celebrities on a neighbouring table: is that Kylie Minogue kissing Jason Donovan?

Then there came a point, there had to come the point, when he felt concerned by his companion's absence and questions came to his mind, 'Is she OK? Why is she taking so long?' He was also feeling uncomfortable: he had finished gawping, but now everyone was staring at him, wondering whether his date had departed. He was compelled to go and investigate her disappearance. He put his napkin on the table, stood up and started walking towards the stairs, the stairs which took customers from the restaurant to the toilets.

Tinkle, tinkle. The phone rang on my desk and continued ringing. It was the internal ring tone. I answered in the grumpy, aggressive tone of a bloke who has just been interrupted in a moment of passion. On the other end of the line was Jean-Christophe Slowik – JC from hereon in – and he relayed the grim news: 'The husband is on his way up.'

'Do you have a husband?' I asked the lady who had been on the other end of my lips.

'He's downstairs,' she replied.

'No,' I said. 'No, he's not.'

Abort mission, abort mission. The brunette and I rocketed into reverse. Clothes on, zips up. She could hardly escape via the door marked 'Private' because her husband would spot her. It was just too dangerous and risky. There was no alternative. I opened the hatch door which led from my office onto the roof and quickly helped her squeeze through the space. Once on the roof she positioned herself, crouching out of sight, three storeys up from the pavement but with a terrific view of the common. Just as I was re-adjusting my apron and lighting a Marlboro, I heard footsteps at the top of the staircase. I opened the door, assumed I was talking to the husband, and asked, 'Can I help?'

'I'm terribly sorry,' he said, apologising for being out of bounds, 'but I'm looking for my wife. Have you seen her by any chance?'

Seen her? 'What does she look like?' I inquired. Brown hair, black dress. I pouted and shook my head as he gave a description. I scrunched my face, hoping to send out a signal that I was bemused. 'Nope,' I said. 'Can't help.' He turned and trotted off back downstairs, and I opened the hatch door, tugging the shivering woman back into the warmth. She rushed back to her table and her mystified husband, and in time for dessert; the Soufflés of Chocolate with Chocolate Sauce, possibly, or the Crackling Pyramide, I don't know.

The reason for telling this story – an anecdote entitled Brief Encounter in a Michelin-Starred Restaurant – is to give a taster, an amuse bouche, of where Harveys would take me.

Everything that happened at that restaurant – and what happened to me – seems like a dream. It is as if I am witnessing a fantastic rollercoaster ride during which the traveller zooms along at a dizzying, reckless speed yelling, 'Faster, faster, faster ...'

And who is this man in the dream? He is in his twenties but just a kid, really. He is socially inept and, twenty years on, still troubled by the death of his mother. But he has a burning obsession with his restaurant because it is the thing that will bring him acknowledgement and he thinks acknowledgement will bring him happiness.

He is there in the kitchen seventeen hours a day. Late at night he says farewell to the last customers, the stragglers, and then he works on the menu, drawing pictures of the dishes, pictures he will turn into reality in the kitchen come morning. Sleep is a hindrance. When he does allow himself some shut-eye he might curl up under the tables or, if it is particularly cold, he'll kip in the restaurant's boiler room.

Then, not long into the dream, his passion is well rewarded. The customers like his food – and so do the restaurant critics. He is awarded a Michelin star. Then he gets another. How odd, he thinks, that the dyslexia that made him feel stupid as a schoolboy is now an irrelevance. He is acclaimed as the 'genius' at the stove of 'London's best restaurant'.

He is different from the chefs the world has known until now. Gastronomy has been dominated by pot-bellied, good natured souls with ruddy jowls and tall, white hats. But here is a lanky, hollow-cheeked youngster who, like his long, dark, curly, hair, is in need of some discipline. Who let this anarchist in?

He wears a blue-and-white striped apron – the apron traditionally worn by an apprentice – as opposed to chefs' whites. And he even dares to come out of the kitchen. He crosses the divide to kick out customers. And customers come to be kicked out by him.

Gossip columnists sniff out stories about his hectic love life. Who will he marry next? When will he get divorced? Feature writers arrive with photographers to observe him in the kitchen and then disappear to write thousands of words about the foul-mouthed bollockings he gives his brigade of young protégés. They call him the enfant terrible of the culinary world. They call him the Byron of the Backburner and the Jagger of the Aga. He becomes known as the Rock-Star Chef. And almost every move and each bizarre, mania-filled episode of his life is picked up by the press and fed, morsel by morsel, to newspaper readers who, with cornflakes and breakfast tea, digest the latest developments of the chef's life.

He is the so-called working-class hero, the poor little lad from a Leeds council estate who has worked his arse off to win fame and celebrity. Or is he Italian? Or is he French? Is he, in fact, posh – the little rich kid who became the original Yuppie chef?

And the dream goes on for six, nearly seven years – 'Go
faster, go faster' – ending in a blur with the young chef
rollercoastering into the distance, towards more excitement. You
can just hear his voice; you can just make out the words, 'Why
aren't I happy?'

Think Harveys, think pace. Imagine you are running a marathon …
at sprint speed. Now imagine what you might look like halfway
through and it will help you get a picture in your head of what I
looked like during Harveys: gaunt, debauched and knackered.

I suppose I was trying to kill myself but sacrificing your health
for your career was all the rage. Harveys opened against the
backdrop of Thatcher's greed culture. People talked about City types
being burnt out by the age of thirty. Young men and women didn't
stop to question the damage that can be caused by chronic
obsession; we didn't pause to consider the consequences of the
pace. *Wall Street* was the big movie of 1987, the year in which
Harveys opened, and it was a film about greed and self-indulgence,
about hunger for success. Its underlying message was that greed is
destructive but the sub-text was totally missed by most cinemagoers
of my age. Instead everyone was reciting Michael Douglas's line,
'breakfast is for wimps', as if it was a mantra for anyone who wanted
to get to the top. My own breakfast, by the way, has always consisted
of the same three courses: a cough, a coffee and a cigarette.

Others of my generation may have been driven by money but it
was not a concern for me. My success would be measured in
Michelin stars. One was not enough, I always wanted more.
Meanwhile, in Harveys I had found my adrenaline heaven, a pain
paradise. Customers may well have gone there to fill their stomachs,
but I went to feed my addiction to work, my addiction to adrenaline
and to pain. At Harveys something was always happening.

Actually, it's wrong to say that something was *always* happening.

Harveys: step inside and enjoy the show.
You can see me in the office at the top.

During those first couple of months after opening nothing happened. Things were bad and they certainly weren't helped by the brutal winter weather. We could cater for forty-four covers, but most nights the restaurant was virtually empty. One evening it was completely empty, so I came out of the kitchen with Mark and Simple Simon and we stood with Morfudd and her front-of-house team of two, looking out of the window watching the blizzard rage across Wandsworth Common.

Through the snow two scarfed-up, sludge-covered people suddenly appeared, trudging bravely in their boots and anoraks towards Bellevue Road as if it were the peak of Everest. It turned out to be the head jailer of Wandsworth Prison, bringing his windswept wife for 'a treat'. When they had finished their meal I joined them for coffee and a chat.

I was so overwhelmed by their Hannibalesque trek to Harveys, impressed by the effort they had put in, that I found myself saying, 'Don't worry about the bill.' They wrapped themselves up again, in that cheerful sort of way the British do before throwing themselves into a snowstorm. Stiff upper lip. Then they stepped out of the restaurant and into the blizzard and vanished.

That was the worst night. Two covers, zero takings and I don't think Mr and Mrs Jailer ever came back.

FOURTEEN

The christening

THEY CAME to Harveys for the food and they came for the Marco Pierre White show. It was a lively act, a sort of circus of tension, drama and unpredictability. It was the big top within a small restaurant. There they were, eating this sophisticated food, while some poor cook was being murdered in the kitchen. It was hell out the back and heaven in front. And then out came this creature – me – looking like he'd crucified himself, all ready to kick out a customer. You could come along, have a good dinner and see the person at the next table get slaughtered by the chef. Punters were fed, amused and shocked.

But let's deal with the food first, because without it there would never have been the circus.

I wasn't expecting an easy ride to Michelin heaven. After all, I was taking over what had been an upmarket burger bar in Wandsworth, rather than an elegant dining room in Mayfair. The interior design was horrific – it was done up like a country house hotel – but there was no money to re-decorate. The kitchen was tiny, and again there were no funds for improvement.

My business partners, Nigel and Richard, lurked around in the background; the former looking after the wine list, the latter dealing with the accounts. Understandably, they wanted to see a return from their investment, but my motivation was to serve the finest food in the world.

How could I deliver a high standard of cuisine with the restraint of limited resources? If Harveys was going to work I would have to be smart and draw heavily from my not insignificant experience of serving alongside the Michelin masters. I would need to use every trick I had learned on my nine-year journey from Harrogate to Wandsworth Common.

I had always admired the Box Tree's clever technique of rotating stock (ingredients rather than chicken stock), because it meant they could reduce their waste. Reduced waste equals increased profits. Stock rotation therefore became a rule at Harveys, and this is the way it worked: one day I might do pigeon with fresh thyme-scented roasting juices and champagne braised cabbage. But if the customers didn't go for it then I would re-think the dish because I couldn't contemplate the prospect of chucking the pigeons into the bin. The next day I might put Pigeon à la Forestière (with wild mushrooms) on the menu and, fingers crossed, that would do the trick.

I also had to find a way to work in such a small, cramped kitchen. I had worked in a few big kitchens by now, including the Gavroche powerhouse where there might have been four chefs on the Sauce section, three on Fish, four on Pastry, two on Hot Starters and two on the Larder. At Harveys kitchen space was a luxury, so, just like Pierre Koffmann had done at Tante Claire, I put a massive table in the middle of the kitchen. The table became the work surface and in those early days we were like a pack of wolves; three or four of us darting around, surface to stove, stove to surface, each of us doing a bit of everything.

There wasn't enough space for a separate garnish section, so to overcome this, I tried to incorporate vegetables as ingredients served on the plate with the main dish, rather than served on separate side plates.

I'd serve young leeks, roast button onions and girolle mushrooms on the same plate as a guinea fowl, roasted on the bone, skin taken off, legs split, thigh bone taken out, skin taken off, drumstick cleaned up, the whole lot put together, breast carved and laid across the top with jus blonde. Likewise, the Pigeon en Vesie was served on the same plate as a Tagliatelle of Leeks. And the roast pigeon de Bresse did not come with side plates of vegetables, but was garnished with potato rösti, young turnips, lentilles du pays and a single ravioli that contained mushrooms, garlic and thyme. Harveys dishes were filling and substantial.

The kitchen at Harveys was also too small for the traditional French-style chefs' hierarchy. At Gavroche hierarchical ranks were important and the system was respected by every man in the kitchen, but my Harveys brigade would only ever be as large as ten – I wouldn't have the real hierarchy until I had The Restaurant at The Hyde Park Hotel. I had two chefs on Pastry in a poky kitchen annexe and the remaining eight of us were packed into the overcrowded main kitchen, not on sections, but working together to compensate for our lack of staff. In other words, we all mucked in to do garnish, hot starters, main courses and fish. If there was a table of five, eight cooks worked on five plates, which might mean two people working together on one dish, then I'd piece it all together.

So I was the head chef and every other member of the brigade was an 'assistant' – there was no sous chef. I told my assistants to call me Marco, rather than Chef. I was still in my twenties and didn't consider myself old enough to be called Chef. However, when I gave Kevin Broome, a cook from Manchester, a job at Harveys he started to call me Boss, which stuck. Thereafter, I was either Marco or Boss until my retirement from the kitchen in 1999. Although I didn't go for Albert's hierarchy, I certainly adopted his high regard for discipline.

As far as I was concerned, consistency would have to be crucial at Harveys. At Le Manoir, you'll recall, I had watched the system fall apart when the pressure increased and the number of covers rose above forty, when dishes left Raymond's kitchen minus an ingredient, or with a sloppy presentation. With this in mind, I wanted to ensure that each and every Harveys dish was good. One

I would draw pictures of the dishes before
they made their way to the next day's menu.

of the problems at Le Manoir was that not every chef could copy Raymond's artistic style. Quite simply, they didn't have his flair. Somehow, I had to find an easy-to-follow way of enabling my chefs to imitate my desired presentation of dishes. I devised a simple method – the plate became a clock. The top of the plate was twelve o'clock and the bottom of the plate was six o'clock; three o'clock was to the right and, of course, nine to the left. So if a chef was dressing pigeon with a petit pain of foie gras I could shout across the kitchen, 'Foie gras at twelve, confit of garlic at four ...' You can never go wrong, as long as your cooks can tell the time.

———

One of the problems, incidentally, with the world of gastronomy back then was that all the top chefs were using twelve-and-a-half inch plates that were big and clumsy. The perfect plate size is eleven inches.

Then there was the food itself. I began questioning everything that went on the plate. Why am I doing this? Why serve this with that? Why serve that with this? Why cook this for so long? Why, why, why? I remember serving a vinaigrette with a terrine of leeks and thinking the vinegar was too harsh. It often is, isn't it? So I just cut the vinegar and diluted it with water; you still get the strength but you've taken away some of the acidity and made it palatable. I called it water vinaigrette: oil, water and garlic into a large bowl, add garlic, salt and pepper, and then stir very gently so the vinaigrette doesn't emulsify. It looks beautiful on the plate – separate pearls of oil and water.

When I wasn't in the kitchen, I would sit down with pen and paper and draw pictures of dishes that came out of my imagination and were intended for the following day's menu. Sometimes, in a search for inspiration, I would resort to my trunk, which contained French cookery books and menus I had collected over the years from other restaurants. Then I might deface my books by drawing my own sketches of dishes straight onto the books' illustrations. Years later, at the Hyde Park, I still did my late-night sketches, then handed them in the morning to my head chef Robert Reid, saying, 'Copy these.'

At other times I might pick a main ingredient – sea scallops, lamb or whatever – and create a long list of other ingredients that would go well with it. I would sit there, studying the list, allowing my imagination to go, and then … I would start to see it visually. With so many of the dishes I would start at the end, if you like, and work my way backwards, but the process always began with drawing that picture on the plate.

We live in a world of refinement not in a world of invention. That's the way I see it. People who claim to have invented a great dish are only fooling themselves. Someone has always done it before. Customers and critics used to rave about my Harveys dish, the Tagliatelle of Oysters. They thought it was a great 'invention'. But I'm sure I didn't invent it. Centuries before we were born, people were eating pasta with shellfish, weren't they? It was simply the concept I had created.

Again, the Pigeon en Vesie – pigeon in pig's bladder – might have seemed new to Harveys customers in the late eighties, but Fernand Point was serving chicken in pig's bladder in his French restaurant in the forties and fifties, and Le Gavroche did its own version of Point's classical dish.

Pig's trotter, another Harveys favourite, was inspired by a similar dish that was done by my former boss Pierre Koffmann at Tante Claire. And Pierre's pig's trotter, if you take my meaning, was his own version of the one done by the French chef Charles Barrier. So I took it from Pierre, who had taken it from Charles, who doubtless took it from someone else.

Pierre's version involved stuffing the trotter with chicken thighs and sweetbreads before dropping it into boiling water. I got rid of the chicken, which I felt had been put there to pad out the more expensive ingredient, sweetbreads. I would gently poach the trotter in water at 85 degrees Celsius for ten minutes and then rest it. Pierre's technique, in contrast, was to cook the meat for double that length of time. To my palate, my method produced a more succulent taste.

From day one at Harveys I did the Pied de Cochon Pierre Koffmann, my own version of his pig's trotter dish and a tribute to him. It would stay on my menu, from one restaurant to another, for the next twelve years until I retired from the kitchen. I had not invented the pig's trotter dish, just like I hadn't invented the Tagliatelle with Oysters. I had refined it.

Whatever you do, never underestimate the might and strength, the power and force of the restaurant critic. It was only after Egon Ronay delivered a superb review of Harveys, a couple of months after we had opened, that the restaurant became a massive success. In fact, it was, quite literally, an overnight success. On the Saturday night we were catering for the usual small crowd. The next morning, the *Sunday Times* came out. The paper contained Egon's critique, and that was it. Bang! The bookings never stopped from that day on. Egon, though short, fragile and getting on a bit, was the man with the Midas touch. For decades his guides had been telling British restaurant-goers where to eat out and now here he was, in the Spring of '87, enthusiastically advising his followers, via a *Sunday Times* column, to head for Harveys. The impact was quite extraordinary.

I had never met Egon but he had, of course, played an instrumental part in my life. It was when I was a teenage chef at the Hotel St George that I came across a Ronay guide and realised that: 1) restaurants can win awards and 2) there was a beautiful restaurant called the Box Tree – it was as a result of that that I applied for a job there.

I say I'd never met Egon, but we had spoken on the telephone two years earlier when I worked at Le Manoir aux Quat'Saisons. It was one of those Manoir days when I had picked up the ringing kitchen phone pretending to be an answer machine. 'Please leave a message and we shall come back to you,' I said, before delivering an ear-splitting shriek, 'Bleeeeeep!'

Then the voice at the other end of the phone, a gentle voice with a foreign (it was Hungarian) accent, said, 'This is Egon Ronay. I would be most grateful if Raymond could call me when he picks up this message.'

———

There I was in the kitchen at Harveys, totally unaware that Egon Ronay had visited my restaurant, eaten my food and was about to write a review, when the phone rang. I answered and a voice said: 'This is Egon Ronay ...' I got a flashback to Le Manoir. '... May I speak with Marco White?' He explained that he had been in to eat at Harveys and had enjoyed his meal tremendously. He intended to write a piece for the *Sunday Times*, but beforehand he wanted to know a bit more about me. 'I can tell from your accent that you are not Italian,' he said to me. 'So how did you get a name like Marco?'

'Well, that's only part of my name,' I casually told Egon. 'My full name is Marco Pierre White. My father was English and that's where the White comes from. My mother was Italian, hence the name Marco. My aunt Luciana, my mother's sister, came up with the name Pierre, but don't ask me why.' When Egon's review appeared I was thrilled by his comments about the restaurant but alarmed to see that he had referred to me as Marco *Pierre* White. My middle name, for so long a well-kept secret, was now revealed, and on the pages of a broadsheet. Pierre stuck, of course.

Before Egon's piece I had been Marco White, but from that Sunday on I became Marco Pierre White. MPW. Quite posh. Quite confusing. Some people would think I was Italian while others would say I was French. And there would be those who thought I had made the whole lot up because, after all, who do you know with an Italian-French-English name? Egon, I suppose, had refined me.

Overnight success is a strange experience. Where there had once been virtual silence, now there was noise. Up until that point, we had all jumped when the phone rang. But after Egon's article, when the pace picked up, the ringing phone became a continuous background noise at Harveys. All you could hear was ringing, chopping, hissing, frying, ringing ... and me shouting (which, as promised, I shall come to).

A few months after Egon's review came the Catey Awards – organised by the industry's trade magazine, *Caterer & Hotelkeeper*. I still shudder at the memory of attending the Cateys. I was sitting there in the audience and Lord Montgomery was called onto the stage to present an award.

I thought, what am I doing here? I should be back in the kitchen, cooking. This is not my thing. Then suddenly a dishevelled, skeletal face appeared on a giant screen alongside Lord Monty. I thought, Eh? Jesus. That's me. What am I doing up there? Before I knew it, I was being pushed up onto the stage and Lord Montgomery was presenting me with an award for Newcomer of the Year. It was one of the worst nights of my life. I didn't like it one bit and saw it as Catey PR. As far as I was concerned, it was a ridiculous award: Harveys had only been open for five months. It was the first and the last time I went to the back-scratching Cateys.

———

But the PR, of course, was picking up and my old friend Alan Crompton-Batt was out there somewhere, pouring booze down journalists' throats and encouraging them to review Harveys. Meanwhile the punters continued to flood in, coming to taste the food. They came for the Blanquette of Scallops and Langoustines with Cucumber and Ginger; the Feuillantine of Sweetbreads; the Hot Foie Gras, Lentils and Sherry Vinegar Sauce; the Noisettes of Lamb en Crepinette with Fettucine of Vegetables and a Tarragon Jus. They came for the Hot Mango Tart; the Passion Fruit Soufflé and Lemon Tart.

I borrowed a quote from Oscar Wilde and put it at the top of the menu: 'To get into the best society nowadays one has either to feed people, amuse people, or shock people – that is all.'

The high-class restaurant industry – a profession dominated by middle-aged lardy chefs – was as shocked by me as the snooty critics. But restaurant-goers – the punters, the customers, the payers, the diners, the eaters – were not only fed by me but also apparently amused and sometimes shocked. The media was amused. Indeed, everyone, except for Establishment food figures, was ready for a change and I was becoming gastronomy's symbol of Thatcher's greed, the young chef who had crossed the North–South divide when it still existed. Make way for the long-haired, gangly cook who had won the heart of Egon Ronay. Word spread.

———

As well as the Yuppies south of the Thames, punters crossed the bridge to dine at Harveys. They came from Chelsea, Westminster and Mayfair.

Celebrities came as well, and not just any old celebrities but the young, good-looking, sexy ones, the sort who are shadowed by the paparazzi and who appear in newspapers alongside the caption: 'XXXX pictured last night, emerging from Harveys.' They all wanted to be fed by the undernourished chef who was passionate, obsessed and intense. Denice Lewis, the beautiful Texan model who featured daily in gossip columns, would turn up with her boyfriend, 'Green Shield stamps heir' Tim Jefferies. Koo Stark, Prince Andrew's former girlfriend, became a regular. Kylie Minogue and her then boyfriend Jason Donovan were others who made the trek across the Thames.

Mavericks seemed to identify with me as like-minded. I was at Harveys one day when I answered the phone to Oliver Reed. That's Ollie Reed, the film star, scrapping hell-raiser and all-round icon. He introduced himself, booked for dinner, and when he arrived with his wife, Josephine, he was everything you could have hoped for ... and more. He sat on the floor, and that's where he drank his aperitif before heading to the table. From that night on he became a regular. He had to come to Harveys, he used to say, because he was barred from everywhere else.

I adored Ollie. I saw him as a kindred spirit; someone who did things his own way. Whenever I knew the Reeds were coming, I'd always try to get away from the kitchen, if only for a minute or two, to greet them at the door.

———

One night Ollie walked into the restaurant and looked around before saying grandly, 'I'd like to commend you on the decor. It is the finest.' (He always spoke like a character out of a Sherlock Holmes adventure.)

I said, 'But Oliver, you've been here a hundred times.'

'Yes,' he said, 'but it's the first time I've arrived sober.'

His evenings at Harveys followed a pattern. He'd drink his aperitif while sitting on the floor, then after his starter he would leave the table, sprint into the kitchen and, without saying a word, rip off his tie and throw it at me before running out. He'd return to our chaotic kitchen a dozen times each night, for a chat or to do something crazy. He must have spent as much time in the kitchen as he did at the table. In the restaurant he would summon the wine waiter and when asked what he would like to drink, Oliver would reply, 'Bring us three more bottles of what we just had.' He was rarely seated when his main course arrived; instead, he'd be on the landing upstairs, arm wrestling another customer. After service one night, he challenged me to an arm wrestle, and we sat at a table with the TV magnate Lew Grade acting as referee. Puff, pant, puff, pant. After about ten minutes Lew declared a stalemate.

For years afterwards, when Christmas approached, Oliver would phone to ask if I had a good recipe for turkey and I would patiently talk him through it.

———

Afterwards I'd get a note from him, on paper headed: 'From under the desk of Oliver Reed', along with one of his cartoons of a turkey. More often than not he would also call on Christmas Day to wish me well. The staff loved him – he was a big tipper – and the customers loved him, too. He would start chatting to groups on neighbouring tables, and before long the tables would be rearranged until Oliver's table had grown to four times its original size. He wasn't happy unless he had met everyone in the restaurant and kissed their hands. Booze famously played a major role in his life, although I once watched him have an argument, a heavy discussion, and it was hard to believe he'd had a drink because he was so articulate and clinical in his delivery.

Harveys became a party when Oliver was in the house. He'd walk in and everything would rev up a gear – the only other person I've seen have that effect is Frankie Dettori. One night I was in a rush, dashed past Oliver, and was half-way up the stairs when I noticed he was chasing after me. I stopped, turned around to him and said, 'Oliver, why are you running?'

'Where's the fight?' he said.

And among the celebrities and the politicians, supermodels, pop stars and gossip columnists ... somewhere among that fascinating cast of customers there must have been a Michelin inspector.

———

The Michelin Guide is published every January, and in December 1987 I picked up the phone and called Derek Brown, the UK's head inspector. I had never met him but, like Egon Ronay, he had the power to do amazing things to my career.

I introduced myself and we had a short conversation. I said, 'Mr Brown, I am coming to the end of my first year in business and was wondering whether I will be awarded a Michelin star.'

He replied, 'We never reveal information like that prior to publication of the guide.' Oh well, I thought. It was just a cheeky call: I thought I'd chance my luck. I would have to wait another month before finding out if I had won a star. Or would I ...? Just as I was about to put down the phone, Mr Brown added, 'But I can tell you that you won't be disappointed.'

I really would like to say that it was one the happiest days of my life. But by now you know me well enough to know that it did not bring me happiness. There was no celebration, no knees-up. Somehow it didn't register as a great achievement because I wanted so much more. I wasn't used to congratulating myself and I didn't know how to reward myself. I didn't have time to organise a party, let alone attend one.

I went to a little party on 1 January 1988. A crowd of us gathered at the publisher Anthony Blond's house to toast the New Year and Jonathan Meades was there. Previously, Jonathan – the restaurant reviewer for *The Times* – was the one critic who terrified me. He could destroy a place. But I didn't need to be scared of him: in the Easter of 1987 he had booked into Harveys, using the alias Hogg, and he later phoned me to say, 'My name is Hogg. I was in the other night and had jelly of calves' brains. It was sensational. How did you make it?' Only when I saw the article did I realise that Hogg was Meades and vice versa. Then, in an end-of-year round-up for *The Times*, Jonathan had given the Newcomer Restaurant of the Year award to Harveys.

The gathering at Anthony's house was a few days after Jonathan had given me the Newcomer award. Apart from Jonathan, his girlfriend Frances Bentley (who worked for *Tatler*) was there as well as three other chefs: Nico Ladenis, my former boss; Rowley Leigh of

Kensington Place; and Simon Hopkinson who had just opened Terence Conran's Bibendum, and whose cookery book, *Roast Chicken and Other Stories*, has more recently been voted the most useful recipe book ever written. The evening was memorable for two reasons:

Firstly the food, or rather the simplicity of the food considering there were four chefs in the house. It was 10 p.m. and everyone was starving, but everywhere was closed and the host had not thought about catering for his guests. 'My cupboards are bare,' said Anthony. I volunteered to cook, partly because I found it easier to cook than socialise.

I went into the kitchen and searched around. He had a couple of onions, some pasta, a tin of tomato purée, a few rashers of bacon and a clove of garlic. I did a spaghetti sauce the way I'd been told my mother used to cook it – sweat off the onions with the garlic without colouring them, then put in the diced bacon and sweat that off, then add generous amounts of tomato purée and that was all sweated off in more olive oil. Then take the cooked pasta and put it straight into the sauce. It was very simple but Jonathan said it was one of the greatest pasta dishes he'd ever eaten. And I was too shy to say, 'Well, it's not me, it's just the way my mother used to cook it when I was a boy.'

The evening was also memorable for the squabble between Nico and Simon, who had a silly argument about food. If I remember rightly, it was Simon who started it when he began criticising Nico's brioche. Serious chefs take their brioche seriously. So Nico said, 'I don't make my brioche. I buy it.' Simon might have thought he had scored a point but then Nico said, 'The brioche I buy is better than the brioche I can make.' It was Nico's way of saying he would only serve the best. 'And when I first started in Dulwich,' he continued, 'in Lordship Lane, I used to buy fish soup because it was better than the one I could make.'

'You do know,' added Nico, who was angry but still eloquent, 'that I'm a self-taught chef.' To be self taught is a big put down in the premier league of chefs. In the outside world it is a bit like calling someone a cunt. And then Simon started crying. I don't know if it was the words 'self-taught chef' that produced the tears; perhaps it was the strength of the criticism. I felt sorry for him being savaged and slaughtered by the great Nico who, incidentally, had won Restaurant of the Year in Jonathan's awards. I stepped in, telling Nico to forget about it. Mind you, the proof was in their puddings (and starters and main courses): Nico went on to win three stars from the Michelin. Simon, meanwhile, retired from the kitchen in the mid-nineties before he had the chance to win a star. The pressure was too much for him. During service one day he had what he now calls a 'mini-breakdown', and to save his sanity he stepped away from the stove of the professional kitchen.

———

At the beginning of this chapter I mentioned that I hated the interior design of Harveys, and then later on I said that Ollie Reed loved the decor. In between me hating it and Ollie loving it, the restaurant was re-decorated. But during that period when I still hated it, something else happened. There was an episode, if you like.

Morfudd came into the kitchen during service one day and told me about a certain customer in the restaurant. He said he had played a role in designing Harveys in its days as a burger bar, before I took over. This man had told Morfudd that because of his contribution to the restaurant he and his five guests should be entitled to a meal or drinks on the house.

What he had done to my restaurant was ghastly. It was chintzy, mediocre, charmless and lacking in imagination. It really bothered me. Morning, noon and night I would look at Harveys' decor and silently pray for the day when we had enough money to have the place done up properly. So you'll understand my reaction when I learned that this bloke was not only sitting in my restaurant but had the audacity to ask for a free meal or drinks.

'No, Morfudd,' I said. 'No, no, no. And please go and tell him that

I am not prepared to cook for him because I dislike the way he furnished the restaurant.' She was reluctant at first. I can see why now. But I was adamant, and so she went back into the dining room to have a quiet word with the designer. 'What?' he screamed as she relayed the news to him. He was outraged, furious and probably very embarrassed in front of his friends. He stormed towards the kitchen. From the stove, I could hear him shouting, ranting and raging. I stopped whatever I was doing and went into the corridor that led down to the restaurant. He was at one end while I stood at the other.

He had made a mistake. The punch-up that followed was a release, in a way. For months I'd been staring at the chintz thinking, I'd like to meet this bastard and now he was charging towards the end of my clenched fist. Every swipe I delivered – and I delivered a few – was a blow for good taste. The kitchen brigade had to pull me off him. Ask Morfudd if you don't believe me. He staggered out of Harveys, minus a tooth or two and nursing a perforated eardrum. I had partially stripped him, as well. During the scuffle, I ripped an entire sleeve from his suit jacket, and it was left lying on the corridor floor, a casualty of battle. As his friends helped him out of the restaurant, he stepped onto Bellevue Road, looked down at his arm and wailed, 'This is Gucci, for Christ's sake.'

FIFTEEN

Beautiful doll

I MET my first wife at the fishmonger's in the summer of 1987, some six months after the opening of Harveys. My relationship with Lowri-Ann, the one-time Queen of the King's Road, hadn't worked out. I can't remember how it ended – these things fizzle out – but I had removed myself and my trunk from her place in Battersea and resettled in a flat close to Wandsworth Common. The location of my new home meant that when I wasn't sleeping in Harveys, I was at least bedding down a few hundred yards from the restaurant and my cherished kitchen.

I was living with a bloke called Benedict, who was another member of the King's Road set. Benedict had been a heroin addict and I only moved into his place after he promised me he'd managed to kick the habit. He hadn't. Most nights I would return from Harveys, shattered, burned and cut, and walk into the flat to find Benedict and his friends drugged up, lolling and slumping. I may as well have been living in an opium den. In the mornings I'd be awoken by a shaky hand knocking on my door. 'Yes,' I'd say. Then one of Benedict's junkie mates would stumble into the room and ask to borrow a mirror – not to apply make-up, you understand, but to snort a line of cocaine. I got back one night to find a girl, off her face and wilting on the sofa. She asked if I could roll her a joint. 'I'm sorry,' I said politely. 'I can't.' As in, I don't know how.

'Christ,' she replied, her eyeballs swivelling. 'Are you that stoned?'

Benedict was unperturbed by my reluctance to take drugs. As far as he was concerned, I was a dependant just like him. 'You're an addict, Marco,' he once told me, with a junkie's beam of confidence. 'You're an addict to the warmth,' by which he meant the stove, the cooking, the kitchen, the work.

It was all of those things which took me one morning to Johnny the Fish, who happened to introduce me to his secretary. Her name was Alex McArthur and she was blonde, blue-eyed and pretty. In fact, she looked like a beautiful doll. She was, I later found out, a surgeon's daughter and was as middle class as I was working class. We chatted and established a connection, the Oxford connection. She had studied in Oxford at the same time as my friend Piers Adam, and they had known each other briefly, and I had worked at Le Manoir. We said farewell and off I went with my lobster and sea bass. But when I got back to Harveys Alex was still on my mind. I was far from self-assured and still not good with girls, but I obviously found the courage to call Alex and ask if she fancied dinner.

'When?' she said.

'What about tonight?'

'What time?'

'Eleven,' I said, explaining, 'I have to finish service first.' I couldn't let a good relationship stand in the way of work. That night she arrived in her little Fiat Panda and I squeezed my six-foot-three-inch frame into the passenger seat. We went to Chinatown, in London's West End, for late-night noodles, and after dinner we went back to her flat in Kensington. I did not leave. Our relationship had been cemented, as they say, in less than twenty hours. One morning I had met Alex and by bedtime I was living with her.

She tolerated my addiction to work. I think – I thought – she was happy to go along with it. In fact, she would come and collect me when I was done for the night at Harveys. We were young and infatuated. I was twenty-five years old and Alex was twenty-one, and we managed to keep the relationship going for a year, long enough for me to propose. One day in June 1988 we were married in Chelsea Register Office, the place where rock stars tie the knot. We did it discreetly. My

Escaping from the kitchen
to see Alex, a beautiful girl.

best man was Bob Carlos Clarke, the photographer who had been virtually living at Harveys so that he could take photographs for my book, *White Heat*. Bob's wife Lindsay was the other witness. That was it – just the four of us. We emerged from the register office onto the King's Road and felt a celebration was in order, so we trotted down to Dino's and the four of us sat there eating poached eggs on toast. I had a Michelin star by then but hadn't considered cooking a sumptuous feast for the occasion. When the meal was finished I had my own speech to deliver, which was, quite simply, 'I've got to get back to work.' I have no recollection of the bride being bothered about her groom vanishing, but that is precisely what I did. Buggered off, back to my kitchen. A honeymoon? What do you think?

At some point during our brief marriage we did have a holiday in Yorkshire, where we stayed with Tom and Eugene McCoy, the cheffing brothers who ran the superb McCoys restaurant in Staddlebridge. Alex slipped on the landing in Tom's house and when I got to her, she said she couldn't move her leg. At the hospital the doctors said she had a fracture and she was promptly trolleyed off to a hospital bed. Every day I would go in to visit my injured wife, taking platters of food which I had cooked in McCoys' kitchen. I used to turn up with huge lobster salads and that sort of thing, and when I heard the elderly woman in the bed opposite Alex whinging about the hospital food, I got the hint. On future visits I'd take in two portions of everything – one for Alex, the other for the old lady. It transpired that the elderly woman was the grandmother of Mel Smith, the comedian-turned-businessman who co-founded the extremely successful Talkback television production company. Small world that it is, I met Mel Smith a few years ago when he asked me to do his fiftieth birthday party at my restaurant in Holland Park, the Belvedere. We had a good chat about his grandmother, a wonderful character, who by then had passed away.

When Alex gave birth on 20 September 1989, I finished my lunch service before heading off to see our new baby at the Chelsea and Westminster Hospital. We named our daughter Letitia Rosa

(Rosa being my mother's middle name), which was shortened, of course, to Lettie. I was delighted at becoming a father but emotionally I was all over the place. I wasn't prepared mentally for fatherhood. I was so involved in my work, but Harveys had become a form of escapism.

Truth be known, I was lost within myself. How could I take on the responsibilities of fatherhood if I could only just manage to deal with myself? I couldn't really settle into the potentially blissful environment so many new parents enjoy. It was easier for me to be in the kitchen at Harveys, grafting away, sweating and toiling, and dishing out the bollockings. Once again in my life, I wanted pain.

Lettie's birth prompted me to get in touch with my dad. I hadn't spoken to the old man for a decade – there had been no contact with him since the late seventies, when he had remarried after I left home. On the day Lettie was born I felt compelled to phone him. It was a brief conversation, and I cannot recall it verbatim. I said something about how he had become a grandfather for the first time; how I wanted to be the one to break the news to him and didn't want him to learn about it from the papers. And that was it. Another two years or so would pass before we came face to face.

It was never going to last with Alex, and a couple of years after marrying we were divorced. Two people need to have the same dream. Mine was winning three Michelin stars, and that ambition came before everything else in my life. Alex's dream ... well, I don't quite know what her dream was. Even on paper we weren't a good match. I came from a hard, working-class world which, since my mother's death, had been dominated by men. As you know, I wasn't good with women, perhaps because I'd missed out on any female influence during my childhood.

Following my mother's death I hadn't been encouraged to talk about the burden of grief and because I was severely under-developed when it came to sharing my emotions I mustn't have been the most communicative husband. I'm not asking for sympathy, that's just the way I was. I felt unable to articulate my feelings and communication is a necessity if a relationship is to survive. All of a sudden there I was, married to a nice middle-class girl. I couldn't take it in. Pain junkies don't like things to be too good or too easy. They don't like things to be perfect. I didn't want pleasure. I was driven by my insecurities and a fear of failing, and to some extent a fear of dying before achieving my ultimate goal. The kitchen was the only place where I felt comfortable.

One of my problems was that when good things happened to me I just didn't know how to accept them.

———

The same two questions always crop up about Harveys. First, was I really so nasty to my chefs? Second, did I really kick people out of the restaurant?

Sometimes I bump into hugely successful, talented chefs who were my protégés and they say, 'You were really nasty to work for but it made life easier afterwards …' And they say that without a hint of irony. I've also come across punters who tell me they came to Harveys and add, '… You kicked me out, but I suppose I asked for it.'

Dealing with the staff issue, first. Yes, I was a hard boss. Even without my insistence on discipline, finding staff was difficult enough. At that time the majority of young chefs aspired to work north of the Thames, rather than south. They'd rather have done Belgravia than Bellevue Road. When they accepted the job they were in for the shock of their lives. My unmanageable desire for perfection brought out the tetchiness in me. I expected my chefs and the waiters to match my commitment, and I let them know that. My addiction to work, my constant craving for an adrenaline fix, set the pace, both front and back of house. I was working a hundred hour weeks, but they weren't slacking, either. If joining Gavroche was the culinary equivalent of signing up for the Foreign Legion, then taking a job at Harveys was like joining the SAS. We were a small unit of hard nuts.

In the early days, I allowed staff to sit down for a meal before service, but that didn't last long. Egon Ronay's glorious review a couple of months after we opened started off the non-stop bookings which pretty much finished off the custom of staff lunches. There just wasn't time to eat. Jean-Christophe Slowik, or JC, replaced Morfudd as maître d', and one day he asked for a quiet word. He explained in his engaging, diplomatic and charming way that he had a problem. What is it, JC?

He said that he was having to take money from the petty cash box, nip to the deli a few doors down and buy sandwiches for his ravenous waiters. He asked, 'Is it not odd that we work in a restaurant but have to buy lunch from somewhere else?' JC is good when it comes to making good points. From then on I allowed staff to have a meal, but not too often, before service.

I survived on a diet of espresso and Marlboro – my nutritional intake came from the morsels, nibbles and sauces I tasted during cooking. Most members of the team found that Mars and Twix were ideal for energy bursts. Then there were the plates that were returned to the kitchen from the dining room totally clean. For ages I thought the customers were so impressed with the food that they were devouring every last speck on the plate. In fact, it was the starving waiters who were responsible for the spotless dishes. As they left the restaurant and walked along the corridor to the kitchen they would polish off the customers' leftovers, guzzling the remains like famished vultures. There was a look of horror in the eyes of JC's new waiters as they arrived for their first day at work. The sight that greeted them was one of waiters and chefs suffering chronic fatigue and hunger, all set to the soundtrack of a screaming boss.

Even before service started and the first customers arrived, a new waiter would often make an excuse about getting something from his coat, only to scurry off and never return.

————

These new waiters couldn't work a single hour, let alone an entire shift. Eventually JC accepted that many of the recruits would evaporate as fast as their enthusiasm and he worked extra hard to compensate for this problem.

In the kitchen, the first three weeks was the toughest period for the new boys. By the end of it they were usually fucked, having lost a stone in weight, gained a dazed expression and cried themselves dry. That was when the shaking started – and when many of them left. One day they were there, the next they were gone. If they could make it into the fourth week they were doing well and those who, like Gordon Ramsay, lasted longer than a year at Harveys were by and large destined for acclaim. Six of them went on to win Michelin stars of their own, so I must have been doing something right.

I make no apologies for my strict leadership methods and I have no one to blame but myself. However, I was of course the product of disciplinarians who included my father, Albert Roux, Pierre Koffmann and good old Stephan Wilkinson, my first chef at the George and the man who called me cunt as if it was my Christian name.

Step now into my theatre of cruelty.

Normally only one person was allowed to speak during service, and that was me. Kitchen visitors said it was a bit like watching a surgeon in an operating theatre.

Me: Knife. [Knife is passed to me.]

Me: Butter. [Butter is passed to me.]

Me [through gritted teeth]: Not that fucking butter. Clarified fucking butter, you fucker.

Poor timing always upset me. If we were doing a table of six, for instance, and only four of the main courses were ready then I was prone to flip. That's when I might send a chef to stand in the corner. 'Corner,' I'd say, jabbing a finger towards the corner of the room. 'In [finger jab] the [jab] fucking [jab] corner.' The chef would stand not with his face to the wall but facing me; that way he could pick up some knowledge while enduring his punishment. I remember one night, when I was in an intensely irritable mood, four chefs pissed me off so each of them was sent to stand in a corner. When the fifth chef did something to annoy me I shouted, 'Corner. In the fucking corner.'

'Which one, Marco?' he asked. I had run out of corners.

I went berserk if brioche wasn't toasted correctly. Toasted too quickly and you can't spread the foie gras on it; toasted too slowly and it dries. It has to be toasted at the right distance below the grill, so it's crispy on the outside and soft on the inside. You don't scorch it and you don't dry it. Insignificant to you, maybe, but the difference between life and death to one of my cooks. If the brioche wasn't right, or if the vegetables had been chopped incorrectly, then someone was in for a nasty bollocking. 'Do you really want to be the best?' I'd tell them. 'If you do that's fantastic, if you don't then don't waste your time.'

In order to achieve my dream I reckoned I needed a brigade with army-standard discipline and, as I had learned at Gavroche, discipline is born out of fear. When you fear, you question. If you don't fear something, you don't question it in the same way. And if you have fear in the kitchen you'll never take a shortcut. If you don't fear the boss, you'll take shortcuts, you'll turn up late. My brigade had to feel pain, push themselves to the limits, and only then would they know what they were capable of achieving. I was forcing them to make decisions. The ones who left, well, fine, at least they had decided a Michelin-starred kitchen was not for them.

Take a look at the ones who stayed, the ones who could take it and even appreciated it. Today, they are considered to be among Britain's finest chefs and they all came from that cramped kitchen at Harveys. The Michelin star winners include Gordon Ramsay (three); Philip Howard (two); Eric Chavot (two); Stephen Terry (one). Meanwhile, Tim Hughes is now chef director of The Ivy, Le Caprice and J. Sheekey. And Tim Payne was another who went on to win acclaim. Interestingly enough, some members of the Harveys kitchen brigade – just like me – were the product of a tough upbringing. They might have lost a mother or a father. They would have grown up on council estates. They were working class; from the wrong side of the tracks.

Cheffing was still predominately a working-class profession then, and there was one cook who for a long time pretended he was working class just to fit in. It was a while before we discovered he was the son of rich parents and a public school boy to boot.

Gordon, Stephen and Tim shared a flat in Clapham, a couple of miles from Harveys, and I used to scream at them (earmuffs on), 'Did you bunch of cunts go home last night and conspire against me? "What stupid things can we do to wind up Marco?" Is that what you all said to each other? Did you sit down together like a bunch of plotting cunts and say, "What can we do tomorrow that will really piss him off? What can we do to really irritate him?" Did you, Gordon? Is that what you did, Stephen? Did you conspire against me, Tim? Because you are all being so fucking stupid today ...'

Other times the bollockings included physical abuse. I might severely tug a chef's apron, or grab a chef by the scruff of the neck and administer a ten-second throttle, just to focus him. One night I lifted Lee Bunting and hung him by his apron on some hooks on the wall. The cooks never knew what to expect from me ... and neither did I. A film crew arrived for the series *Take Six Cooks* and happened to walk into the kitchen as I was throwing bottles of sauce and oil at an underling. The producer had to duck down to avoid being hit by flying glass. 'I don't know if we can film in there,' he told JC. 'War zones are less dangerous.'

Chefs who weren't sent to stand in the corner, throttled, or forced to duck to avoid flying sauces might even be chucked in the bin. We had a great big dustbin in the kitchen, which was filled with the usual waste produced in professional kitchens. The boys who were too slow, or simply too annoying at that particular moment, were dumped inside it. Arnold Sastry, the brother-in-law of comic actor Rowan Atkinson, was known as Onion Bhaji and he was regularly binned.

'Onion Bhaji in the bin,' I might say, and the rest of the brigade would obey orders.

There are Harveys stories which will have you asking yourself –

if the question has not occurred to you already – 'Why did these poor young men continue to work for that bullying brute, Marco?' Good question. And many of them not only continued to work with me, but stayed with me for years, right up until the day I retired in 1999. The thing is, a bollocking isn't personal. It's a short – sometimes not so short – sharp shock. It's an extremely loud wake-up call. It's smell the bloody espresso time. In the heat of service, I didn't have time to say, 'Arnold, would you mind speeding up a little, please?' I couldn't stop cheffing, couldn't take my mind off the game in order to say politely, 'Gordon, when do you think you might finish the guinea fowl, old boy?' I had to be heard to deliver the message and the message was: 'Do it now and do it right'. They all knew this and they all understood it. That is why, when a chef is receiving a bollocking, none of his colleagues jump in to defend him. The rest of the brigade look down and carry on with the job. Each one of them knows that sooner or later he will be the one getting a bollocking. I created fear but I don't remember anyone ever saying, 'Marco, enough is enough. Pack it in.' I'm convinced that a mile-wide streak of sado-masochism ran through the Harveys brigade. They were all pain junkies, they had to be. They couldn't get enough of the bollockings.

During the summer the tiny kitchen, with its glass panel skylights, became blisteringly hot, and we all wore sweat bands on our foreheads and wrists. One day Jason Everett moaned that he was too hot, so I did something which, on reflection, was rather hazardous. Carving knife in one hand, I held his jacket with the other and slashed it. Then I slashed his trousers. Both garments were still on his body at the time. 'That should provide a bit of ventilation,' I told him, and when he asked if he could change out of his chopped-up clothes I said, 'Yes, at the end of service.'

One day the whole sweaty bunch got together to grumble about the heat. 'Right, that's it,' I said. I was annoyed and couldn't stand their moaning. I marched over to the air-conditioning machine and turned it off. 'We'll all roast together,' I said. From that night on they kept their complaints to themselves. If the boys couldn't stand the

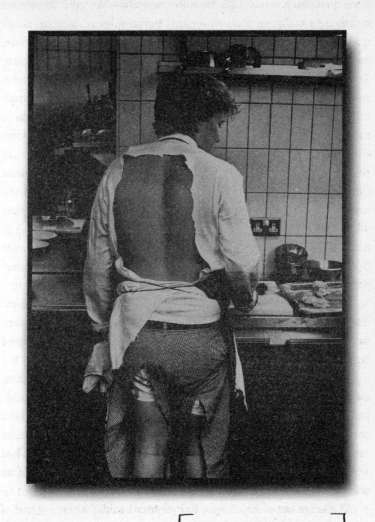

Air-conditioning, Harvey's style.

heat, well, that was tough because they couldn't get out of the kitchen.

When I was feeling charitable I'd give the instruction to remove the kitchen's skylights, thus allowing some of the heat to escape. Gordon was in the kitchen one morning, skylights off, and he was rolling out pasta when he felt water on his head and assumed it was rain. He was wrong. A dog had wandered onto the roof terrace, cocked a leg and promptly urinated through the roof and onto Gordon and his ravioli. Gordon was enraged, if not a little embarrassed in front of his cackling colleagues. He ran outside with a knife. I don't think he was going to stab the dog; he just wanted to *look* like he was going to stab the dog. As it turned out, the beast was too fast for him.

When Gordon wasn't chasing dogs, he was usually rowing with Ronnie, his younger brother, who has spent years fighting another battle, an addiction to heroin.

When I gave Ronnie a job as kitchen porter I hadn't reckoned on the bickering it would entail. The two brothers loved each other dearly but had ferocious squabbles. I once asked where Gordon had got to, only to be told to look out of the window. I glanced across the road and there was Gordon on the common, sprinting away from an angry Ronnie, who was trying to catch him waving clenched fists.

They were hugely competitive. One day I saw Ronnie at the sink and, after examining his sparkling plates and cutlery, I told him he had the most talented hands I'd ever seen. I was winding him up, but for weeks after he boasted to Gordon that I had praised his hands, as if he was the more gifted of the Ramsay brothers.

There was another kitchen porter, Marius, and when I think of him it makes me realise how unskilled I was at handling certain situations with my staff. Marius turned up for work one morning saying he had a sore throat. I didn't send him home to bed like a sympathetic, experienced employer might have done. Instead someone or other mentioned that the best cure for Marius was Armagnac and Port, so we filled a brandy glass with the concoction and told him to drink it. Half an hour later, when Marius collapsed unconscious on the kitchen floor, we carried him outside to the freezing cold, dumped him in the courtyard and forgot about him. A snowstorm came and went before someone said in a shocked way, 'Marius.' We rushed out to recover his trembling body. Two hours after complaining of a sore throat, Marius was suffering from alcohol poisoning and the onset of hypothermia.

Marius took some time off sick (recovering from the world's worst hangover) and the stand-in kitchen porter pitched up. On his first day I gave him a few hundred quid and told him to go to the bookies and put the money on a horse which was racing that afternoon. He left with the readies, muttering the horse's name to himself so as not to forget it. We never saw him again.

Anyway, you now have a clearer picture of me as the boss. I was nasty, vicious, aggressive and blunt. I put my hands up to all of that. But, hey, don't get me wrong, along the way I had earned the respect and loyalty of the brigade. My style of leadership was harsh but it was necessary if I was going to achieve my dream of winning three Michelin stars. All of the chefs who went through Harveys will say they have never worked in a more pressurised environment, but I doubt any of them will say they regret the experience. Chefs love mania.

Away from the kitchen, I like to think I had my moments of compassion, too. I helped out those with financial problems, and when Gordon went to work in France I lent him the money for the trip. I was also there with the rest of them when they played football on Wandsworth Common. In fact, I was often the one who dragged them out to play when they said they were too tired to exercise.

The boys would do anything for me, and that included beating up my rivals. In the summer of 1990 I was asked to cook at a polo event and Antony Worrall Thompson, by then an established name in the restaurant world and the head chef at 190 Queensgate, kindly said he'd come along to help out.

I arrived at the Royal County of Berkshire Polo Club with my brigade and everything was going well until my boys decided Antony deserved a pummelling. Aristocrats and rich polo lovers were happily enjoying their food in the marquee, but behind the scenes in the attached kitchen, Antony was being pelted with lemon tarts.

Lemon tart has to be served warm. You make a pâté de sable and line your mould with it, let it overlap to cover for shrinkage and blind bake so it's perfect. Then you put your lemon custard in and cook it. Then you cut the excess off so you have a perfect wall of pastry, and you keep the tart warm.

At Harveys I used to make lemon tart fresh for every service. You can't make it in the morning and then serve it in the evening because it won't have that magic and the perfume from the lemon zest.

The other day I was in Luciano, my restaurant in St James's, and the girl who was making the Tarte au Chocolat was allowing it to set. I said, 'Keep it close to the oven so it's like eating a fondant that melts in your mouth. If it sets it goes like a soft bar of chocolate.'

Antony was quickly coated in sweet yellow goo. He tried to make a run for it but thought better of charging through into the marquee because he looked ridiculous and it would cause too much of a scene. So he sprinted out of the makeshift kitchen and into a field, and that's where Antony was tackled by one of my boys, the wildebeest brought down by a leopard. He was then subjected to the humiliation of having a dozen eggs cracked on his head by the Harveys brigade. Antony, whom I've always liked, didn't take it very well.

Another incident that illustrates the vicious rivalry at the time involved my boys and the ones who worked for the Roux brothers. It was during the restaurant world's annual trade fair at the Business Design Centre, in Islington, north London. The boys from Harveys were taunting the Roux brigade by calling them Roux robots and Boil-in-the-bags, a reference to the line of pre-cooked food that was produced by the Roux brothers. There was an air of tension and then, as I was on stage in the middle of demonstrating how to cook fish, a scuffle broke out in the audience between the two brigades. A couple of the lads had to be escorted from the building – fine, if they had been drunk at a nightclub, but they were haute-cuisine chefs at a trade fair, for heaven's sake. Newspapers got hold of the story and had a lot of fun writing about 'Michelin Star Wars'.

As it was, there was more than enough scrapping going on at Harveys. We had to contend with the Wandsworth yobs who thought it hilarious to wander up to the restaurant window, drop their trousers and do moonies at my customers. I'd send out chefs to deal with the bare-arsed idiots and chase them off. The Wandsworth louts might have thought they were tough, but the Harveys brigade was the toughest of the tough. One day a trio of young hooligans pushed open the front door, produced a can of Coke, shook it up, opened the lid and threw the exploding can into the restaurant. According to witnesses, it was like a gas bomb. Customers dived for cover, hoping not to be soaked by the foam as it fountained out of the missile. The yobs then legged it, stupidly unaware that their escape route was taking them right past the kitchen door at the back of the restaurant. 'Get them, Gordon,' I shouted.

Just as the yobs were running past the door, Gordon and a couple of other chefs greeted them in the courtyard. From my place at the stove, I could hear the biff, bang, wallop sounds of a good old scuffle. Then Gordon reappeared clutching his hand. During the fight he'd punched one of the yobs in the mouth and had somehow managed to end up with a tooth wedged in his knuckle. He extracted the gnasher, but was clearly in some pain, moaning and groaning; there was some speculation as to how long it would be before septicaemia set in and killed him. 'For Christ's sake,' I said. 'Am I the only bastard cooking?' At this point JC dashed into the kitchen, his eyes wide with terror. 'They've got a hand grenade!' he screamed.

Hand grenade? Who? My maître d' spluttered something about the yobs' dads appearing on the scene for a bit of score settling and bringing with them a hand grenade. We were so exhausted and run down that none of us thought to question JC's suggestion that our little restaurant by Wandsworth Common was about to be blown up by a hand grenade. I gave the command, 'Bolt the fucking doors and get down.' My SAS unit searched for cover, sheltering under pieces of furniture and in kitchen cupboards. When it was all quiet on the Western front, everyone re-emerged and continued with the job in hand, be it chopping veg, making pastry or trimming cheese for the evening service.

SIXTEEN

No bill, no mink

MY MANAGERESS came into the kitchen and she was nervous. The man on table two was complaining about the cheese, she said. I don't know what was making her nervous: his complaint about the cheese or my potential reaction to his complaint. I was curious. 'What's wrong with the cheese?'

'He says he always chooses his own cheese,' she replied.

'Well, tell him that's not the way we do it here,' I said. 'Just tell him that we do a plate that contains a selection of seven cheeses – they are all perfectly ripe – and that's how we do it. Go and tell him that.' She scurried off, but returned a minute later saying the customer was still insisting he wanted to choose his cheese rather than have the seven-cheese selection. 'Can you deal with it?' she pleaded.

I walked from the kitchen to the restaurant and up to the customer in question. You'll have to take my word for it when I say that I was extremely polite, even though he was a particularly ugly, short-arsed idiot. I told him that we serve a selection of seven cheeses, 'And that's the way we do it here, sir.'

'But I don't like two of those cheeses,' he said.

'Well, that means there are still five of them that you do like, sir. And each cheese is served as a substantial, generous portion.'

He was having none of it. 'I always choose my own cheese.'

'That's not how we do it here,' I repeated, not quite knowing where we were going with this one.

Slowly, with a hint of menace in his voice and a pause between each word, he said, 'I always choose my own cheese.' I don't know what happened in my head. I just decided that I wasn't going to tolerate it. The job's hard enough, I thought, why do I want someone like that in my restaurant? Even if there is an issue and we're wrong, there's no need to be an arsehole. And don't patronise me – and that's what he had done. He was patronising me.

Of course I wanted to kick him out, but when you work your way up through the kitchens of Michelin-starred restaurants they forget to teach you how to deal with rude and difficult customers. Albert was a strict boss and Pierre was notoriously hard on his staff, but I had never seen either of them give the punters what for. Raymond, of course, was charm personified, so probably would have conceded and let the bloke choose his own bloody cheese. And what about Nico? It would infuriate him when customers booked a table and then did a no-show, so Nico would make his wife phone them to ask what had happened and then, with his hands on his hips, he would stand close by her – close enough for the person at the other end of the line to hear – and bark loudly, 'Tell them to fuck off ... we don't need their fucking money ... Fuck them ... Put the phone down on them.'

Staring at this dwarfish, patronising man who was slowing down the smooth-running operation of the restaurant for my valued customers, I found myself saying, 'Why don't you just fuck off?' Pause. The smug smile didn't leave his face. 'Forget the bill,' I said. 'Just fuck off.' He stood up and walked out of Harveys.

The choose-my-own-cheese story is one of those anecdotes which, according to most people, would be told to illustrate the claims that I was an angry young man. After all, what kind of a chef kicks out a customer whose only offence is to ask if he could choose his own cheese? Yet what is fascinating about the above story is that I have since heard the customer *intended* to be kicked out. It was all premeditated. He came to the restaurant with the sole intention of getting a free meal by being obstinate. I can't think of many men who would put themselves through the humiliation of being told to eff off just so they could have a free lunch. But then, I suppose I should take it as a compliment.

Harveys had earned a terrific reputation for its food but, as I have previously mentioned, punters also came for the show. One element of the show was provided by the celebrity clientele: star-struck customers could sit just a few feet away from them and ogle. I mean, if Ollie Reed had asked you to join his table you'd remember it for the rest of your life, wouldn't you? Food is food, but a great restaurant is an experience. And the tension was heightened by the thought of the volatile, moody chef who was supposedly skulking in the kitchen. Customers had this image of me: the long-haired wolf lying in wait, ready to pounce on his prey, be it the customer who dared ask for salt or the one who returned his plate because the meat was undercooked.

The truth is that if customers wanted salt they could have it. If they wanted their meat well done, let them have it that way. That's their choice. Everyone has a different palate. What bothered me was when customers started swearing and being loud, causing a scene in the restaurant and abusing the waiters, spoiling the enjoyment for neighbouring tables – that's when they were asked to leave. I say *asked* to leave, though the five-step eviction process was perfected to such a degree that often not one single word was necessary. This is how it would work:

1) JC tells me about the irritating customers and I emerge to check them out before giving JC the OK.

2) JC rounds up his waiters and nods towards the table where the offending customers are seated.

3) On JC's command the squad of waiters zooms in and clears everything – plates, glasses, cutlery, wine bottles, you name it – from the table in about fifteen seconds, so only the tablecloth remains. The customers are left sitting there, thinking the table is being cleared for the next course and marvelling at the fantastic service.

4) JC swoops in, eagle-like, and snatches up the tablecloth. He disappears with it without a word, just whoosh. A few minutes

earlier the customers were sitting there, drunk and imperious, now they're embarrassed. There is nothing but a wooden table in front of them.

5) The customers get the message – they have been humiliated – and they grab their coats and hurry out onto Bellevue Road. And no, they did not have to pay a bill.

It was a spectacular sight. However, one night the victims – a barrister, his mate and a woman – sat there for 15 minutes, stunned by JC's performance but puzzled as to what would happen next. Nothing happened, absolutely nothing – actions speak louder than words. The message could not be ignored: table number nine, your time is up. That's the end. Please leave.

I used that particular eviction technique – 'the whoosh' – in subsequent restaurants that I owned. At the Canteen a customer tried to pay his bill by American Express, even though the menu clearly stipulated that we did not accept that particular credit card. The manager came to me and said: 'The man says Amex is all he has. He says, "Take it or leave it." What shall we do?' Well, that's rich isn't it? The bloke had enjoyed a nice dinner with his wife and two friends but now he couldn't pay for the meal. So I gave the instructions to clear the customer's table, whoosh-style. Once it was cleared the customer and his companions walked out of the restaurant, having enjoyed a free meal but looking extremely embarrassed to have been whooshed in front of the other diners. Before he got to the door, the man came up to me at the bar. He was red-faced, sneering and angry and had something to say to me because he felt belittled. 'I run rings around dickheads like you,' he said. He may have been the most important man in the outside world but he was in my restaurant and I used my standard but effective line (delivered in a quiet but firm voice), 'Your evening is over, sir.' He left.

I was at the stove in Harveys one night when JC came into the kitchen and said a customer was refusing to pay his bill. Why? Because he waited twenty minutes for his soufflé. Well, what can you do about people like that? A soufflé has to be cooked to order because it starts to deflate as soon as it comes out of the oven. You can't say, 'Here's one I made earlier.' The customer was trying to take advantage, hoping for a free meal, but he had upset me in the middle of service. I asked JC if the customer's wife had a coat in the cloakroom and he disappeared and then returned saying, 'She has a mink, Marco.'

'Bring it to me,' I said, 'and tell the customer to come and see me.' When he appeared in my sweatshop with his wife alongside, he was looking cock-sure, as if he'd told his wife to observe how he would handle the situation. He said, 'Who is the chef?'

'I am.'

'You wanted to see me.'

'Please stand there,' I said in my best headmaster's voice, telling them to position themselves by a wall. 'Wait until I have finished preparing this dish.' He and his wife stood silently for a minute or two, watching me while I finished chopping or searing, then I turned to them and inquired, 'What's the problem?'

The man puffed himself up. 'We waited twenty minutes for our soufflé and we're not going to pay our bill now.' I said, 'That's fine. No bill, no mink.' I pointed towards an underling in the corner who was holding the coat. The customers looked over. I had kidnapped their coat. I repeated the terms of the ransom. 'No bill, no mink. Make your choice.'

I had hardly finished the sentence when his wife perked up, 'Pay the bill, darling.'

I wasn't chippy, I don't think. It wasn't a case of a working-class lad having an issue with his upper-class customers. I didn't have a problem with the world I came from and I've never tried to hide from it. I was brought up on the belief that no man can choose what he's born into, but every man can choose to better himself. I tried to show customers the same amount of respect they showed my staff, although obviously there were exceptions.

JC told me the man on table twelve was being obnoxious.

I said, 'What's his problem?'

'He's just obnoxious. He's not very nice.'

So I stopped cheffing, went out to table twelve and said to the man sitting there, 'Good evening. The maître d' tells me you've got a little problem.'

The customer said, 'I haven't got a problem.'

'Strange,' I said, 'because the maître d' tells me you're being obnoxious.' At that point the man sitting on the neighbouring table interrupted, 'I can vouch for him. He wasn't obnoxious.'

I thought, What's it got to do with him? Why can't he just eat his meal and keep his nose out of it? So I said, 'And you can fuck off, too.' Two birds with one stone.

Other customers must have found this sort of behaviour extremely exciting, because a lot of the observers on neighbouring tables tended to come back. So much so, in fact, that certain people actually thought I was hamming it up for effect. They reckoned my irritable nature was part of an act, designed to get more PR for Harveys. The reality is, I didn't like it when people interrupted my intensity. I was so passionate about the food and the restaurant that any criticism was destined to wind me up. A customer questioning the cheese dish was criticism. A customer saying he wouldn't pay his bill was criticism. And then there were the moments when I just happened to be in the wrong place at the wrong time.

I was at reception one evening, going through the following day's bookings, when I heard a voice and said, nose still in the book, 'I'll be with you in a minute, sir. Can you hang on?'

Then I heard the same voice say to me, 'Are you going to insult me?'

I looked up and there, in front of me, was a mountain of a man. He was about six foot seven and broad as well. He had been in for dinner with a mate and had clearly drunk too much.

'Sir,' I said. 'If you're looking for insults then you've knocked on the wrong door.'

'Is that the best you can do?' he asked. He was itching for a fight.

'Look, if I decide to insult you I'll choose my time and place to do it,' I said. 'And now is not the time or the place, so please enjoy your dinner, sir.'

He went back to his table, and an hour or so later the big bruiser and his mate left Harveys, took a right and were walking up St James's Drive. It was about midnight and I decided that now was the time. I told one of my chefs, Lee Bunting, and another one of the boys to fill two buckets of water. Then I sent them off to soak Man Mountain. They hurried off and returned, mission accomplished. I was having an espresso a while later when Man Mountain reappeared, perfectly dry but clutching two carrier bags full of soaked clothes. He must have gone home, changed, and then returned to the restaurant to show me the sodden garments.

'You threw a bucket of water over me,' he said.

'I didn't,' I replied. 'I know nothing about this. Did you try chasing the people who did it?'

And his response was, 'Have you ever tried running in a wet suit?'

Great line, that.

I could smell the Michelin inspectors a mile off. The most important ones were the two at the top of Michelin UK; Derek Brown, the head inspector, and his number two, Derek Bulmer. They were the two Dereks. Or rather, the two Mr Bs. I was not on first-name terms with the highly influential duo.

Inspectors tended to book a table for two early in the evening, let's say seven o'clock. You'd instantly smell a rat as seven was rather early for dinner in Wandsworth – then they would order a half bottle of wine. Again, that's suspicious, because people going for dinner to an upmarket restaurant usually order by the bottle. Then there was the fact that we knew what they looked like. After winning my first star I had met both Mr Bs, but when booking they would still use an alias because obviously they didn't want me to know they were coming.

They didn't arrive in disguise, wearing false beards and wigs, but although I knew they were in the restaurant they were too clever to be outwitted.

There wasn't the opportunity to make their meals more special because they ordered dishes you couldn't change, such as a fish soup or terrine, which had been made earlier in the day.

After winning my first star in 1988 I had retained it the following year. Then, in the last few months of 1989 it crossed my mind that I might be up for promotion, because the Michelin men visited half a dozen times.

By now I had done several things to improve Harveys since winning my first star. During the summer of 1989 I closed the restaurant for six weeks so that it could be totally refurbished. The provincial, unexciting decor I had inherited and despised was stripped away. I had taken on the services of interior designer David Collins, who would go on to design many of my restaurants. David made Harveys far more stylish, elegant and chic, basing his design on New York's Waldorf Astoria.

One day I saw Derek Brown in the restaurant and asked him what he thought I could do to win two stars. 'It's not for me to tell you how to run your restaurant,' replied the man I called Mr Brown. 'But if you start serving amuse bouches and improve your coffee you won't be a million miles away.' That day I started serving amuse bouches or amuse-gueules – little tasters to entertain the mouth. The following week I bought the best coffee machine and ordered in a brand of delicious coffee. Harveys started serving the finest coffee in London. I could see where Mr Brown was coming from. Amuse-gueules provide the first impressions of the meal while coffee provides the final mouthful.

I also asked my former boss, Albert Roux, what I could do to win another star, and he said, 'Your menu is right, the balance is right; just refine the dishes and you will win two stars.'

I've mentioned the refinement of classical dishes. There's another name for it – nouvelle cuisine. The phrase probably sends shivers down your spine if you were a restaurant-goer in the eighties and remember the horrendous dishes involving small portions of food and crazy combinations – an assault on the palate of punters who seemed happy to pay for the stuff. What a great shame that so few chefs – and most restaurant-goers – do not understand the true meaning of nouvelle cuisine. In fact I'd say that 99 per cent of chefs haven't got a clue what it means. Nouvelle cuisine is classical cuisine with the concept lightened. It is what Fernand Point did in France in the forties and fifties and then explained perfectly in his book, the book I found while working in the kitchen of the Box Tree as a teenager.

At Michel Roux's Waterside Inn they used to do a veal cutlet with caramelised bananas and raspberry vinegar sauce. No, not very clever. At Albert Roux's Gavroche they did tournedos of beef with mangoes, oranges and lemons with a rum sauce served with a timbale of rice with a fried banana on top of it. Again, it doesn't sound particularly palatable. You'd probably describe both of these dishes as nouvelle cuisine and you wouldn't be blamed for doing so. But neither of them are true nouvelle cuisine because neither can be described as a classic dish which has had the concept lightened.

At Harveys it was all about lightening the concept. So I'd take flour out of sauces and use natural juices. A mousseline of scallops – a classic – is traditionally made with eggs and cream. But if you use eggs then you have to use the cream to lighten the

flavour, and before you know it, you've diluted the taste of the
scallops, which is what you really wanted to eat in the first place.
You don't need eggs because scallops have their own natural
protein. Simply get rid of the eggs and there you have it –
nouvelle cuisine. Classical cuisine ... new.

The Michelin men would always host a press lunch to coincide with the annual publication of the guide, and usually the meal would take place in a restaurant that was up for promotion. Of course, Michelin needed to book a large table, and surreptitiously, so no one sussed them.

Every January chefs would phone one another to see if anyone had received an unusual booking for the day of the guide's publication lunch. In January 1990 I didn't need to phone around. A booking had been made for a table of twelve and the organiser was very cagey about who was hosting the lunch. I felt confident it was a Michelin lunch, which, more than likely, meant I had won my second star.

I was in the kitchen at about twelve thirty, preparing for lunch service and awaiting the mysterious guests, whose table was booked for 1 p.m., when JC came in and said, 'Mr Brown from Michelin is here to see you.' And there was Mr Brown, standing right by the kitchen door. I went to shake his hand and he held up the freshly printed *Michelin Guide*. He flicked through the pages and then stopped on the entry which read, 'Harveys: two stars ...'

It was an achievement. I was 28 years old, the youngest chef to win two stars from Michelin. It had been six years since a British restaurant had been upgraded from one star to two. I now joined a clique of two-star chefs, all of whom had been my bosses: Raymond Blanc, Nico Ladenis and Pierre Koffmann. The only three-star restaurants at the time were Gavroche, run by another mentor Albert Roux, and The Waterside Inn, overseen by Albert's brother, Michel.

On top of that, Harveys was doing well, considering the slumping economy and high interest rates, which had been imposed to stop the boom. Maggie Thatcher's popularity was in decline and she wasn't doing herself any favours by introducing the poll tax. She had won her third term in office in 1987, the same year I opened Harveys, and the way business was going my restaurant would still be open for business long after Maggie left Number Ten.

Yet Mr Brown's good news did not encourage me to leave Harveys and go off to celebrate. Instead I retreated back into the kitchen and the comfort of hard work and discipline. Mr Brown's guests from the press swanned into Harveys, took their seats, filled their glasses and cheerfully awaited the meal. I served them Tagliatelle of Oysters with Caviar as amuse-gueules; leeks and langoustines in jelly; pig's trotter and then the Crackling Pyramide. And they finished their banquet, Mr Brown would have noted, with the most pleasant coffee money can buy.

A week or two after I had won my second star, the French chef Michel Leron was in London and booked a table at Harveys. Michel was the proud owner of three stars and he wanted to bring three or four fellow Frenchmen for lunch. The table was booked for 1 p.m. but by one fifteen there was still no sign of him. Keith Floyd, brilliant chef and close friend, was in for lunch and could see that I was agitated. I kept popping out of the kitchen, through the restaurant to look out of the window for Michel's car. 'Where is he?' I kept saying to Keith as he told me to calm down. Bad traffic had held them up, but by the time the French contingent arrived at 1.45 p.m. I was in no mood for pidgin English excuses or apologies. Michel and his entourage, draped in expensive cashmere overcoats, hovered by the reception. By now Keith had given up on his own meal and was in the kitchen. I said to him, 'That's it. I won't serve them. They can't take the piss out of me like this. Let's see how a three-star Michelin chef reacts when a two-star chef tells him to fuck off.'

Keith may well have had a few famous dramas in his time, but on this particular day he didn't want a scene. He had come in for a nice lunch but now he was being dragged in as peacemaker, the Kofi Annan of gastronomy.

He dashed out to the restaurant and in his fluent French tried to placate Michel and his crowd. Once he had got them seated, a glass of champagne in their hands, he hurried back into the kitchen. 'You just can't be like this,' he said. 'Cook for them. And when you have cooked for them, you get out there and you sit and try to talk to them. You can't talk French and they can't talk English, but you can still enjoy the experience of their company.'

I remembered that this was not the first time Keith had played the peacemaker. About a year earlier he had been in the middle of lunch at Harveys when a film crew turned up to film me. Halfway through filming, I got shirty for some reason or other and told them to get lost. As they headed out of the restaurant to load their equipment into their van, Keith came into the kitchen. 'You may not like these people,' he said. 'They are, after all, television people, but it's terribly important that you are nice to them because they can help your business.' I went outside and had a chat with the crew and within a few minutes they were back in Harveys, cameras rolling.

Keith says that while he still loves me, I am like a petulant child at times. But remember, I was just a young man in his twenties. I was trying to be a great chef, not a celebrity. Keith had made a conscious decision to become a television star, and at that time he reigned as king of the celebrity chef pack.

If I was away from the kitchen, doing an interview or making a programme, who would be in the kitchen cooking? I was chasing a Michelin dream which had more than enough pressures attached to it. Now I was being followed by photographers and journalists who relayed my every movement and conversation to the British public. I didn't have a team of managers like the celebrity chefs of today. Alan Crompton-Batt worked as my publicist but unlike the modern-day celebrity chef, my life was not one long day of meetings with potential sponsors, TV producers, book publishers and agents. I didn't zoom from one television studio to another to sit on a sofa or stand in a mocked-up kitchen doing a Baked Alaska demonstration for the viewers at home. If you are a chef today and want to become a TV personality then you'll have some idea of what to expect because others have gone before you. But I wasn't in a position to look around me and think, There's another young cook who's in the limelight; I'll ask him how he copes with being a celebrity. There were no other young celebrity chefs. What's more, I was a working-class lad, and the big name at the time was Keith, who was posh, highly articulate, witty, and distinctly middle class.

When I gave rare interviews to newspapers the journalists would have to come to Harveys and stand by the stove, firing questions while I fiddled with the gas, chopped, ladled, seared and poached. Away from the kitchen, it was a struggle to keep my private moments my own, and I was constantly trying to outwit the Fleet Street pack that lurked so close behind me. When I started going out with Nicky Barthorpe, the *Daily Mail* gossip columnist Nigel Dempster sniffed out the story and sent one of his team, Kate Sissons, to the flat in Tite Street, Chelsea, where Nicky and I had set up home together. Kate rang on the buzzer wanting an interview. Would Nicky and I pose for a picture? I ignored the requests. Half an hour later I looked out of the window down onto the street a couple of storeys below and could see Kate sitting in an open-top sports car with a photographer, another woman, at the wheel. They knew I would have to come out sooner or later and they would sit and wait all day if necessary. I was imprisoned, there was no way out other than through the front door and into the *Mail*'s clutches, but somehow I had to escape.

I phoned the kitchen at Harveys and asked to speak to Lee Bunting, by far the most loyal of my henchmen and the one who truly appreciated my sense of mischief. I said, 'Lee, listen closely. There are two people outside my flat waiting to get a picture of me. They're from the *Daily Mail* and they're in an open-top sports car. I want you to get a couple of the lads and give them a bucket each. Fill the buckets with flour – be generous with the flour – then add some water and mix it to a good paste. Once you've done that get over to Tite Street and chuck the contents of your buckets over the two people outside my flat. Got it?'

'Yes, Marco.'

I sat by the window waiting for the show to start and waved at Kate, who waved back. Then I saw Lee and his little gang appear, their car screeching up beside the photographer's sports car. Lee and the others jumped out and – splat – three buckets of paste were thrown over Kate, her snapper and the leather interior of the car. Goo all over them. They jumped out of the car and stood there, white statues on the black tarmac. On the other side of the road was an old people's home and the elderly residents gathered and gasped. The next thing that happened was not meant to have happened. From nowhere a red car zoomed into the picture and four large men with guns leapt from it. 'Police!' they yelled. Lee and the other cooks were pushed up against a wall while the police put away their guns and produced batons and handcuffs. A couple of squad cars arrived and my chefs were put into it and whisked away.

It all could have gone badly wrong had I not phoned Kate and asked her not to press charges. 'Come for dinner as my guest at Harveys,' I said. She saw the funny side of it, but the photographer wasn't happy. Nigel, meanwhile, ended up with a good story and eventually Kate got her interview. A couple of nights later I was there at the stove, with Lee and the other miscreants by my side, cooking a Michelin-starred dinner for the journalist we had pasted. Paying penance has never seemed more peculiar.

SEVENTEEN

Banged up and Butchered

I WOKE from my sleep with a start. There was a nasty stabbing pain in my chest, which intensified, making me gasp for breath. It was as if I couldn't get any oxygen. What was happening? What the hell was going on? The last thing I could remember was returning home from Harveys at 2 a.m. and crashing onto the bed, fully clothed, clutching my house keys. Now I looked down to my hands and couldn't see the keys. The pain in my chest wasn't easing. Had I swallowed them? Was it possible that I had swallowed my house keys? My sleep-deprived, adrenaline-fuelled, thousand-meal-an-hour, workaholic existence was certainly manifesting itself in strange forms. I couldn't die now, not before I'd won my third Michelin star.

I staggered from the bed, out of the house and into the street, grabbing a spare set of keys on the way. I grabbed a spare set because it occurred to me that the keys in my gullet might remain lodged there for ever, like the cowboy sheriff with the rusty bullet in his body, and I'd be unable to get back into the house.

I clutched my chest with one hand while using the other to hail a cab. 'Chelsea and Westminster, please.' What a wretched sight I must have looked to the medical team at A&E: a big, pallid, panting creature with wild hair. 'What's the problem?' asked the doctor.

'Swallowed my house keys.'

You hear those apocryphal stories of people limping into hospital because strange objects have been stuck into their orifices during kinky sex games. The story about the wild-haired man who turned up with keys in his chest was destined to become another classic yarn in the staff canteen at the Chelsea and Westminster.

I was taken to a room and X-rayed and then the doctor stood and studied the picture in front of me. 'As you can see,' he said, running his finger down the X-ray, 'there are no keys inside you.' Reassuring news. He reckoned I'd suffered a panic attack in my sleep – there were more of those to come. My blood pressure was something crazy like 210 over 180. If I'd been an older man I would have suffered a heart attack. I didn't ask for a second opinion and I'm glad that I didn't – I later found my house keys on my bedside table.

My God, what had I done to my poor body? I didn't really accept it at the time, but I was undoubtedly messed up, physically, mentally and emotionally. The frightening thing was, I didn't feel tired or exhausted because my craving for the next fix of adrenaline kept me going. I had this ability to drive myself beyond myself, if you get my drift. My mind was stronger than my body. My body was saying, 'Give me a break,' but my mind was saying, 'Let's go faster.' Most mornings, I would leap out of bed and dash around the house, putting on my shoes while simultaneously brushing my teeth, making the coffee and reaching for a Marlboro red.

That pace continued throughout the day, in the restaurant from nine in the morning until two the following morning, and then back home for three or four hours' sleep. It was absolutely relentless. Rumours circulated that I was a coke fiend – understandable, I suppose, when you consider the mania whirlwind that engulfed me. However, I couldn't have done the job or worked those hours if I'd been on drugs. Sitting in Harveys once, aware of the gossip, I amused myself by lining my forearm with salt and sniffing it up my nostrils. Onlookers would have thought I was snorting cocaine, but I won't try that joke again. I wasn't much of a drinker either and wouldn't really take up drinking until I was thirty-eight.

I was in the kitchen one afternoon, probably jabbing an incompetent lackey, when JC poked his head through the doorway and said, 'Your doctor is here.' Eh? My doctor?

Don't try this at home.

'How weird,' I said. Wandsworth was a bit off the beaten track for her. 'Has she ordered?' I asked JC.

'No, she's not eating,' he replied. 'She says she wants to see you.' I went through to the restaurant and, sure enough, there was my doctor at a table. I was surprised by her presence but sat down and joined her. She explained that Nicky Barthorpe, my girlfriend in between my first and second wives, was very concerned about my health and had requested she come and see me. How peculiar.

I lit a Marlboro, swigged a double espresso and mumbled something about feeling fine. My doctor explained that I was an adrenaline junkie (I'm paraphrasing, of course) and that I was pushing myself too far. She said I was exhausted and depressed.

She certainly had me sussed. 'You need to be sedated,' said the doctor and she gave me a prescription for some pills. 'Take the pills, go to bed and stay there for three days.' She made me promise to obey her orders. I took the pills, climbed into bed and had an extremely good night's sleep. But it was no use. The following morning I jumped out of bed and zoomed back to Harveys, my beloved comfort zone, my adrenaline heaven.

Nicky and the doctor meant well, but the prospect of taking it easy for three days was utterly incomprehensible to me. My desire for perfection was so dominant that it had become a massive negative in my life. It would take me years to accept the damage that can be caused by determination.

Just in case anyone was unaware of my intense obsession with food, *White Heat* was published in 1990. It wasn't just a cookery book with recipes and photos of the Harveys dishes. It also contained dozens of moody, black and white snaps by Bob Carlos Clarke, the photographer who had been my best man when I'd married Alex. Bob had spent months at Harveys photographing me and my team. (In fact, there were times when he was assigned to do an advertising shoot and would ask me – then unknown – to be his model. I remember, for instance, posing in Levi jeans for one of Bob's ad shoots.)

Alongside the photos of the brigade cooking dishes, smoking and fighting there are quotes illustrating my outlook on life at the time. Flicking through the pages today, I'm struck by a massive quote of mine which reads, 'I can't work in a domestic kitchen; it's just too confined. There's no freedom and there's no buzz. At home I'm not hit with forty covers in half an hour, so there's no real excitement.' In a strange way, it may have explained why I was rarely at home, let alone in the kitchen at home.

I was engulfed by tension, and the whole world, it seemed, was conspiring to keep me in this bizarre state. There were rarely moments of normality. Nicky Barthorpe, who had been a friend and work colleague of my wife Alex, collected me from Harveys one night and was driving us home to Chelsea when we heard a police siren behind us. We pulled over and the cops asked Nicky to step out of the car, so I got out at the same time. After accusing Nicky of taking an illegal left turn, the police then asked if she'd had a drink. Nicky said she hadn't had a drop (which was true) and then she was asked if she'd been smoking drugs (again, she hadn't). Having done a tough night at the stove, I found it all a bit too demanding. It was wrong time, wrong place stuff again. I lurched forward when the drugs question came up, most likely looking haggard and sweat-drenched. 'That's an unnecessary question,' I said to the copper, 'and I think you should retract it.'

The cops turned from Nicky to me, the monster in the darkness. Let's be honest, I don't suppose there was the slightest possibility of the question being retracted. One of them sneered, 'Come again?'

I said, 'I think it's unnecessary to ask her if she's been smoking drugs, and I think you should retract the question and apologise for asking it.'

They told me to get back in the car. They didn't want trouble. 'No,' I said, 'not until you apologise.' I think it was probably three seconds later that I found myself face-down on the warm bonnet of a police car, handcuffed and heading for a cell at Battersea nick. They locked me up for seven hours, then released me and told me to be in court at 10 a.m. I failed to keep the appointment. Instead I went to my solicitor and told him what had happened, but when I said I'd failed to present myself at court he was sick with worry and angst. 'You can either become a fugitive or surrender yourself,' he explained.

'This is all a bit serious,' I said. 'I mean, all I've done is ask a policeman to say sorry to a lady.' Anyway, I surrendered myself, got banged up for another couple of hours, and then made my appearance at the magistrates' court. I was bound over to keep the peace for six months. One of the three magistrates said, 'We'd like you to sign the book on the way out, Mr White.' I assumed she was referring to *White Heat* as it had only recently been published.

'I'm terribly sorry, Your Honour,' I replied, 'but I didn't bring a copy with me.'

The magistrate in the middle was puzzled. She turned to the judge on her right and they whispered for a bit before turning back to me. 'Not *your* book,' she said impatiently, '*our* book.' She pointed towards the clerk's office where reprobates have to sign various court documents.

My tortured life – with its extremes, conflict and encounters with coppers – may have been difficult for me to deal with, but the press couldn't get enough of it. I was in the papers every day. One minute I was 'the enfant terrible of haute cuisine', the next I was 'the enfant terrible of British cooking', then I acquired global domination by becoming 'the enfant terrible of the culinary world'. I was the 'anarchic Byron of the backburner', who was 'almost psychopathic'. Most of them saw me, unequivocally, as 'London's rudest chef', which had no detrimental effect whatsoever on business.

When you become famous you become sexy. I might make a flirtatious remark to a woman customer and then, well, one thing would lead to another, which led to my office. The ladies' loos were also used for brief, casual intimacy, and there was even action in the courtyard outside the kitchen, weather permitting. Women who had seen my picture in the papers, or observed my mug on the telly, felt compelled to raid their drawers and send me explicit letters along with their knickers. Chefs aren't supposed to receive knickers in the post, no matter how many Michelin stars they've won. If I'd kept the contents of those Jiffy bags I could have opened an underwear shop.

Instead I used to auction the knickers in the kitchen before service. I'd start the bidding at a pound and invariably it was the young Gordon Ramsay, emotionally battered and bruised by my bollockings, who outbid the others and ended up with these mementoes – perfumed, lacy souvenirs of his life with the man he later described as his mentor.

———

My adrenaline addiction dictated that when I'd finished a seventeen-hour day at Harveys I didn't particularly want to go home and sleep. I was both an early bird and night owl. Several years earlier, when I'd first come to London, I had headed to the King's Road and hooked up with the post-punk crowd. But during my Harveys days I went from socialising with the Chelsea set to mixing with the Mayfair mafia (affluent young people, rather than gangsters) and I moved into a flat in Pavilion Road, Knightsbridge.

I would go to Tramp, the renowned rock star-crammed nightclub in Jermyn Street, just off Piccadilly, which was owned by the so-called King of Clubs, Johnny Gold. I didn't dance and I didn't drink, but I liked the place, nevertheless. Johnny was very kind to me, and although I wasn't a member he allowed me to come and go as I pleased and always invited me to join him on his table of beautiful people.

Even in this star-studded environment I feared slumping into boredom, so in order to maintain my adrenaline rush I would flick French fries across the room at famous people, though obviously not when Johnny was sitting beside me. One night I spotted the Rolling Stone Bill Wyman and I thought I'd chip him. He was moving in to chat up a blonde and just as he put his arm around her waist I flicked the chip. It hit him hard on the hand. Bill snatched his hand back and scarpered, probably thinking the girl had smacked him.

Tramp was the setting for an encounter with Lisa Butcher, the woman who would become my second wife. I was walking into the club one night when there were three young ladies getting a hard time at the door. Tramp didn't like to be seen as a pick-up joint – it was there for couples and friends – so single-sex groups were usually turned away. As I passed reception I felt sorry for the girls and said, 'They're with me,' and as a result they were allowed in. I carried on walking down the stairs when one of them said, 'Hello, Marco.'

I turned round and stared at her face, but I couldn't put a name to it. In fact, I didn't recognise her at all. 'Who are you?' I asked.

She said, 'We met at Harveys. I'm Lisa Butcher.'

Then she reminded me how she had been one of the guests at photographer Norman Parkinson's birthday party, held at Harveys in 1990. Bob Carlos Clarke, who was also at the party, had brought her into the kitchen to introduce her. I remembered the occasion now. She was an eighteen-year-old model, dressed glamorously in a sailor's suit. She was a big name; people had been talking about her. At school she had won the Elle Face of the Year competition and when she arrived at Harveys she was something of a celebrity, because Parkinson had recently photographed her and publicly predicted that she was 'the face of the nineties'. I suppose Parky had done for her what Ronay had done for me. It had been a brief introduction at Harveys and now, on the stairs at Tramp, our conversation was equally short. I didn't see her again that night.

At Harveys the next day Lisa phoned. She wanted to say thanks for helping her and her friends get into Tramp. She suggested coffee sometime. 'I'm at Harveys all afternoon,' I said. 'If you want to come over, I'd love to have coffee with you.' I couldn't let a beautiful girl get in the way of Harveys. That afternoon we had coffee at my restaurant, followed by a walk on Wandsworth Common. It was all quite romantic. A dinner date was fixed and the next thing I knew we were partners.

Lisa was undoubtedly one of the most exquisite-looking women in the world. I was enchanted by her beauty and that was the problem.

I was a young man who was visual and found her looks intoxicating, the mere sight of her was so amazing that I completely forgot to think about her personality. But if I'd thought about it, it would have dawned on me that we weren't a good match because we had so little in common. Within three weeks of meeting her at Tramp I had proposed with the line, 'Do you fancy running off and getting married?'

What on earth was I playing at? I thought I was happy, but I was lonelier than I had ever been. If I'm honest with myself, I never had any emotions for Lisa. It wasn't her fault. Apart from having nothing in common, there was also a big age difference – she was twenty-one and I was thirty. Of course, I didn't step away from my one true love. I continued to work like a dog at Harveys while Lisa set about organising the wedding, a Catholic number at Brompton Oratory in Knightsbridge, followed by a reception for seventy guests at the Hurlingham Club, beside the Thames in Fulham.

The night before the wedding I had a memorable meeting with a man called Rafiq Kachelo. Rafiq had been a regular at Harveys since the early days and was such a big spender that he was single-handedly responsible for keeping us going in the days before Egon Ronay's glorious review. We all adored him because of his ability to torch money like no other person I've known.

I think I'm right in saying that he was the world's richest mango grower and his wealth was obvious. He would arrive at Harveys and order a £2,000 bottle of Petrus '55 – and that was just as an aperitif. Most people might have a five pound gin and tonic before their meal, but Rafiq's pre-dinner drink cost him 400 times that amount. There had been weeks when Rafiq alone was accountable for 50 per cent of Harveys takings. When I was married to Alex, Rafiq took us and another couple for lunch at Michel Roux's Waterside Inn. The bill for five was an astonishing £10,000. He spent big, seven days a week. He looked the part, too and was always immaculately dressed. There was something odd about him, though. Although he could drink huge quantities, Rafiq never appeared drunk and the waiters used to say he never left the table to go to the loo. He gave new meaning to the phrase hollow legs.

Anyway, the night before my wedding, I was sitting with Rafiq and for some reason he asked me what sort of cufflinks I would be wearing for the wedding ceremony. 'Oh my God,' I said. 'I haven't got any cufflinks.' I'd never needed cufflinks before. Rafiq removed the ones he was wearing and handed them to me. They were monsters; heavy, large and with fifty diamonds in each of them. They were beyond vulgarity because they were so beautifully crafted.

————

I promised to return them to him after the wedding but when that moment came he refused to take them back, saying, 'I meant them as a gift.' (Months later, when I asked Lisa to rummage through my belongings and give the cufflinks back, she said they were lost.) Before I left Rafiq that night, he said, 'Are you sure you're doing the right thing?'

Of course I was doing the wrong thing, but I didn't have the courage to accept it, so I replied, 'Yeah.'

Rafiq was continually spouting words of wisdom, one of his favourite sayings being, 'Never let an illusion turn into a delusion.' Those words came back to me in the Brompton Oratory on 14 August 1992, as my bride walked down the aisle towards me and my best man, Albert Roux. It was all so showbizzy, the rock-star chef marries the upmarket young model. The illusion that I could be as successful in the home as I had been in the kitchen was rapidly turning into a delusion.

I do remember thinking I shouldn't be there, but there was something inside me which said that rather than cancel the whole thing, it was better to go through with the wedding, let Lisa have her big day and then let it break down naturally afterwards. It seemed like an easier blow, though I accept that many people might be appalled by my rationale.

It didn't take long for it to break down. Right from the start the signs were obvious to the outside world. A reporter had asked for my opinion of the bride's dress – a floor-length, backless white dress designed by Bruce Oldfield – and I mumbled something about how she looked like she had dressed to go down the catwalk rather than the aisle. My unkind remark spawned newspaper features along the lines of, 'How would you feel if the man you were marrying hated your dress?' Even at the reception, as guests relaxed and chatted over champagne, I disappeared into the kitchen of the Hurlingham Club to check up on my brigade of boys, who were preparing the wedding breakfast: Terrine of Salmon and Langoustines in a Sauternes Jelly followed by a Fillet of Scotch Beef en Croûte with Pommes Fondants, haricots verts and the Madeira-based sauce périgueux. Amid the heat, the smells, the noise and the pressure, I felt secure. I don't remember blazing rows with Lisa; it just fizzled out. I was at Harveys much of the time and Lisa was working abroad a good deal. Within fifteen weeks we had separated. Let it break down naturally, I had told myself before taking my vows. And it did.

About eight years ago I was in the Pharmacy, in Notting Hill, with my wife Mati, the only woman, apart from my mother, I have ever truly loved. We were having dinner with Jane Proctor, then editor of *Tatler* magazine, and Jane's husband Tom. A woman walked into the restaurant and all heads turned to observe the apparently striking blonde. She was with a group of friends and they walked over to a table and sat down.

Customers were transfixed by the woman, muttering 'Wow, who's she?' and that kind of thing. I glanced at her but couldn't see it myself; I didn't understand what all the fuss was about. But then I found myself studying her and thinking, I know those expressions, I know those looks; I've seen them before.

A few minutes later the woman who'd caused the commotion walked towards our table. As she got closer, she said, 'Hi, Marco.' It was only at that point that I realised it was Lisa, my ex-wife. Just like that night on the stairs in Tramp, I had failed to recognise her. Had she really played such an insignificant role in my life that I didn't have a clue who she was until she spoke?

She said, 'Do I get a kiss from you, Marco?' and bent down to kiss me, but my immediate reaction was to recoil. I moved my head to avoid her pouting lips and said, 'Please don't, Lisa.' My marriage to her had been a mistake and I don't have many good memories of the experience. Lisa didn't say another word, she just walked back to her table and that was the end of it. A couple of minutes later, though, I felt a thud on my chest as I was hit by a missile. Someone from Lisa's table had chucked an ice cube at me. Mati, Jane and Tom were horrified. You don't expect ice-cube throwing in civilised restaurants. In the old days, the days when I did spontaneous things like marrying Lisa, I would have responded rock-star style by charging over to the table with a bucketful of ice. But then I did nothing. Lisa – or another good shot at her table – had finally exacted her revenge.

EIGHTEEN

Not a lot of people know this

MICHAEL Caine was a father figure to me. I couldn't see it at the time but I can see it now as I reflect on our relationship. I remember Michael's friends saying that he regarded me as the son he never had, although if that was the way he felt, he never said it to me.

I met him in the spring of 1991 and we clicked. Michael was a charming and chilled movie star in his late fifties who'd done well in Hollywood. He'd already won his first Oscar and was on his way to winning the second one. I was the Leeds chef, hot-headed and driven, about thirty and not appearing to give a flying fuck about anyone as I roller-coastered towards three Michelin stars. Apart from becoming good mates we were also business partners and opened a seriously successful restaurant called The Canteen. When it all went wrong with a big falling out and a horrible legal battle – it went wrong in spectacular style. I often think that had we not been in business together we would still be great friends.

I owe him immensely. Michael was my mentor, I suppose. He was the man who brought me out of my shell and out of my kitchen. He took me away from Wandsworth and across the river, towards three stars and a restaurant empire. He was confident and charismatic, and he was an established restaurateur who could teach me a few tricks. Without Michael I might never have met Rocco Forte, as it was Michael who introduced us, and without that I might never have won three Michelin stars. Michael's influence on my life was massive.

He was a warm man with simple tastes and a funny, witty, great raconteur. When you sat at his table you didn't want to leave because he had that ability to make everyone in his company feel special. He was full of great lines, including the one he wrote as an inscription to me in his autobiography: 'To Marco, Never let them see you sweat and you'll win.' Perhaps he'd have chosen different words had he known then that we would go on to have a big legal fight, but he described me in his memoirs as his 'new protégé ... brilliant chef'.

Michael wanted me to be rich. Early on in our friendship, he and his wife Shakira took me for dinner to Odin's, one of the restaurants Michael owned with the chef Richard Shepherd. I don't remember much about the meal, I think we were celebrating Shakira's birthday, but afterwards we came out of the restaurant and were standing on the pavement saying cheerio when Michael said something that has stuck in my mind. 'If you are going to be my friend, Marco,' he said, 'you've got to be a millionaire.' When I asked why he replied, 'Because all my friends are millionaires.'

There is an interesting story of how we came to meet. Michael's London home was a penthouse flat overlooking the Thames in Chelsea Harbour, on the other side of Wandsworth Bridge and only a ten-minute drive away. He had been in for dinner at Harveys a few times, but I had always been too busy in the kitchen to go into the restaurant for a handshake and to say hello. However, I knew he was friends with a Harveys regular called Steven Saltzman, the son of Bond movie producer Harry Saltzman. A series of unusual telephone conversations got me and Michael together. What follows is an illustration of how crossed wires can lead to big business with mega stars.

It was March or April 1991 and I was in the kitchen at Harveys when Steven phoned. Steven, by the way, had been a Harveys regular since the day he'd phoned to book a table after reading a *Sunday Times* article about the restaurant. In the article I was quoted as saying something controversial like, 'Everyone who eats at Harveys is fat and ugly.' So when I told Steven there were no free tables, he'd replied, 'What if I tell you I'm fat and ugly?' After that amusing remark I found room for him on that evening and any subsequent evening.

On this particular spring day Steven called for a chat and, apropos of nothing, he asked what I'd been up to. I mentioned that I'd nipped over Wandsworth Bridge to look at a potential restaurant site in Chelsea Harbour and we talked for a minute or two about the area, how it was up-and-coming, with luxurious, expensive apartments, a few boutiques and a couple of so-so restaurants. Princess Margaret's son, Viscount Linley, and the aristo photographer Patrick Litchfield, had opened a burger bar called Deals, which seemed to be doing well and was getting heaps of publicity. There was also a nice hotel where punters could sit and have a cocktail on the terrace while admiring the yachts in the marina.

I finished the chat with Steven and ten minutes later he phoned again saying, 'You're going to be getting a call from Michael Caine.'

'Whatever for?' I asked.

Steven explained that following our conversation he had phoned Shakira Caine and mentioned that I was planning to open a restaurant in the harbour. Michael Caine had been milling around in the background and overheard Shakira mention my name. His ears pricked up and when she came off the phone he asked, 'What was that all about?' So Shakira told him I was going to open a restaurant on their doorstep. Michael was really interested. In his time, he'd made a bit of cash from restaurants and he saw the opportunity of making more with me. Remember though, I wasn't going to open a restaurant in the harbour; I'd only been to look at a site, nothing more than that. My remark to Steven had been embellished wonderfully in the re-telling.

As a kid I didn't watch much TV because I was too busy poaching and nosing around the Harewood Estate rather than sitting at 22 Lingfield Mount when BBC1 showed its Monday night movie after the nine o'clock news. But I had seen two of Michael's movies, *Get*

Carter and *The Italian Job.* So when he rang the voice was instantly familiar.

'May I speak to Marco Pierre White?' he said.

Feeling mischievous I asked, 'Who's speaking?'

'My-cool Caine,' he replied and then swaggered straight to the point, 'I hear you're opening a restaurant in Chelsea Harbour.'

Fifteen minutes ago I hadn't been opening a restaurant in the harbour, but now I was. 'What if I am?' I replied.

'I want in,' said Michael – pure Harry Palmer stuff.

That was how it started. We must have had a meeting, but I don't remember it, and then we hooked up with Claudio Pulze, who'd made a few quid out of the Italian restaurants he owned in London. Claudio owned the lease to the site – it was the same site I'd seen that morning before speaking to Steven – so he was in, as well. This was the set-up:

Michael is the man with the vision. He has wanted to open a restaurant in the harbour because he quite likes the idea of owning a restaurant that's virtually next to his living room. He's just been waiting for the right thing to come along and now it has. Michael has the cash and he's going to give me – yes, hand me – a stake in the business.

Claudio is the guy with the property and he knows about the catering business. He was a bellhop in Turin before coming over to England and, in 1975, opening his first restaurant, Montpeliano in Knightsbridge, which, incidentally, is still there.

I am the one who is passionate about food and has the reputation for being a workaholic. And Michael likes me, so there you go.

The three of us go to see the site. It's a monster. It's going to be bigger than any top restaurant London has ever seen. We're looking at a 200-seater, which means about 3,000 covers on a good week, and when it eventually opened we reached that target. And the more punters we got in, the more money we would make. This place is going to revolutionise restaurants. From now on, size matters. The phrase *gastrodome* had yet to be coined, but what we had in mind was a gastrodome, nevertheless.

There was a hitch, however, which prevented us from opening quickly. The trouble was, Britain was hobbling along in one of the worst recessions of the twentieth century. The restaurant industry was really suffering and there we were, talking about opening a huge restaurant and expecting it to be filled every night. People were skint, for Christ's sake. The Yuppies had done their bollocks, as my old man would have said. John Major was the Prime Minister but there was an overwhelming feeling that he was on his way out, and then there would be a hung Parliament or an end to Labour's years in the wilderness. 'We'll wait,' said Michael. Come again? And he explained his strategy: we would wait for the outcome of the General Election and take it from there. He didn't want to invest until he felt comfortable that he was on to a winner. He was asking himself the crucial question: If Labour win will the economy sink so low that it kills all hopes of opening our Chelsea Harbour monster? It was, then, a Major hitch.

So we waited, and during the pause Michael and I underwent a bonding process. He was a gourmet who liked good food cooked well, no fuss, and he liked to talk about restaurants. The Canteen trio was the second threesome in which he had been involved. Michael was a partner of the chef Richard Shepherd and that restaurateur extraordinaire, the Irishman Peter Langan. He was still Richard's partner, but Peter had died in 1988 in horrific circumstances. Drunk at his home in Essex one night, he had managed to set fire to himself before leaping from his bedroom window. The fire brigade arrived and found him sitting on a bench in his garden, stark naked and suffering from fatal burn injuries. He did five weeks in intensive care before dying.

I never knew Peter, but like everyone in the restaurant industry during the seventies and eighties, I knew *of* him and appreciated his ability to make the headlines. It's worth talking about Peter for a moment or two because Michael saw me as another, younger, Peter. And Michael was not the only one who drew that parallel. One of the first newspaper articles written about me said, 'White behaves like Peter Langan and cooks like Pierre Koffmann.'

Like Peter, I was known as a bit of a character and maverick. But while Peter had been a big drinker – customers went to Langan's to see him crashed out at the table – I wasn't interested in getting drunk. While Peter was an incoherent hell-raiser, I was a coherent one. I respected Peter's love of art – he had magnificent pictures hanging in his restaurants – and I liked his trademark off-white canvas suits, one of which he shows off in the famous portrait of him by David Hockney. The way I see it, Peter was a man who gave himself, and in doing so destroyed himself. He was ruled by emotion, by spontaneity, by romance, by wanting to make people happy.

At times Michael felt let down by Peter, on other occasions he seemed to be extremely fond of him. Perhaps I was becoming the Langan replacement and certainly Michael and Shakira were very kind to me. Michael invited me into his confidence, his home and the world of the glitterati. He didn't need to be so good-natured because we were, after all, simply business partners-to-be. But as our restaurant site sat waiting for the General Election outcome Michael and I started to spend time together. The Caines would come for dinner at Harveys and I would go for lunch at their house near Wantage, in Oxfordshire.

Lunch *chez* Michael followed a pattern. He was the one, rather than Shakira, who would do Sunday lunch, and he was more than capable of the job. He is what I would describe as *a proper cook*: he did what he did – usually simple stuff, nothing too aspiring – but he did it very well. We'd sit down and have a good roast with all the trimmings. There were times, certainly at the beginning of our friendship, when I felt slightly intimidated by Michael, not only because he was a legend but because I wasn't used to sitting down to a meal with people thirty years my senior.

When the food was finished he'd produce a bottle of that ghastly herbal alcoholic drink Fernet-Branca. Then we'd leave the table and go for a stroll in his beautiful garden. Michael and I would walk ahead of the rest of the lunch party like Hitler and Goebbels stepping out of the wolf's lair. And as we ambled through the garden, Michael would recount amusing stories about the people he had met during his fascinating life as well as a Langan story or two.

He'd smile nostalgically while reminiscing about Peter's custom of staggering from his restaurant to collapse on the pavement outside, his legs extended over the kerb so his feet were in the gutter. Michael was at the restaurant once when Peter stumbled in and said in his Irish brogue, 'I don't know why but me feet are fookin' killin' me.' Michael said to me, 'I looked down at his spats to see bloody tyre marks on each shoe. Some bastard had driven over his bloody feet. And Peter didn't even know it …'

We'd continue ambling through the grounds, Michael and I ahead of the herd, until we arrived at Michael's carp pond. Before wandering back to the house, we'd stop and stare at the fish in the water. Michael cherished those carp. One Sunday, after the roast lunch and Fernet-Branca, during the stroll and Langan anecdotes, we arrived at the pond and stood there gazing into the water. It took a minute or two before it registered there wasn't a single fish in the pond. 'Michael,' I said. 'Where have all your carp gone?'

His eyes were misty: he was like the man standing on the church steps after a funeral. 'Bloody flood,' sighed Michael. 'The river flooded, came right up to the pond, and they all swam away.' I offered condolences and as we turned to make the return journey to the house, he took a last look at the pond and moaned, 'Bloody flood, eh?'

While the Canteen was still waiting to see what would happen in the General Election, Michael invited John Major for lunch at the penthouse. 'Will you cook for us?' Michael asked me, and of course I said yes. I was something of a hired gun at that time. Celebrities and anyone who was wealthy enough to have outside caterers at their home would call me in and I'd pitch up with a few of the Harveys boys. I arrived at Michael's penthouse with my mini team of cooks and got to work on the meal. I don't remember what I cooked apart from the main course. Remember, Michael is a straightforward eater who doesn't like fuss, so there were no surprises when he asked for a roast chicken with all the trimmings.

In at least a million homes every day a chicken is put into an oven, left to sit there for a couple of hours and removed when it's brown.

That's not how to roast a chicken. This is what I would do at Harveys and in the restaurants I had afterwards, and this is what I did for Michael:

I'd get the best chicken, a poulet de Bresse, and then I would sous-vide it – cook it under pressure. Sous-viding is a process by which the bird is sealed in a bag, almost vacuum-packed, and poached for ten minutes at eighty degrees Celsius so that the heat gently penetrates from each side. Then it's lifted out of the water and allowed to rest. After that you cook the skin by browning the bird on each side in a pan of clarified butter, sitting it on its back and putting it in the oven for thirty minutes, depending on how big it is. Done – you have a golden brown chicken, cooked to perfection.

If you just put a chicken in the oven it's cooked before it's brown. In my restaurants I had sous-viding machines but you can do the same thing at home by wrapping the bird in heat-proof cling film until it's perfectly sealed. The beautiful juices will collect in the cling film and can be poured over the cooked meat.

The sous-viding process means you don't need to stuff the bird. Stuffing is an important part of roasting a bird, and when I was a boy it was traditional to stuff ducks and geese and then sew up the arse before roasting. Why were they stuffed? To slow down the cooking so the bird cooked from the outside in. If you don't stuff them, the heat gets into the cavity and cooks from the inside out so the skin isn't cooked and the bird is very fatty.

Michael greeted his guests at the door and John and Norma Major came in. Then Mick Jagger and Jerry Hall. And finally, Bryan Forbes and Bryan's wife, the actress Nanette Newman. I was in the kitchen with the boys and we were cooking and chatting – it must have been one of those rare occasions when I allowed conversation – about *The Italian Job*. We were talking about that classic scene in the movie when Michael's team blow up a mini and he delivers the classic line, 'You were only supposed to blow the bloody doors off.' As we were chatting we found ourselves in our own drama. Smoke erupted from the cooker and the air-conditioning wasn't working. So before we knew it we were all coughing and spluttering, engulfed in a fog of smoke, then the fire alarm went off. One of the choking boys opened the kitchen doors to get a bit of oxygen and a thick, dark cloud of smoke poured out of the kitchen and into the living room, where Michael was standing with the PM and a cluster of stars, no doubt telling them how they were about to be fed by a Michelin-starred chef. Through the smoke I could see Michael with a look of shock on his face – he knew the fire brigade didn't have hoses long enough to reach his penthouse – and then he became the action hero we all know and love. Michael dashed in with the window key, yelling, 'You're supposed to open the windows, not the bloody doors ...'

John Major survived that lunch date and went on to beat Neil Kinnock and win the election in April 1992, stretching the Conservatives' winning streak to four general elections in a row. The pollsters and pundits were alarmed by the victory but Michael, Claudio and I were delighted. Major might not have halted the recession but we opened the restaurant anyway, perhaps because Michael felt we had escaped the worst-case scenario, which was a Labour win.

Jonathan Meades, *The Times* restaurant critic, was responsible for the name of our new restaurant. He said, 'Compared with posh little Harveys, the new one sounds like it's going to be a great big canteen.' He was right, I said. 'Then call it the Canteen,' he replied. I have since learned that the famous artists Hockney, Lucian Freud and

Francis Bacon referred to Peter Langan's Odin's as their canteen, so in naming the Chelsea Harbour restaurant I inadvertently paid tribute to the great Peter Langan.

The Canteen opened in November 1992, just as Bill Clinton was about to beat George Bush Senior in the U.S. Presidential Elections. It was heaving, just as we'd hoped, and was bright, spacious and busy, clocking up a few thousand meals each week. Another gastrodome was opened shortly after we appeared on the scene, Terence Conran's Quaglino's. The nation was still in recession but that couldn't stop us. We were a destination restaurant, by which I mean punters travelled to Chelsea Harbour just for a meal at the Canteen. Superb ingredients cooked to perfection.

We cooked dishes like Roast Wood Pigeon with a Perfume of Ceps and White Truffle Oil, Roast Saddle of Lamb with Juniper Jus. There was poached salmon and there was sautéed salmon, served with savoy cabbage leaves which had been cooked, liquidised to a purée and then blended with chicken stock and cream and infused with white truffle oil. The Canteen won a Michelin star and I can't think of another restaurant that size that has achieved that.

I didn't step away from Harveys. I was still there during lunch and evening service, but the rest of day was spent at the Canteen, where I had installed former Harveys chefs Stephen Terry and Tim Hughes. It wasn't until the following year, 1993, that I baled out of Harveys. I sold my stake and Mark Williams, who had been my Harveys assistant from day one, became the restaurant's head chef. Eventually, my little gem on Wandsworth Common was no more. Harveys had played such an influential role in the career of so many talented chefs, but now it was gone. Today it is still a restaurant and a good one at that. It's Chez Bruce, which has one Michelin star, where Bruce Poole is the chef. I have never been back to eat at that restaurant, though. You move on, don't you?

When Michael was in town I would see him at the Canteen and we'd sit at the bar, the king and prince surveying their kingdom. One day a waitress who was quite a large lass walked past carrying a tray of puddings. Michael said, 'What's her name?' I told him and then he turned serious. 'Marco,' he said, 'we've got to stop her serving the food. She makes the portions look small.'

Customers would spot us sitting there and they'd often come up and ask us to autograph their menus. One day a girl approached us and handed the menu first to me. I signed it and was about to pass the pen and menu to Michael when the girl said, 'Thank you very much,' grabbed the menu from my hands and walked off. Maybe she hadn't recognised the man sitting next to me. Maybe she hadn't realised it was Michael Caine, the Hollywood movie star. Or maybe his presence alone had made her go a bit wobbly and she hadn't been able to muster up the courage to ask for his autograph. I was embarrassed for Michael and I think he was a bit put out.

NINETEEN

The best thing that ever happened to me

GIVE ME a rule and I'll probably break it. As a boss I had one sacred rule, which was never to go out with a member of staff. I managed to keep to it from the day I opened Harveys in January 1987 right up to the final days of 1992. Business was business, and I reckoned a fling with a waitress or manageress would be an unnecessary distraction. You can appreciate the dangers, can't you? Think of all those horror stories about the office boss who has a romance with his secretary. I resisted the urge to date attractive women on my payroll for five years, a full half decade, but when I broke the rule, I did it stylishly. What started out as a fling with the bar manager at the Canteen progressed slowly to marriage, and today Mati and I have three adorable children, Luciano, Marco and Mirabelle.

However, our story begins not in 1992 at the Canteen, but a year or so earlier. Antony Worrall Thompson was a mate of mine and would often phone up, asking me to go along to the Char Bar in Chelsea. 'There's a beautiful Spanish bird who works there,' he used to say, as if that was enough to make me charge over the river. Antony's intention was not to set me up with 'the Spanish bird', but he didn't want to turn up at the bar on his own, otherwise he risked looking like a lonely bloke. Despite Antony's pleading phone calls, I don't think I ever went with him, so I never met the woman in question, and I'm sure he was never so precise as to mention that her name was Mati.

Then one night I finished service at Harveys and went for a drink at

Antony's trendy restaurant 190, Queensgate. Antony's charm offensive had reaped dividends. Mati was no longer serving him drinks at the Char Bar, but sitting at his table having enjoyed a long dinner. I don't remember the encounter particularly well. He brought her over to my table, introduced us, she ponced a cigarette and that was it. You might want a bit more detail, so I've asked Mati for her recollection, which goes like this:

It was my birthday and Antony had invited me and a few of my friends for dinner. My friends left and I stayed to have a coffee with Antony and I needed some cigarettes. The cigarette machine was broken so Antony said, 'I'll ask my friend, Marco.' He had mentioned Marco loads of times but I'd never paid much attention and didn't know who the hell he was, which sounds strange now because he was such a big name in the industry.

So Antony took me over to this table and there was this huge guy, slumped forward on the table. I couldn't see his face, only the mass of curly hair on his head. He was wearing a white T-shirt and white chef's jacket. He had one arm draped around a girl and the other arm draped around another girl who was wearing a bustier in order to show off her huge bosom. On the table, there was an overflowing ash-tray as well as scattered packs of different brands of cigarettes. Antony said, 'Marco, this is my friend Mati. Can I have a cigarette for her, please?' This huge man didn't move but said, 'What do you smoke? Marlboros are for hardcore people, Bensons are disgusting, Silk Cuts are for wimps.'

I said, 'I'm afraid I'm a Silk Cut person.' He didn't have any, so I took a Marlboro Light. That was it. He didn't raise his head

once; no eye contact. He must have left some sort of impression
because I remembered the encounter, but it wasn't a particularly
good impression.

Mati knew the Canteen's restaurant manager Torquil, and he called
her to say this fantastic new place was about to open – mentioned the
fact that Michael Caine was behind it – and offered her a job as a
waitress. She didn't want to do waitressing and turned down the job.
Two weeks later Torquil phoned to say the bar manager had dropped
out so would she prefer that position? She said yes. Amid the buzz
of getting the Canteen up and running I didn't really notice her. But
in those first few weeks after opening the Canteen I became
entranced. There were scores of good-looking female punters
coming in each night, dressed to the nines and being friendly to me,
but I was more interested in the woman serving the drinks than the
ladies drinking them.

Mati Conejero was olive-skinned and beautiful. My two wives had
both been English, but I must confess that I much prefer the Latin
look to the English one, and that's probably why I considered Mati to
be stunning. She was born in Majorca, the daughter of Spanish
parents, but she grew up here, so her accent is London rather than
Palma. My initial seduction technique with Mati – my own little way
of telling her I was interested – did not involve conversation. At the
end of evening service I would sit at the bar, flicking matches and
rolled-up pieces of paper in her direction as she took care of the
customers. Feeling the gentle stab of a match in her neck really
annoyed her, but I figured that at the end of the night, when she
came to sweep the floor, she would be forced to think about me.

Within a month or so I must have moved on from match-flicking
to conversation and we became friends. If I saw Mati going for a
break, I would follow her out of the restaurant and jump out behind
her. 'Fancy a coffee?' She'd agree and we'd take a cab from Chelsea
Harbour to Pucci's café on the King's Road.

At first, neither of us remembered that we had already met at 190, Queensgate. Then one night Antony Worrall Thompson came into the Canteen, headed up to the bar and asked Mati if she would like to join him for a glass of champagne. She said she couldn't because she was working, so he said, 'Don't worry. I'll ask my mate Marco if it's OK.' That's when Mati realised that I was the 'huge guy' with the cigarettes at 190. And when Antony came up to me to see if I would allow Mati to have a drink, that's when it dawned on me that Mati must have been that 'Spanish bird' he was always going on about.

One of the things I liked about Mati was that she came from the same humble beginnings as me. Her mother, Lali, was a seamstress (and I would later learn that she is also a magnificent cook) and her father, Pedro, was a waiter. I'd been out with posh girls – hell, I'd even married a couple of them – but I reckon you can only really love your own. In my opinion, if you're from the poorer side of society you can't marry into upper-class circles because you'll never be understood.

There were two obstacles that threatened to stop us turning from friends into lovers. The first was that Mati had a boyfriend; the second was that Lisa Butcher, my estranged wife, wanted to get back together with me.

Mati had been seeing this bloke, on and off, for about two years. She told me, more recently, that her boyfriend had asked her one night, 'Are you in love with Marco?' She had said that no, of course she wasn't in love with me and told him off for asking such a ridiculous question. But I suppose it got her thinking. Shortly afterwards she split from her boyfriend, moved out of his house and into her parents' home in Holland Park. She then had a row with her father, Pedro, about her lurcher's non-stop farting, so she and her dog moved out of her parents' house and into a friend's flat in Tower Hill.

I gave her the keys to my flat in Pavilion Road, Knightsbridge, and said, 'Go and stay there if you need to.'

She said, 'I've got a lurcher that farts.'

'That's fine,' I said, but she declined the offer and handed back the keys a few weeks later.

Some nights Mati would give me a lift home to my flat, and one evening I kissed her before leaping out of the car and hurrying into my flat. She didn't see me for two days afterwards, and even then I didn't mention our snog – is that evidence that I was shy with girls? So Mati was now young, free and single ...

Enter Lisa, stage left. Between the spring and summer of 1992 I had managed to charm Lisa, get engaged to her, marry her in Brompton Oratory and then separate. People make wedding speeches that last longer. Occasionally Lisa would pop into the Canteen for a chat, and then at some point in December, she said, 'Why don't we have another go? Let's give it a try.'

Looking back it seems crazy that I even considered reconciliation. I'm sure I knew by then that Lisa and I were not suited and that our marriage had been a mistake. Meanwhile, Mati and I hadn't done anything more intimate than the occasional kiss, but there was a feeling that we were growing closer. However, for some strange reason I found myself agreeing to Lisa's suggestion.

Lisa and I spent Christmas together at the Manor House Hotel, in Wiltshire. Surrounded by a few hundred acres of parkland, the setting was romantic enough, but our attempted reunion was disastrous. It just didn't work, put it that way. I was reminded of all the reasons we'd broken up, one of the major ones being that we had nothing in common. I just didn't know her and she certainly didn't know me.

It's never going to happen between us, I thought, so I said to Lisa, 'I have to get back to London.' We cut short our stay and a friend of mine, Gary Bentley, came and collected us and drove us back to London. He dropped Lisa at her flat and me at mine. That's it, I thought. I've got my freedom now. I had promised to spend New Year's Eve with Lisa and it was a promise I kept, but before she turned up at the flat I spoke to Mati on the phone.

'What are you up to tonight?' she asked.

'I'm spending the evening with Lisa,' I told her.

'That's nice,' said Mati sweetly. 'You're going to try and make it work again, then?'

I said, 'Well, I'm not in love with her. I'm in love with somebody else.'

'Who?' asked Mati.

I didn't tell her and she later said she didn't think I was referring to her. I ended the conversation by telling Mati, 'I'm very fond of you.'

The dilly-dallying with Mati couldn't go on for ever, though. My uncertainty, indecision and hesitation were proving too frustrating for her. Our relationship was cemented in early January 1993, when we sat alone in the Canteen in the early hours of the morning. The customers had long since paid up and gone and the staff had cleared up and headed off. It was just the two of us together in this massive restaurant at a table at the end of the bar. We were talking about this or that when Mati suddenly stood up, climbed over the table and kissed me. We spent the night together and then I gave her the keys to my flat again; this time she held onto them.

Michael Caine kept his nose out of it. I can't recall him expressing an opinion about me breaking my never-date-the-staff rule. He had not been enthusiastic about my marriage to Lisa, although he'd never said, 'You're making a mistake.' Michael was too polite to say something like that. But then again, when I told him I was going to marry Lisa, he hadn't said 'Great stuff, Marco' either.

When word leaked out that Mati and I were seeing each other, newspapers despatched their hacks and hackettes to trail us. One of the most persistent reporters was Deborah Sherwood of the *Sunday Express*. She was on my case morning, noon and night and arrived with a photographer at the Canteen one evening asking if she could speak to me. Deborah was thinking to herself, It could go one of two ways: Marco might want to have a drink with us or he might tell us to get lost. When she saw me walking in her direction with a glass in my hand she thought, he's obviously decided he wants to have a drink with us. I was not in that sort of mood. Instead, I removed the photographer's camera from his hands and smashed it into tiny bits by hammering it hard on the Canteen's tiled floor. They got the message and left the building, but not before Deborah, ever persistent, fired a few questions at me. I later paid for the camera. Like I said, she caught me in the wrong mood.

Mati fell pregnant, and in December 1993 Luciano was born. A couple of months before his birth, Mati and I and a couple of friends went off for a break in Yorkshire. We were driving back down the A1 when I nodded off in the back seat. I must have had a nightmare and woke screaming, 'Please stop the car. Get this car off the motorway.' I came to my senses and apologised for the outburst, then about fifteen seconds later we were overtaken by a lorry which pulled into our lane; the next thing we knew our car became lodged between the lorry's trailer and cabin. We were dragged down the road, smoke all over the place and sparks flying, then our car was catapulted across the road. We freed ourselves from the wreckage and wondered how the hell we'd survived, and when the police arrived at the scene they were just as shocked that we were alive. They dropped us off at some motorway café and we called a taxi to take us back to London. When we arrived home the house was freezing because the louvre windows had been left open. I stood on the window ledge trying to shut the window when it suddenly jolted upwards and my head was crushed between the window and window frame. I was half dead. Weird that I should survive a horrific car crash then nearly killed myself trying to close a window.

———

I don't keep press cuttings about myself, but when I was in my twenties I would study the newspaper and magazine articles and wonder why I was described as an 'angry young man'. According to the psychologists of Fleet Street, I was angry because my mother had died when I was a kid. Of course, there were times when I was angry, but I saw myself more as confused and hurt by my mother's death.

It was around about the time that I met Mati, when I was about thirty-one years old, that I started to think about what I was all about. Dad had raised me, but now I found myself asking who my mother was. Dad had always said simply that she was 'a wonderful person'. That's much the same response that I'd expect from anyone else who knew her. My logic told me to write down all the memories I had of my mother and break them down, in an attempt to get a sense of who she was. And that is what I did. So, for instance, I remembered what had happened once when she took me on our usual Saturday walk into town, following the side of the river as we made the journey. The river, on this particular Saturday, was low, and a few feet away from it was a small pool of water that had previously been part of the river. There were about six or seven little fish trapped in it, and my mother stopped and put the fish back into the river, one by one. From that memory, I wrote down 'Aware' and 'Detailed'.

I also remembered how, during a holiday in Italy, my mother would light the stove only after checking whether any birds had fallen down the chimney. If they had she would let them go, and only then would she light the stove. From that memory I got 'Compassion'. If there is a spider in the house I won't stamp on it. I will catch it, take it outside and let it go. So it seemed that I'd inherited my mother's compassion because I wouldn't describe the old man as compassionate, but now I realised that I had some of my mother's characteristics. Once I'd finished this mathematical approach to self-analysis I studied the single piece of paper that had helped me understand who my mother was but, more importantly, enabled me to understand who *I* was. For the first time since my mother's death, I was me. I was the product of my mother, not just of my father.

TWENTY

The dream becomes reality

THE restaurant at the Hyde Park Hotel was the big stage. It was the platform that would enable me to win three stars in the *Michelin Guide*. It was the place where my dream could – and indeed would – come true. It was Forte's flagship hotel, a magnificent Victorian building that sits imposingly on that stretch from Knightsbridge to Hyde Park corner. At the back, the hotel overlooks the park and across from the front entrance you'll find Harvey Nichols and Harrods.

The hotel is now The Mandarin Oriental and remains one of the capital's most beautiful hotels. I wouldn't have come by it had it not been for Michael Caine. He was the instigator, the one who introduced me to his friend Rocco – that's Sir Rocco – Forte, who had taken over the helm of the company from his father, the great hotelier Lord (Charles) Forte. Michael and Rocco met for lunch one day in 1993 and my name cropped up.

Rocco liked the idea of teaming up with Michelin-starred chefs. He had recently done a deal with Nico Ladenis, renting him the restaurant of The Grosvenor House Hotel, which Nico called Nico at Ninety. It went on to win three stars – so Nico had done well out of the deal. There were also benefits for Rocco, though. Firstly, he got the glorious PR that comes with having an outstanding chef on the premises, and secondly, Nico's restaurant provided an alternative for hotel guests who didn't want to use the main dining room but didn't want to travel too far to eat. Rocco is blessed with vision, and I think he was the pioneer of this clever idea of renting hotel space to chefs.

So the deal with Nico had worked very well and having sorted out The Grosvenor House, Rocco had turned his attentions to the Hyde Park. The old grill was on its last legs, perhaps because the punters were dying off. Nothing lasts for ever.

Michael brought me and Rocco together for a meeting. Rocco was a real gentleman, very charming and courteous, and he asked me, 'How do you fancy taking your two stars from Harveys to the Hyde Park?' Transferring Michelin stars was possible. Others had done it, including Raymond Blanc, who had transferred his two stars from his city-centre restaurant to Le Manoir. I would need approval from Michelin, but it was certainly doable. What's more, I liked the prospect because I had outgrown Harveys and Wandsworth. It was time to move on. I had been there for seven years and could go no further. With its forty-four covers, Harveys had brought me two stars, but it was too small to win me another. I had started to see it as little more than a shop front with fifteen tables. On top of that, thanks to Michael I was beginning to appreciate that there was life beyond Wandsworth Common. I was only thirty-one years old but here I was – a mere cook – mixing with legends like Michael Caine and Rocco Forte. One door had closed and as I moved on another was opening. Mati, meanwhile, shared my dream of winning three stars, so she accepted the time and commitment I needed to give to the job.

I visited the site with Rocco, did the deal and it all came together pretty quickly. In July 1993 I left Harveys, and two months later we opened Restaurant Marco Pierre White at the Hyde Park Hotel. At Harveys there had rarely been more than eight in the brigade, but at the Hyde Park I had about twenty cooks. My team included five chefs who had been with me in the final days of Harveys: Robbie McRae and the aptly named Donovan Cooke, both of whom had worked at Michel Roux's Waterside Inn before joining Harveys; Mikey Lambert, who had also worked at the Waterside and L'Ortolan before Harveys; Roger Pizey, who had won Pastry Chef of the Year Award while at Harveys; Lee Bunting, who had joined me at Harveys when he was a kid of sixteen or seventeen, after an unsuccessful and brief career as a waiter. Donovan and Mikey, by the way, later moved to Australia where they have been voted the country's best chefs.

Others in the Hyde Park brigade included Robert Reid, who had just left Robuchon in Paris, Spencer Patrick who'd come from Hambleton Hall, Richard Stewart and Robert Weston. Thierry Busset had worked at Gavroche and came in to join Roger on Pastry, while Charlie Rushton, who'd done time at Harveys, was brought back into the fold.

The average age of the chefs was twenty-five. They weren't kids. They were strong people whose heads were full of experience and culinary knowledge and whose bodies could stand the pace and physical demands of working sixteen or seventeen hours a day in a kitchen. I also introduced the sort of classical hierarchy I'd seen at Gavroche. There was me, my head chef, four or five sous chefs, three on Fish, three on Meat/Sauce, three on Pastry and four on the Larder. There were the chefs de partie, the premier commis chefs and the commis chefs. Each of them was a head chef in his own right.

This kitchen was big. The one at Harveys was so small that we had to store the vegetables in a shed in the courtyard. The size of the kitchen at Wandsworth prevented me from winning three stars because I was unable to show off different cooking techniques. You need to have the right number of staff and the right amount of space to do that, and as the kitchen was so cramped, I couldn't fit in the staff or the techniques. At the Hyde Park, however, we had braised dishes, confit dishes, dishes *en cocotte*, dishes *en vesie* – an array of dishes that we couldn't have done at Harveys. At Harveys there had been just a few dishes on the main course, but now, on the fish section alone, we'd have six or seven dishes and the entire menu might contain fifteen main courses. The food stemmed from classical French but veered towards simplicity. Pigeon with Foie Gras, wrapped in cabbage and served with pommes purée and crushed black pepper, was a favourite. Lobster was grilled and served with a little truffle butter, pig's trotter was served with sweetbreads and sauce périgueux, while the menu also included a French fillet of

Teaching a young lad called Ramsay.

steak with horseradish as well as guinea fowl with risotto of white truffle.

On the top of the menu I used a Salvador Dali quote, 'At six I wanted to be a cook, at seven Napoleon and my ambition has been growing steadily ever since.' The pudding menu contained the quote from the eighteenth-century food writer Brillat-Savarin, 'To know how to eat well, one must first know how to wait.' That was a message to all those customers who kicked up a fuss when their food took time to prepare.

Later, when I had an investment in a restaurant called Sugar Reef, I put on the menu 'Be blonde,' and attributed the remark to General Custer. It was made up, of course, and was really a tribute of sorts to the captain of the *Titanic*, who apparently shouted, 'Be British,' as his ship was sinking. On the pudding menu at the same restaurant, we used the quote, 'Yes,' and attributed it to the man from Del Monte – orders for desserts have never been better.

To start with we struggled. The trouble was we weren't used to doing big numbers at lunchtime. At Harveys we'd been busy every night, but because we were in the middle of nowhere we only did fifteen or twenty covers for lunch on a good day. At the Hyde Park we were doing three times that amount, maybe fifty or sixty for lunch. Then just as we were recovering from that service, we had to do up to a hundred covers for dinner. Cooks who had been strong enough for Harveys were now not so strong. They couldn't grow. They couldn't move on and up their game. I suppose it's like a football team that gets promoted. If they don't up their game then they're not going to stay in the premiership.

Consistency remained a priority. Derek Brown, head inspector of Michelin UK, had visited the Canteen one day and I'd chatted to him. I had asked him why Gavroche had been demoted, going from three stars to two. 'Well,' he had replied, 'three of the four meals I had that year were not up to a three-star standard.' Mr Brown did not like compromise. And his remark underlined my belief that every dish heading from the kitchen to the table would have to be of a three-star standard. I said to him, 'I have always dreamed of winning three stars and what I do is look at the other three-star restaurant in London, Tante Claire. I look at its amuse-gueules, I look at its Fish section, I look at its Meat section and its Pastry. I look at their puddings. If I can beat them on all levels you cannot deny me three stars.'

'Very clever,' Mr Brown replied.

And that is what I did. I studied every aspect of Tante Claire's menu and made sure we were stronger.

The pace was relentless. We worked six days a week and had little life outside the kitchen. I was living in Pont Street, a ten-minute walk away, and would leave home every morning at 8.45 a.m. In the kitchen I might do a bit of butchery, perhaps the mise en place, and then talk to the chefs de partie about dishes that were coming up. I'd talk through dish ideas with my head chef Robert Reid. At 11.45 a.m. Mati would come in with Luciano and our new baby, Marco, and she would sit them on the passe while she had a cup of coffee. I was on one side of the passe and my family was on the other. Fifteen minutes later lunch service would start and we'd finish about 2.30 p.m. Then I would do whatever paperwork was required, or perhaps meet with suppliers. People came to me; I would rarely leave the restaurant. Late afternoon, Mati might come back and we'd have a coffee while the boys sat on the passe, then after service I'd talk through the evening with my brigade before going home. My head would hit the pillow at about one in the morning, so it was a fifteen- or sixteen-hour day Monday to Friday. Other members of the kitchen staff would start at seven thirty or eight in the morning. On Saturday I would go in at two o'clock in the afternoon and work until midnight, then on Sundays I slept. Lots of famous chefs today don't look fucked because they don't work. They have a healthy glow and a clear complexion. There is blood in their cheeks. They haven't got burns on their wrists and cuts on their hands.

During all this I tried to spend time with the kids. One day I was walking with Luciano and Marco along Beauchamps Place in Knightsbridge when we saw a mob of paparazzi ahead of us, taking pictures of a woman. 'Who's that?' asked Luciano. 'That,' I said, 'is one of the world's most famous women.' It was Madonna. Bizarrely, the very next day I got a call from Madonna's assistant, asking me if I would like to join the icon for afternoon tea. I accepted. It would have been rude not to. We had tea at the Hyde Park Hotel, where she was staying, and have been friends ever since. She and her husband, Guy Ritchie, have been very special people in my life. They come to my restaurants and we go shooting together. They are exceptionally kind.

When I finished tea with Madonna I went back down to the kitchen, where the phone rang. It was Mati who said, 'I've been trying to get hold of you. Where have you been?'

'I've just had tea with Madonna,' I said in a casual way, as if I'd just been chatting to a next door neighbour.

'You've had tea with Madonna?'

'Yes.'

She said, 'You've had tea with Madonna while I've been going round the supermarket with the kids.' Then the line went dead. Mati didn't talk to me for three days. She broke her vow of silence by saying, 'What was she like, then?'

I also met Sylvester Stallone at the Hyde Park Hotel. He shook my hand, squeezed my bicep and said, 'I don't usually eat your kind of food, but for you I ate it.' I haven't got a clue what he'd eaten but he was impressed enough to ask me to do his wedding feast when he married Jennifer Flavin at Blenheim Palace and I cooked them Ballotine of Salmon with Herbs, Salad of Langoustine and Wild Sorrel, and for the main course they had Contrefilet of Aberdeen Angus garnished with marrowbone and a confit of shallots and garlic, and served with a sauce a la Bordelaise which has a red wine base.

The Duke of Marlborough, who I didn't know at that time but now know well, came in as I was cooking and said, 'Hello, are you Marco Pierre White? How lovely to have you in my kitchen.'

I said, 'It's a pleasure to be here. It's a lovely kitchen, isn't it? Very Victorian, your Grace.'

I was friends with the Duke's son, James Blandford, first, but nowadays I get on with the whole family. I'm the boy who grew up on a council estate and has been accepted by toffs. The first time I was invited for lunch at Blenheim Palace, I sat down with the Duke and said, 'Tell me, your Grace, how many acres is the Blenheim estate?'

'Fifteen thousand, five hundred.'

'That's interesting.'

He said, 'What's interesting about that?'

'The estate I came from had about the same number of houses on it.'

The Duke told me that he didn't allow any vegetables larger than his little finger to enter his kitchen. 'Now what do you think about that, Marco?' I told him I disagreed with that because young (please don't call them baby) vegetables are quite tasteless. I like something that's got a bit of size to it, then it has real flavour. He asked, 'What about a Jersey Royal?'

I said, 'You can't exactly chip them, can you?' And he gave me a funny look. We had a barmy lunch and then all of a sudden the Duke, a giant of a man, stood up and said, 'Right, I'm going salmon fishing now,' and vanished.

———

Mentally, I was all over the place in January 1995. *The Michelin Guide* was due out on Monday and by the Thursday before finding out whether or not I had won three stars life was intolerable. In fact, I was so preoccupied that one day I couldn't cope with the pressure any longer and had to go off fishing with a couple of friends, Tim Steel, my oldest mate who I have known since childhood, and Edgar Barman. At about 11 a.m. I got a call to say that Mr Brown and Mr Bulmer had dropped into the Hyde Park to see me. They said they would nip back at 2.30 p.m.

I hurriedly packed away my fishing gear, loaded it into the car and drove back into town. By then I had sussed that I'd won three stars. Why else would they want to see me? But I would have to wait a little longer to find out for sure. Bang on two thirty they arrived back at the Hyde Park. 'Have you got anywhere private?' asked Mr Brown. We went into my office, where some coffee arrived, and then Mr Brown said, 'In the 1995 *Michelin Guide*, Restaurant Marco Pierre White will have three stars.' Three stars. Two words that established me in the history of British gastronomy as the first British chef to win three stars. At the age of thirty-three, I had become the world's youngest ever chef to achieve such an award (a record I still hold, incidentally). My old friend Nico Ladenis also won three stars in the same year. This meant that Rocco had a pair of three-star chefs in his hotels.

I can't really tell you what went through my mind. I was confident that I had done enough to win them, but it was still a bit of a shock. I felt as though I'd finished my race. Boxers win Heavyweight Champion of the World and lose the hunger, so to speak. Why should chefs be any different? I can understand why chefs get to the top and then go off and do other things. The simple reason is probably that they become bored in the kitchen.

Shortly before Mr Brown retired from Michelin UK I got a call from Derek Bulmer, who would be his successor. He said, 'I am taking Mr Brown for a farewell meal and have asked him where he would like to go. He wants to eat at the Hyde Park.' I was touched that Mr Brown had chosen my restaurant for his last supper. It confirmed my feelings that we had won the award for all the right reasons. After dinner I walked Mr Brown from his table down the hotel steps. I wanted to say goodbye and thank you. It was late at night and as we stood on the pavement a doorman hailed a taxi. The Michelin man shook my hand and said, 'Never forget what made you great.' *Great* might be an overstatement, but the theme of his remark was that my success was down to the time I'd spent in the kitchen and what I put on the plate. His message was: stay behind the stove.

Things went wrong at the Canteen in the summer of 1995. There was a disagreement of sorts and Michael and I decided to go our separate ways. A legal battle erupted and the consequences resulted in a settlement that prevents me discussing the reasons behind our fall-out. What I can tell you is that Michael and I did not have an argument – there was no screaming match – and the end of the partnership had nothing to do with Michael wanting to put fish and chips on the menu, as is widely believed.

Michael and I have only seen each other once since then. It was a few years ago when I was invited to Liz Taylor's birthday party at the Café Royal. I walked into the room and saw Michael sitting at a table with Harvey Weinstein, the man behind Miramax. I thought, this is ridiculous, I've got to say hello, so I went over to the pair of them and said, 'Good evening, gentlemen.'

Harvey shook my hand and, clearly unaware of the difficulties Michael and I had been through, pointed at Michael and said to me, 'This guy here is the toughest guy you'll ever meet.'

Michael looked at his movie-making friend and said, 'Harvey, if you think I'm tough, try dealing with him.'

I had lost Michael as a business partner, but Rocco had big plans. We did a deal to buy the Criterion, a massive restaurant in Piccadilly Circus. It was to be a joint venture between the two of us, but before the paperwork had been signed Forte became victim of a hostile takeover by Granada. Forte's business ground to a halt because of it. Once a hostile takeover begins everything stops. I felt desperately sad for Rocco and thought it was wrong that he was about to lose the company. It was a particularly rough ride for him.

There was a clause in my unsigned contract which stated that if the management of Forte changed I would have a right to buy its 50 per cent of the Criterion, and that is how I thought things would end up. When Granada took over I was called in to see the company's chief executive, Charles Allen. Not so much called in, actually, as we had dinner at Le Gavroche. During the meal I said to Charles, 'Well, you know I've got my contract and it's not signed. But the Criterion is open now and it is certainly implied in the contract that I have an option to buy you out.'

Charles said, 'We don't want to sell. We want to do more with you.' Oh.

I then had to go and see Granada's chairman, Gerry Robinson. He was charming and polite, and when the tea was carried into his office he looked at me and said, 'Shall I be mother?' The night before the meeting I had asked myself, why does Gerry want to see me? I reckoned he wanted to suss out my relationship with Rocco. Granada was a plc, and the last thing they wanted was a loose cannon like Marco Pierre White running around saying all the wrong things. About eight minutes into our cup of tea, Gerry said, 'What do you think of Rocco Forte?'

'Sir Rocco Forte', I replied, 'is the only man who ever gave me everything he promised.' Despite my words of support for Rocco my relationship with Granada continued. The deal was that I would have the lease to the restaurants in their major hotels – The Meridien, The Piccadilly, The Capitol, The Regent Palace and The Waldorf. The deal also included The Queen's Hotel in Leeds, the hotel where my father had worked as a young chef. I travelled up to Leeds with a Granada executive and we were greeted in the foyer by a manager who said he wanted to show us round.

How interesting, I was thinking, to be in the hotel where my old man had toiled with his friend Paul La Barbe, the cook who had trained in France and was the subject of so many of my father's stories. I tried to visualise the grandeur of the hotel when it was in its prime, and as we walked into the bar the manager said, 'What you're about to see is the biggest mini bar in the world.' The biggest mini bar in the world? What on earth did he mean? The Granada executive and I stood in silence, transfixed by the gruesome sight of a Mini car suspended from the ceiling above the bar. The manager was really proud of his Mini bar, but I can tell you that it was one of the naffest things I've ever seen and the Granada executive wasn't impressed either.

In the end I didn't do The Queen's Hotel because I wanted to concentrate on the restaurants in the London hotels. I talk about some of them in forthcoming chapters, but this is a good point at which to say that the Granada relationship ended in 2002. It was my first experience of the corporate world and I thought it was horrible. You think blue-chip companies are run perfectly, but in my opinion they are worse than private companies. Board meetings are painful. We'd have an hour-long meeting about the price of coffee with them wanting to produce coffee for five pence a cup and spending sixty minutes talking about how every penny counts. 'You can get spectacular coffee for twelve pence a cup,' I'd say and then emerge from the meeting brain dead. It was all about percentages rather than working out what's going to make the customer happy. I handed back everything, but kept the Criterion.

There were amusing moments. I went to Charles Allen's fortieth birthday at the Meridien and the cabaret was provided by a Shirley Bassey lookalike. An executive high up in the organisation leaned over to me at one point and said, 'That's influence and power for you,' pointing towards the stage and the prancing drag queen.

I said, 'I'm sorry. What's influence and power?'

He said, 'Getting Shirley Bassey to come and sing for your fortieth birthday.'

TWENTY-ONE

Just another day

PEOPLE found it peculiar that I had won Michelin's coveted three stars without ever setting foot on French soil. Journalists would arrive to interview me and ask me to tell them about my favourite meal in a French restaurant. 'I haven't got one,' I'd tell them, 'I've never been to France.' Oh, they'd say, and we'd move on to the next question. The other big players – Albert, Michel, Raymond, Pierre – had all come from that side of the Channel, but there I was, serving some of the finest French food in Britain, without having visited the great Parisian restaurants whose dishes had set me on the path to Michelin stardom. I'd simply say, 'Well, there you go. Proof that you don't need to go to France to win three Michelin stars.'

When I finally crossed the Channel I didn't have a passport and had to be smuggled into the country by my old friend, the chef Jean-Christophe Novelli. I first met JC back in the late eighties and he tells a ridiculous story, of which I have no recollection. He says that he wanted a job in my kitchen and arrived at Harveys to introduce himself to me. There was a man mopping the floor who apparently told young Monsieur Novelli that Marco Pierre White was not around. JC says it was only later when Nico introduced us that he realised that the man mopping the floor was, in fact, me.

Anyway, as you already know, I had intended to go to France in 1986 after my year-long stint at Raymond Blanc's Manoir. I was going to knock on doors and ask for a job but, what with Alan Bennett's problems, I'd ended up staying in London. As a child of four or five I had been to France, but only to zoom through it on a train, en route to Italy with my mother for a holiday. I have memories of being on the ferry and looking back at the white cliffs of Dover, and of not being able to sleep on the train, perhaps because I was too excited about the trip. But my first *real* visit to France was on 1 October 1995, almost ten months after I won three stars at the Hyde Park. Forte was sponsoring the Arc de Triomphe race and Rocco was hosting an event at Longchamps on the final day. He had chefs on hand in Paris and a few of my boys from the Hyde Park brigade were going to be there as well, but Rocco wanted me to oversee the cuisine for him and his 200 guests.

I invited Jean-Christophe Novelli along, not to help but because he has been like a brother to me and I enjoy his company. I was visiting the world's most romantic city so I wanted Mati to be there as well. As I have never passed a driving test – possibly because I have never taken a driving test – the two of them agreed that they would share the time behind the wheel. Things started to go terribly wrong when we got to the Eurostar terminal in Dover at about 2.30 in the morning, bought our tickets and were ready to drive onto the train. JC was asked to go into an office where there were French gendarmes. He was asked for our passports, so he came back to the car, poked his head in and said, 'Passports.'

I said, 'I haven't got one.' JC looked totally confused. Was I joking? Was this one of my wind-ups? But the passport did not appear. He said, 'What do you mean? If you go abroad, Marco, you need a passport.' I didn't have one. I told him the last time I had travelled abroad was as a ten-year-old when I went to visit Uncle Gianfranco and Aunt Paola in Italy. JC was not in the mood to hear about my childhood adventures. He looked a bit nervous, went back to the office and told the gendarmes, 'My friend doesn't have a passport but he is the greatest chef the world has ever known and I am taking him to cook a banquet in Paris. Believe me, he is a very important person.'

He was informed, 'I don't care if he's cooking for Monsieur Mitterrand.' They were convinced that JC was trying to take me into the country as an illegal immigrant and they even talked of arresting him. Then he glanced back at the car and saw me waving something that looked like a passport. He dashed back to the car, grabbed the document from my hand and hurried back to the office. 'I'm sorry,' he told the gendarmes. 'My friend has found his passport.' But it wasn't my passport; I had given him my fishing licence, which contained a mugshot of me on its cover. They started screaming at him, 'What is this!' From the safety of the Range Rover, Mati and I could hear the word *merde* being used a lot. Somehow JC managed to talk us out of being questioned but we were turned away. It was the middle of the night and at lunchtime I was due to be cooking lunch for Rocco and his 200 guests. JC saved the day. He happened to be well connected with the ferry companies and, don't ask me how he did it, but he drove us to the ferry port, my fishing licence was produced once again and this time it did the trick.

From Calais we motored down to Paris, and when we hit the capital JC announced that he wanted to take us on a tour of the city. We drove to the Eiffel Tower, parked illegally, and then JC dragged Mati and me out of the car and made us stand underneath the tower because 'it is so romantic'. Once that was done, we clambered back into the Range Rover and zipped through the streets, nearly killing the French actor Alain Delon along the way. Alain was crossing the road, clutching croissants and coffee, when all of a sudden he stopped – rabbit in the headlights – as JC applied the brakes and the car screeched to a halt. JC looks a bit like a young Alain, so for a few seconds the petrified actor stood at the tip of the bonnet, gripping his croissants and looking into the window of our car thinking, My double almost killed me.

We had breakfast in La Coupole, which was a great place. There was some nasty art on the walls; it was busy, stylish and … French. Then we went on to Longchamps, where there was an enormous queue to get into a car park . After queuing for what seemed like ages I told JC to drive over the pavement and into the car park, but when he followed my instructions police surrounded the car, screaming and shouting at JC to get the vehicle back on the road. We had to drive back over the pavement into a traffic jam of cars hooting us and furious pedestrians dodging us and yelling, 'Merde.'

Things didn't improve when we finally arrived at our destination. I realised that we were cooking in a tiny, cramped kitchen above a betting shop. It seemed an impossible task, but somehow we did it. The memory of that particular kitchen ordeal has been mostly erased from my mind. We served Terrine of Foie Gras and Ballotine of Salmon, but my strongest recollection is the confined space of the kitchen and having to cook the fish on hot plates.

We headed home exhausted. At Calais the customs officers asked to see my passport. 'I don't have one.' How did you get out of England in the first place? 'We drove.' The irritated officer waved us through with, '*Allez! Allez!*'

At Dover we were stopped and asked to show our passports. I explained that I didn't have one and the customs officer asked if I had any form of ID. I fumbled around in the glove box and confidently produced my fishing licence. The Pierre part of my name would have made him suspicious. 'How did you get out of Britain in the first place?' he asked. 'We drove,' I said for a second time. Eventually we were waved through the barrier with the officer shouting, '… And get a bloody passport.'

———

I wanted to own a restaurant in Mayfair. One night in the summer of 1996 I was driving around London when I found myself heading down Curzon Street and past the door of the Mirabelle. I felt an urge to nip inside, just to have a look at the place, so I asked my driver to stop.

I had been to the Mirabelle only once before, though not for a meal. It was back in the summer of 1981, when I first came to London and was working for Albert Roux. I was nineteen years old, and on my first day off I took a bus across the river and up to Hyde Park Corner, then crossed Park Lane, through the little streets of

Mayfair and into Curzon Street. I had gazed at the Mirabelle for a few minutes. There she was, the grand old dame, once the equivalent in London society of Maxim's in Paris. I walked through the doorway and down the stairs and politely said to someone on the reception, 'I collect menus. Do you have an old menu I could keep?'

At home that night I studied the menu, which contained classical French dishes like Omelette Arnold Bennett, Quenelles of Pike and Cutlets of Lamb Prince William, which is made with truffles. The menu would have been the same for years, influenced by Escoffier and that invaluable cookbook that can be found in every professional kitchen, *Le Répertoire de La Cuisine*. Mirabelle, which opened in 1936, represented romance. Marilyn Monroe, Jackie Onassis (she always sat at table one) and Maria Callas all loved the place and Princess Margaret and Grace Kelly would dine here, as would Elizabeth Taylor. Maurice Chevalier had been a regular. Lord Lucan held his engagement party in a private room at the Mirabelle. Just think of the people who had walked through those doors, the things that had been said, the deals that had been done at those tables. And then there was the romance of the kitchen. Chef de Tries had been the head chef in the days when head chefs were known by their surnames, so you would have had Chef Roux, Chef Blanc and, dare I say it, Chef White. And his menu reflected the romantic tradition of naming dishes after customers and chefs you had worked for. In the case of the latter, it meant that you could give a nod to the man who had taught you your trade. It's a tradition I have always admired and the pig's trotter dish, Pied de Cochon Pierre Koffmann, was on my menus from Harveys up to The Oak Room, not only as a tribute to one of my kitchen mentors but also to let customers know that I did not intend to forget the world from which I had come. By putting Pierre's name on my menu I was saying, I haven't forgotten what you taught me.

Back in 1981 Mirabelle was not a Michelin-starred restaurant, but the AA used to award marks out of three stars, just like Michelin, as well as knives and forks – *couverts* – for aesthetics like service and the feel of the dining room. Mirabelle was the only British restaurant to have three stars and five knives and forks in 1981, in other words, the AA was saying it was the finest restaurant in the UK. I don't believe that was true, but what I do accept is that, like the Connaught under Michel Bourdin, it was one of those few places that gave you an insight into what I call old-world gastronomy.

On that Saturday night in 1995 I walked in just to have a look at the restaurant that had once been so full of romance, mystique and life. It was dead. The menu was – get your head around this – a mixture of French and Japanese food, and the lack of customers told me it was only a question of time before Mirabelle would be up for sale. I introduced myself to the restaurant manager Takanori Ishii – Mr Ishii I called him from that day to this – and we had a two-hour chat. Mirabelle had previously been owned by my friend, that great London restaurateur Nicky Kerman, but was now owned by a Japanese company, and Mr Ishii was good enough to confirm my suspicions that business was not great. He was a charming, polite, softly spoken man, and from then on I stalked him. I would find the time to pop into Mirabelle once or twice a week to let him know that if it ever came on the market I would be interested in buying it. I felt it was only a matter of time before they'd want to sell.

In the meantime a restaurant in the same street caught my eye. Les Saveurs was owned by another Japanese company, although it served only French food and hadn't been so bold as to throw a few Japanese dishes onto the menu. There was no movement on the Mirabelle front and I was still determined to have a presence in Mayfair, so when I heard a rumour that Les Sav might be up for sale I pounced. In fact, I pounced quietly. I didn't want an auction because I couldn't afford to compete with the big organisations, making a bidding war out of the question. So rather than approach anyone in London about Les Sav, I dealt directly with the Japanese company that owned it. Amazingly, I managed to buy the restaurant without any of its staff knowing until that morning, when they discovered their new boss was Marco Pierre White.

About two months after I bought Les Sav, Mirabelle came on the market, but there was a problem: there were others who wanted to buy it, and they were richer than me. People in the restaurant business still remain puzzled as to how I pulled off the deal. Indeed, it was one of those situations where I won against all the odds. When it came to bidding, there were four contenders. There was Anton Mosimann, the renowned Establishment chef. Then there was Jeremy King and Chris Corbin, owners of Le Caprice and The Ivy, who were financially backed by the awesomely successful City figure 'Black Jack' Dellal. The Chez Gerard group was also interested. And there was me – the small fish in a big pond – so if I wanted Mirabelle I would have to use my wits.

In my favour, I had courted Mr Ishii, spending long nights talking food and restaurants, so that could do me no harm. And I had also done the Les Sav deal, which had taught me a bit about the way the Japanese like to do business. I combined those two advantages with my knowledge of serving Japanese customers in restaurants. They are discreet people, not loud and raucous. They come for the meal, and when they order coffee you get the bill ready because you know they're not going to spend any more. Once they order a coffee that's it – they rarely have two.

Sticking with this theme for a moment, Middle Eastern clients like to be served by senior people, so at the Hyde Park Hotel and The Oak Room I would always have six staff in suits – two managers, two assistants, two waiters. The customers didn't know their position, but felt they were getting the best service. These customers didn't mind waiting and tended to stay in the restaurant a very long time – what they really like is service. And when you think about it, it's logical.

Using my knowledge of the Japanese I deduced that they liked quiet deals, didn't like things being on the open market and if something fell through they wouldn't like it to be publicised. The way I saw it, two Japanese companies had opened restaurants in Curzon Street and neither restaurant was doing well, but the companies were too embarrassed to sell. Only when the first one made a move and sold Les Sav to me did the other company feel confident enough to sell Mirabelle. Up until now, pride had prevented them from selling.

Mr Ishii, by now my dear friend, told me to make an offer of half a million pounds less than the highest bid, which had come from 'Black Jack' and the Caprice boys. I took his advice, but my offer included something I felt sure would appeal to Mr Ishii and his bosses. I told him that if the restaurant was sold to me then I would continue to employ its staff and added, 'If I step in and buy the Mirabelle, Mr Ishii, you will have a job for life.'

It is an important aspect of Japanese culture that the boss looks after his employees, or rather does all he can for the people who have worked for him. Essentially, my offer was something Black Jack's money simply couldn't buy. My intention of retaining Mirabelle's Japanese employees suggested I was a man who was not only in touch with the owners' code of conduct but wholeheartedly supported it.

Mr Ishii rang me and said, 'I'm on your side.' Then he spoke to his bosses in Japan, telling them, 'I think Marco should own it because he will look after everyone who has worked here. We will still have jobs.' And with that I was given the Japanese equivalent of the thumbs-up.

Once the deal had gone through, the Caprice boys got in touch and offered to rent Mirabelle from me. I made them put the offer in writing even though I had no intention of doing the deal. It was just me being mischievous and playing with them.

One morning I woke up, horrified by the reality of owning two restaurants on the same street, competing with one another. I thought, fucking hell, this wasn't supposed to happen, what am I going to do? I had put myself in a ludicrous position, but luckily for me Rocco Forte also wanted to own a restaurant in Mayfair and he phoned and asked, 'Can I buy Les Saveurs?' Certainly, sir.

I wanted to take Mirabelle back to what it originally had been. I wanted to reinstate the romance.

I knocked the Tapestry Room, cashier's office and wine cellar into one room, which is now the Chinese Room. A space that had once seated ten people now sat forty. A cloakroom was put in, but when I saw it I was alarmed because it took up part of the bar area, so the cloakroom was knocked down and the bar became massive. Pillars were put into the room but they weren't right – they didn't fit in with the character of the restaurant – so they came down and were replaced. A wooden floor was laid, but a few days later I noticed it was buckling because it had been put down too tightly. The restaurant was about to open to the public, so it was too late to rip up the whole floor. Instead, the builders had to come in after evening service, between 2 a.m. and 8 a.m., and replace the wooden floorboards with tiles. It was a time-consuming, painstaking process, night after night, and took about three months to achieve. In addition to all this I wanted the colour of the ceiling to match the blue in a painting I'd hung on the wall. When the ceiling was painted it didn't match, so it was painted again. It still wasn't right, so it was painted a third time – we finally got there.

The food was restored to its classical French foundations, but with a modern twist of refinement. The Parsley Truffled Soup contained bacon and chicken stock; there was Cappuccino of Mushrooms; Tarte of Endive with Sea Scallops and Spring Lamb Provençale. The chefs included Charlie Rushton, Spencer Patrick, Lee Bunting and Curtis Stone, who today is something of a TV personality. I wanted it to win a Michelin star and it did.

Along the way, there have been splendid meals held at the Mirabelle. It is where I held my birthday party when I turned forty in December 2001. A good evening was had by all. Michael Winner and Robert Earl managed to get Bernard Manning, the stand-up comedian with no regard for political correctness, to provide the cabaret. And then Michael became the butt of Bernard's jokes which included, 'I see we've got Europe's most hated Jew here tonight.' Madonna and Guy – Mr and Mrs Ritchie – were sitting on my table and Piers Morgan was doing his best to interview the couple. While Guy was falling about with laughter at Bernard's act, I'm not sure that style of humour was Madonna's cup of tea. She was wearing a big flat cap so was unrecognisable and Bernard pointed over to the world's most successful singer and said, 'Oh, and who do you think you are in that cap? Lester Piggott's little sister?'

In the same year I had dinner at the Mirabelle with Mati and my friend, the journalist turned PR Damien McCrystal and *Tatler* editor Geordie Greig. It was a famous occasion because, once he had recovered from the evening, Damien wrote about it in his Sunday Business column. We had worked our way through a bottle of 1947 Haut-Brion, a bottle of 1949 Petrus, a bottle of 1961 Mouton Rothschild and finished the meal with a bottle of 1888 Château d'Yquem. The wine bill came to £16,000. The d'Yquem accounted for half that figure and Damien reckoned it tasted like a dry sherry you'd pick up from Tesco for £3.99.

Mirabelle's romance doesn't rub off on everybody, however. My manager came to see me one night, complaining that Marianne, the receptionist, was in floods of tears. A customer had walked into the restaurant where he was meeting his wife and friends, and Marianne had asked him to wait for a minute before taking him through to the table. He didn't have time to wait. 'Fuck off,' he said to Marianne and stormed through to the table, his shocking treatment leaving her in tears.

I went up to the table where the man was sitting and they looked quite flattered that the boss was paying them a visit. I politely said, 'Sir, do you have a problem?'

He looked up quizzically and replied, 'No.'

'I find that very strange.'

'Why?' he asked.

'Because I have a receptionist in my office in tears because of the way you treated her.'

'What did I do?'

'You told her to fuck off, sir. You humiliated and upset her and she feels terribly insulted. Either pluck up the courage to go and apologise to her or leave. I'll give you five minutes to make your decision.'

I was in the bar when the rude man came up to me. He was

'Look friendly,' said Bob Carlos Clarke.

furious and said, 'You just made me look like a cunt in front of my wife and friends.'

I said, 'That's because you are a cunt.'

He said, 'We're leaving.'

But before he could get his coat, I said, 'You must be a cunt, because anyone with any decency would go and apologise. So fuck off.'

Those last two words were important. I had treated him exactly the same way he had treated Marianne. All he had to do was say, 'You're absolutely right, I'll go and say sorry.' If a man comes into one of my restaurants and swears at the receptionist, he is clearly in the wrong restaurant.

What of Mr Ishii? He left Mirabelle, but returned to work for me a couple of years later. He is my chauffeur and assistant. Sometimes his driving is as good as Jean-Christophe Novelli's. Once he fell asleep at the wheel. Another time, after we'd nearly killed a pedestrian, I asked in astonishment, 'Ishii how close were we to killing that woman?' and he replied, 'About six inches.'

He knows I like to wind him up. I've used his mobile phone to photograph my genitals before and applied the picture as the phone's 'wallpaper'. One day we were driving out of a hotel car park and there was this big trailer with two big blokes in boiler suits. I spotted an opportunity to amuse myself. I said, 'Stop the car, Mr Ishii.' He stopped and I said to him, 'Can you ask those two blokes if they're wearing suspenders?'

He wound down the window and said, 'Excuse me, are you wearing suspender?'

One of the bruisers looked perplexed. 'Sorry, mate?'

Mr Ishii asked again, 'Are you wearing suspender?'

'No, we're not.'

'Thank you very much.' Window up and off we drove. I have a laugh at his expense, but Mr Ishii is very dear to me. I spend more time with him than with anyone else and I think he's wonderful. He is gentle, kind and extremely loyal. People ask, why do you still call him Mr Ishii rather than Takanori? I respect him very much, that's why.

TWENTY-TWO

Everything I'd worked for

I HAD won three Michelin stars but my race was not yet finished. I realised that in fact the finishing post was a little further on. As far as stars are concerned, three is the highest you can go, and in the whole of Europe only fifty-four restaurants have three stars. It means that your place serves 'exceptional cuisine' and is 'worth a detour'.

Stars are awarded for what is on the plate, but what about Michelin's *couverts*? In the guides you see them as little pictures of crossed knives and forks, which is why they're known in the restaurant profession as 'knives and forks'. They are awarded for pleasantness, luxury, aesthetics and ambience. To get five of them, and five red ones rather than black ones, became my new obsession. The Oak Room in London's Meridien Hotel would take me there. It would win not only three stars but also the five red knives and forks which, according to the guide, made it the finest restaurant in Britain. Others had won stars, but no other restaurant before or since The Oak Room has been awarded a beautiful, complete row of red. Waterside, Gavroche and Tante Claire have only ever managed four.

The room itself has to have been one of the greatest rooms in the world. With its ballroom grandness, majestic mirrors, gentle lighting and generous space between tables, it's like stepping into an illusion. The Oak Room was a temple of gastronomy. It was about perfection rather than creation – making the greatest Oeufs en Nage, the finest Roast Pineapple. It was perfection, from the amuse-gueules to the starter, from the main course to the pre-dessert, the cheese to the coffee and proper chocolates. It was an *event*. The wine list was the finest in Britain. Every available vintage of Mouton Rothschild was here for you to drink, if you had the money. Other three-star restaurants might have had two or three vintages of Pétrus. Here we had Pétrus that went back a century, seventy or eighty different vintages. The wine list included a five-page list of Château d'Yquem, taking you right back to 1850. The vintages and prices were all beautifully written in pencil so that each page was visually attractive. It used to take a wine waiter about three weeks to write out the list.

Dishes were carried from the kitchen on silver platters and the meat was carved at the table. Previously I'd had neither the space nor the staff to do dining-room carving on this scale. At The Oak Room, a lot of the food was carved in the room, carrying the show into full view. The pigeon would be taken out to the table, where the staff had two minutes to put it on the plate before the vegetables came out. Even if you weren't eating pigeon, you certainly got to enjoy the show.

When a lady took her seat a tiny table was placed beside her for her to put her handbag on so she didn't need to put it on the floor. How many restaurants have a seat for your handbag? If a customer paid in cash, he received his change in brand-new notes and coins. We did not do crushed, creased fivers and dirty fifty-pence pieces. The notes were wrinkle-free, the coins untarnished and sparkling.

I had been inspired by great French restaurants even though I'd never been to one, but with The Oak Room I set out to re-create the sophistication I imagined Parisians experienced. It had to be the ultimate experience and I was fortunate enough to be given the opportunity to pull it off. In August 1997 I transferred my three stars from the Hyde Park to The Oak Room, where I had six weeks to get the place in shape before opening.

I took the brigade from the Hyde Park, loyal boys who had given me everything and who had travelled with me all the way from Harveys. From one star to three stars and now even further. We became an even stronger team. There were probably twenty-five in the brigade, that's twenty-five cooking for seventy customers. Robert Reid was my head chef and there were five sous chefs. If we had a table of six at The Oak Room, six cooks would do six dishes, so timing was crucial. Front of house, I had six wine waiters, four maître d'hôtels and two head waiters in suits – twelve people, six of them in black.

Refining, refining. At the Oak Room, I had reached a level where I would start to wonder where refinement of a dish would end. And of course the road to perfection is never-ending.

For example, in the kitchen at The Oak Room, every morning we would roast thirty-six chickens just for their juices, rather than for the meat.

We'd roast the birds, take them out of the oven and put them into a colander, then press them so the juices flooded out and were collected in a tin underneath. Then the chicken went back into the pan and the whole thing – bird and pan – were covered in clingfilm, because the steam coming from a cooked chicken creates even more juice.

Once all the natural juices were captured, the roasting trays were deglazed, first with a drop of Madeira, which dissolves, then a splash of water is added and the sediment dissolved into it. The juice that had been extracted by squashing the chickens then went into the pan, together with a tiny spoonful of veal stock – not to give flavour but to add body.

The thirty-six squeezed chickens could not be served, of course, because they were too dry, so they would go in the bin or end up as staff lunches. It might seem like a waste to you, but if you were a customer that's what you were paying for – pure chicken juices.

Thirty-six chickens provided enough juices for thirty portions of freshly cooked chicken. In other words, the customer had the juice of more than one whole chicken accompanying his dish. We'd do the same thing with lamb shoulders, roasting them slowly for sediment and then pressing them just for the juices.

It was extreme. As part of that refinement I virtually stopped using veal stock in sauces like jus blond or jus de volaille because I felt it was too big and strong and dominated everything else.

In January 1998, little more than four months after we had opened, *The Michelin Guide* came out. We had retained three stars and been awarded five red knives and forks. I felt as if I was perched on top of the highest mountain. I could go no further.

And what about the boys who worked for me? They were mostly aged about twenty-seven or twenty-eight and every one of them was a fine chef. Each one of them could walk straight into a job as head chef, and many had acquired enough knowledge to run their own restaurant and become a chef-patron. If you look at most large kitchens, there might be two, three, or maybe four who have been there a long time. But now too many of them were talking of flying the nest. Cooks who had come to me as young men were on the verge of launching their own careers and I had to accept that I'd been very lucky to have them, but now it was time for them to move on.

I looked around to see the talent appearing on the scene and was severely alarmed. Young men were coming into the industry because they wanted to be famous, not because they wanted to cook. They aspired to be *celebrity* chefs rather than chefs. Forgive the pun, but there was a distinct lack of hunger out there. There wasn't the energy or the passion. I started to ask myself whether I wanted to start building up a new team? Disenchantment had set in.

The boys, my brigade, may well have worked hard, but they never lost their ability to play hard, too. It was an hour before lunch and I walked into The Oak Room's kitchen, ready for service only to find the place was virtually empty. There were one or two cooks there from way down the hierarchy, but no sign of the others. 'Where the fuck is everyone?' I said. 'We're going to have people at their tables in two seconds' time. Where the fucking fuck is everyone?' And then they told me. It transpired that the night before the boys had finished service and gone off for a few drinks at Break for the Border, one of those overcrowded cattlemarkets where the queue for the bar is ten men thick and punters scream chat-up lines above the thud of the music. There had been a punch-up. One of the chefs had ended up with a broken arm and the others emerged from the scrap as bruised, bloodied, hobbling invalids. I think they were all still down at A&E, being nursed, stitched up and given prescriptions for painkillers. If you were one of the customers who had to wait for your main course that day, then I'm sorry, but the blame lies with the lager at Break for the Border.

———

Outside catering was a nice way to earn extra money, promote my dishes and keep the adrenaline pumping. When I was running Harveys I was asked to cook at lunch and dinner parties, or to provide the catering for someone wealthy who was throwing a bash. The supermodel Denice Lewis held a party and hired us for the day. Using a truck, we transported Harveys to her place in West London, taking tables, chairs, kitchen implements and staff with us, and after the event we brought them all back again in time for the next service.

What I didn't like – what I really hated – was the point at which the host or hostess asked me to come out of the kitchen and meet the guests. Usually that moment – 'Marco, come and say hello to everyone' – came shortly after dessert had been served. I dreaded it. Remember, one of the things that kept me in the profession was the fact that I could hide in the kitchen, rather than spend my time in the real world. The applause as you walk into a dining room, the handshakes and air kisses – I couldn't stand it and it didn't make sense. These people were paying for me to *cook* for them, not paying to have me. Other chefs might thoroughly enjoy the performing-seal bit, but I didn't want to be serenaded and clapped, so I would bale out and do a runner after the main course. I cooked for Fergie at her friend Priscilla Phillips' house, and once the main course was done I baled, leaving Gordon Ramsay to do the puddings. The kitchen door opens. 'Marco, oh Marco. Where are you, Marco?' Gone, in the car roaring back to my restaurant. The hosts began to think my disappearing act was designed to make me mysterious, but the truth is, I was too shy and socially inept to deal with it and I didn't need a pat on the head or stroke on the back.

I remember doing a big corporate lunch in Milton Keynes, and the minute the main course went out, I was off. I jumped into my car and zoomed away without realising that the dining room looked onto the road. The guests must have seen me climbing into my car and they left their plates and gathered at the windows. There were about 200 perplexed people staring at me as I drove past them on my way back to London.

One day in the summer of 1996, Alan Crompton-Batt told me the Prince of Wales wanted me to cook for him. Of course it's a privilege to be asked to cook for a member of the royal family, but it was to be a grand affair and Vanessa Mae would be there, playing her violin to entertain Charles's 200 guests. The menu was not scary – it was summer, so I decided on a very English affair – but the performing-seal prospect seemed even more chilling than usual. I'd have to be very clever with my timing. I'd have to arrive just in time to do the starters – Ballotine of Salmon with Herbs and Langoustines – and escape as the main course – Sorrel d'Agneau à l'Anglaise – was being picked up from the passe. It was crucial that I wasn't there to see out the dessert, Jelly of Red Fruits.

I sat with my driver in my Range Rover on the road outside Highgrove, smoking my way through Marlboros and watching the dashboard clock. I didn't want to be paraded. In the grounds, Charles would be greeting his guests, and in the kitchen adjoining the marquee, my team would be waiting for me to arrive, give the orders and dish out the bollockings. And then, just when the time seemed right, my driver drove us up to the gates and security waved us in. I got out of the car and that's when I was nabbed. One of the Prince's aides grabbed me and I was whisked off to meet Charles. This was what I didn't want. But they knew the gig, didn't they? They knew Marco always did a runner after the main course.

The heir to the throne gave me a confident handshake, smiled warmly and then said, 'Bonjour Monsieur White ...' For three minutes I listened to his monologue, each and every word of it in French. I just nodded along – it would have been rude to interrupt – then when he finished he handed me a little collection of books about Highgrove, each of them inscribed to 'Monsieur Pierre White.'

I had to tell him. 'I'm terribly sorry, sir,' I said, 'but I'm not French. I grew up on a council estate in Leeds ...'

He looked at his assistant as if to say, You've fucking done it this time, boy. You've made me feel like the biggest prick in history. I had my picture taken standing beside a red-faced Prince and then off I went, into the kitchen to cook.

About a year later, in August 1997, I was asked to cook for Charles's ex-wife, Princess Diana. It was to be a lunch the next month held at the tycoon Severin Wunderman's magnificent house in the Vale, Kensington. There would be just a dozen people but the aim was to raise money for a charity. Each of the guests would pay £10,000 a head and Severin would very kindly pay Diana's ten grand as well as his own. I went to see Severin at his home and we talked through the menu. There would be Mille Feuilles of Crab and Tomato followed by Grilled Lobster with Herbs, and as main course Pigeon with Foie Gras. Pudding would be Roast Pineapple, carved in the room.

It wasn't just the pineapple that Severin was excited about showing off. He said, 'After the meal, I'd like you come out and meet the guests. Come out and do your stuff.' Stuff? I didn't do any stuff. I just liked to cook and leave. It seemed rude to say no, though, so I agreed to his request but left the meeting feeling anxious. At home I told Mati about the planned lunch and said, 'The only way I can get out of meeting Diana is if she dies.' The following weekend, the last in August, Diana died in Paris – needless to say the lunch was cancelled.

On the morning of Diana's death I was due to go fishing with Tim Steel. I have known Tim since I was three years old. The pair of us became mates at Fir Tree Primary and then we both went to Allerton High. At some point after school, Tim ended up in TV but we stayed in touch and remained good friends. When I did the Mirabelle deal I ended up with a flat above the restaurant and asked Tim if he would like to live there. He accepted the offer and duly moved in, bringing with him his girlfriend at the time, a certain Heather Mills. She was not well known then, but has since acquired global fame by becoming the wife – and then the estranged wife – of Beatle Paul McCartney.

I think I am within my rights to give my opinion of Heather and say quite frankly that I did not like her. I tried to avoid her company because I found she had a smothering effect. Of course, she had many attributes which Tim found appealing but I couldn't see them.

So on the day of Diana's death, Tim picked me up as arranged and we went off for a fish at Sonning-on-Thames, both numbed by the news. We were at the river bank when Tim's mobile phone went off. It was Heather. They had a chat and when he came off the phone, he said, 'Heather thinks that she could take Diana's role on that land-mine charity.'

TWENTY-THREE

Blue skies over Leeds, again

I GOT a phone call from my brother Clive at about half nine in the morning. 'Dad's had a stroke,' he said. The old man, or Pater as we sometimes called him, was dying. Mati and I put the two boys into the car and headed up the M1 to Leeds and number 22 Lingfield Mount. It was Friday, 12 September 1997, a week or so after the opening of The Oak Room. The sense of accomplishment that comes with launching a restaurant was suddenly drowned, of course, by the numbness that accompanies loss.

A sofa bed had been set up for Dad in the front room and he was lying there, dipping in and out of consciousness. He should probably have been in hospital, but he'd always wanted to die at home, in his small two-bed semi, and it seemed as though his wish was being granted. His wife Hazel was there, as well as my brothers Graham and Clive and a doctor. 'He'd just had his breakfast when it happened,' said Clive.

Luciano went up to Dad, kissed him on the cheek and said, 'Love you, Grandpa.' The old man had been out cold, but at this point he opened his eyes and whispered back to his three-year-old grandson, 'You, too.' He would live to see just another day, but those two words were the last I heard him speak. Mati, the boys and I drove into the centre of Leeds and checked into The Queen's Hotel, where my father had trained as a chef, starting out as a boy. The next morning, a Saturday, I wanted a distraction, so I took Luciano for a stroll in the city centre to buy the newspapers. I stepped onto the street and looked up. The sky was crystal blue and the sun shone brightly, and

I was instantly reminded of that February day – another Saturday – back in 1968 when I last saw my mother. I knew then that this would be the last day of my father's life.

Luciano and I walked along the yellow flagstones and my mind took me back to my childhood and those Saturday mornings when Dad would take me off to Leeds market to do a bit of shopping. For lunch he would buy me a pork pie and mushy peas and we'd chop off the pie's lid, chuck in some mint sauce and put the lid back on. Occasionally on those trips we would bump into one of Dad's friends who would hand me ten pence, and as the coin was offered, Dad would nudge me to take it, saying in his dry way, 'Don't be shy. Your mother wasn't.'

We drove to Lingfield Mount to visit Dad for what would be the last time. Others in Dad's position might have wanted a cosy pillow or some soft music to listen to, but a dose of horseracing was the thing that brought him comfort, so the telly was switched on for that day's big race, the St Leger live from Doncaster. As a lad I had witnessed him crouching in front of the TV, whipping himself with a rolled up newspaper as the horses charged to the finishing post in *The ITV Seven*. Now we all stood around Dad, stretched out on his sofa bed, as the horses galloped along on the screen. I watched him more than I watched the race and I could see life in his eyes as if he was aware of the dramatic commentary. Come on my son. Come on my son. Rather fittingly, the winning horse was called Silver Patriarch.

The doctor gave the old man a final shot of morphine and then he told us, 'He won't last longer than two hours. I'm sorry.' It was time to go, time to leave Leeds. I wanted to take the boys and Mati back to London and leave my father with his wife, so she could have that last bit of time with him. I can't do anything for the old man, I thought. We said our goodbyes and when we were on the M1, driving back down to London, my mobile rang. Hazel said that my father had died. He had passed away at the age of seventy, twenty-five years after a doctor had diagnosed him with cancer and given him six months to live.

We arrived back in London and I asked Mati to drop me off at the Hyde Park Hotel to have a coffee, smoke a cigarette and think things through. A couple of days earlier I had bought a picture on approval – it was given to me so that I could have a bit of time to study it and work out whether or not I wanted to buy it.

It was a painting of lilies in a vase by an artist called Gluck and, dazed by the events of the past two days, I sat there in the restaurant, looking at the picture. I decided that I would buy it and today it hangs in my home in Holland Park as a reminder of that day.

As I sat there, I also a recalled a night at the Hyde Park, back in January 1995; the night I won my three Michelin stars. Michael Winner had come for dinner with some of his journalist friends, who included Rebekah Wade, who went on to edit the *News of the World* and the *Sun*, and Piers Morgan, who was then editor of the *News of the World* and fast becoming the most talked about maverick in the media industry. Piers would become a good friend and on that first meeting he asked me, 'What does your father think of you winning three stars?'

'He doesn't understand,' I said. 'As far as he's concerned Michelin make tyres.'

When I told Piers that he was, in fact, editing my father's favourite paper he said he wanted to send a features writer round to interview Mati and me for an article. My Dad was delighted when, come the following Sunday, he saw his son taking up the entire centre spread – for the right reasons rather than the wrong ones. As far as the old man was concerned, two pages in the *Screws* meant a good deal more than three stars in *The Michelin Guide*. Marco must be worth something, Dad would have thought.

Our father–son relationship had always been unhinged, I suppose. After I left home and he remarried, there was a period of more than a decade when we didn't see each other and didn't communicate. We did a good job of patching it up after Luciano was born, and unquestionably my father was a very good grandfather.

He adored the boys – he'd send them cards and toys – and from time to time we would travel up to Leeds and take him out for the day. We might go to Bridlington, where the old man loved to walk along the harbour top, looking out at the horizon and taking in the sea air. I'd buy him kippers and fresh crab to take home as a treat, and he said to me once, 'I would love to have another ten years just to see the grandchildren grow up.' After our day trips and before heading home to London I would always wait for Hazel to go out of the room and then bung the old man a monkey – any less than that and it would have seemed mean; any more and it would have intimidated him. The five hundred quid went straight into his back pocket. He didn't call Hazel and say, 'Here, love, put that in the teapot.' He was very funny, my old man, but he didn't know it.

We didn't have deep conversations. My father was more interested in what the grandchildren were doing than the developments of my much-publicised life. How's it going? What have you been up to? He didn't ask me those sorts of questions. Without him, of course, I couldn't have achieved what I did in the kitchen. After all, he was the one who had told me to become a chef because 'people will always need feeding'. He was the one who instilled discipline in me, as well as the desire and need to be acknowledged, but when I'd accomplished it all, and more, the accomplishments were never discussed. Maybe he wasn't inquisitive, or maybe he was just one of those northerners who don't like to encourage flash behaviour? Could it have been that the sort of food I was cooking meant nothing to him? He had been a chef in a different world, at a time when cooks got excited about Entrecôte Chasseur or Chicken Cordon Bleu. He was more passionate about dog races than food.

I don't think he had ever been to London and he certainly never came to one of my restaurants, partly because he wasn't in good health and partly because he didn't express an interest in doing so. In other words, I didn't cook a single meal for my father. The man who pushed me into my career, whose influence had such an extraordinary impact upon me, never tasted one of my dishes and never asked me about my restaurants. Sometimes I wonder if he was intimidated by me, but if I'm honest with myself, I don't know what he made of me. I haven't got a clue, not a fucking clue.

As I was looking at that picture of lilies on the night of Dad's death it struck me for the first time in my life that I missed him. I had taken it for granted that he was always there, and though I didn't see him for many years, I knew that if I knocked on his door it would open.

Two or three days after Dad's death I was in a betting mood. There was a horse called Frank, as in my Dad's name, racing at Lingfield, as in the name of the road where the old man lived. I had told myself that I would only have one bet that day and I had already put my money on Cloudy Bay which was in another race. So I never put anything on Frank which is a great shame, not least because it would have enabled me to tell you how I won a fortune.

The funeral took place at Lawnswood Cemetery, the same place where we had said farewell to my mother in 1968. Life, as they say, repeats itself. I had taken Luciano to my Savile Row tailor so that he could be fitted out in a smart suit. Simon, my gigantic younger brother, had flown over from Italy to be one of the mourners, and afterwards he came back to London and Mati and I took him for dinner at the Criterion. We were sitting in the restaurant when Simon said to me, 'Frank wasn't my father really. He did not bring me up. My father is Gianfranco.'

I launched into one. 'Well,' I said, 'if that's the case then Graham, Clive and I are not your brothers. You can't have it both ways.'

I went on, 'Please understand this, my father told me that not one member of our Italian family went to my mother's funeral and not one member of the Italian family has been to our mother's resting place. And before our nonna died she wrote a letter to her two children in Italy, reminding them that their sister had three children in England, so even our nonna saw the failings in her own children.'

As Simon tried to absorb the gist of my outburst, I added, 'One thing about our father, what he did, he gave you a better life by allowing you to go to Italy. And he didn't put my two brothers and me in a children's home, which would have been totally acceptable in the sixties. What he did was sacrifice his own life to keep us all together. And whatever you think of that is your opinion, but I think it takes a man to do something like that.'

I haven't spoken to Simon from that day to this. Nine years. I accept that it's wrong that I don't speak to my brother. It is wrong because he's my mother's son. Today I don't want to do it, don't want to resolve the issue, maybe tomorrow I'll want to deal with it. I also accept that he has got to live with the fact that he never knew his mother, and that must be very difficult for him.

TWENTY-FOUR

Rough seas

IN 1998 I opened a restaurant in Soho called Titanic. It sank – much to the utter delight of headline writers. It wouldn't have mattered what I'd called the place because like the ship it was named after, it would still have gone under. There was one problem after another, and a couple of legal battles that caused more headaches.

For a year or two, however, Titanic was rock 'n' roll and there were signs of promise. On a Saturday night about 3,000 people would come through the doors into what was the biggest restaurant London had ever seen. And it wasn't just a restaurant; there was a bar, a stage and a dance floor. It was wild and buzzing and jam-packed with well-known people.

Will Smith, the movie star, would be up on stage singing, or rather rapping, live. The Spice Girls would be on podiums, dancing away. On a table over there was Hugh Hefner, the Playboy boss, celebrating his birthday with thirteen dolly birds. Damien Hirst would be finishing his food and wiping the plate on his stomach and, hang on, now he's getting his cock out and walking along the bar. Is that David Beckham and Noel Gallagher in the corner? Is that Priscilla Presley who's just walked in, looking around and thinking, Golly, what's this place? And in the middle of it all was Mini Me, the midget from the Austin Powers movies, wandering around and getting lost under the tables. I would finish service at the Hyde Park and head off to Titanic and wow was it heaving.

The site had once been the carvery restaurant of the Regent Palace Hotel in Swallow Street. In other words, it was in Soho but just a few hundred yards from Piccadilly Circus. It came into my hands because it was owned by Granada and I had done a deal with them involving me opening restaurants in the company's hotels. The most enticing aspect of Titanic was that it was licensed to hold 850 customers. Keep in mind that figure – eight hundred and fifty – because it is important in the story of Titanic, and in a minute I'll come back to it and explain its relevance.

As things got under way, I brought in the interior designer Keith Hobbs to model the room on one of those romantic ocean liners from years gone by. He worked from pictures and drawings of the *Queen Mary* and when you walked in you were treated to an array of art deco and massive, slowly rotating mirror balls hanging from the ceiling. *Queen Mary* wasn't a good name for a restaurant, so I came up with Titanic, which in hindsight you could say is an even less appealing name. A lot of people said it was hostage to fortune, but at the time I liked the name and anyway, in the basement beneath us was Oliver Peyton's Atlantic Bar and Grill – Titanic was on the Atlantic, if you get my drift. We even got a phone number that ended in the digits 1912, as in the year the ship sank on its maiden voyage.

I never intended to cook at Titanic, but I'd devise the menus and oversee the running of the venue. It was essential to have a head chef who knew how to push out big numbers while maintaining high standards, so I brought in Peter Rafael, who had worked at one of my other restaurants, Criterion, where he had mastered the art of high-volume service. The food was to be simple: burgers, steaks, grilled fish, squid ink risotto, that sort of thing.

So far, so good. We had an opening night and somehow managed to get Billy Zane, star of the blockbuster movie *Titanic* which had come out a year earlier, to come along. All Saints were there, as well as the Spice Girls, and I remember Peter O'Toole, the legendary actor, being there as I had a chat with him. I'd been looking forward to meeting Peter because I wanted to point out to him that both he and my father had been pupils at St Luke's in Leeds. It was a brief conver-sation and maybe since he became established Peter doesn't like to talk about his childhood in Leeds. Apart from irritating Peter, I think I kept everyone else happy, and after the launch success followed.

On Friday and Saturday nights we had a late licence, which enabled us to stay open until three in the morning, and on each of those nights the kitchen would send out 800 meals. To cater for such a large number, we had twenty-five cooks in the kitchen, dozens of front-of-house staff and about fifteen security men. Titanic was a big operation, a monster, and the concept was good. We did the lunch trade, but things really started at five in the evening when we would open the lounge bar for people who fancied a drink after work. After that the place turned into a restaurant, and then at 10.30 p.m. a DJ would kick off and Titanic became a nightclub. The concept, therefore, was lounge bar to restaurant to nightclub – that way we had money coming in all the time. The celebs produced the PR, the PR produced the punters and the punters produced the cash. 'If the recession is our iceberg then we shall sail around it,' I had confidently announced when Titanic opened, but there was more than one iceberg.

Around about the time I thought I was onto a winner, the troubles started. One of the problems was drugs. Titanic catered for a young, late-night crowd who wanted a party. They also wanted drugs, and so did certain members of staff. Up until now, I was used to working with highly disciplined cooks and waiters who'd work from nine in the morning until midnight. But I was about to discover that the staff who work in Michelin-starred restaurants are an entirely different breed to the bunch who work until 4 a.m. at a restaurant-bar-club. They have a different mentality, and perhaps the desire for perfection was sometimes absent. I'm not having a swipe at everyone who worked at Titanic, please don't get me wrong, but the drugs problem was an eye-opener. An old friend of mine asked if I would give his son a job and I agreed, of course. The lad did about a week at Titanic before I discovered he was selling drugs to other members of staff. I told him to stop and he did. Then there were the punters. We had to have security people in the loos in an attempt to ward off cocaine snorters, and when one of my managers went up to someone he suspected of selling drugs to customers, the man pulled his jacket aside to reveal a gun. It's the romance of this industry that's kept me working in it, but there's no way you can tolerate guns on the premises.

The next hiccup was when I received a legal letter from Harland and Wolff, the ship makers who built the ill-fated *Titanic*. They claimed I had infringed their copyright, which led to a row about whether a company is allowed to have a trademark over a name that's been public property for decades. I got someone to check out the number of businesses called Titanic and found places like the Titanic Café and the Titanic Chip Shop. My point was, why single me out? The action didn't really go anywhere – appropriately it sank without trace – but I was lumbered with big legal costs nonetheless.

Then I got dragged into a legal battle between Oliver Peyton and Forte. Oliver was cheesed off because he claimed his lease with Forte prevented them from leasing the rest of the building to obvious rivals, but the issue had become confused since signing contracts, as Forte had been taken over by Granada.

I have only met Oliver Peyton once, and we had a quite extraordinarily short conversation. One night in the days when I had Harveys someone took me to the Atlantic. I was standing there when a man came springing up to me and said, 'Hi.'

I replied, 'Hello.'

He said, 'Oliver.'

I said, 'Marco.' Then he disappeared. I don't know if he knew who I was but I certainly didn't have a clue who he was until later someone said, 'That was Oliver Peyton, you know,' and I said, 'Oh, right.' Hi. Hello. Oliver. Marco.

Years after this highly intellectual, stimulating conversation, Oliver was furious to discover that I had just opened a place above his, catering for the same young, fashionable crowd. He thought I would steal business from him because punters would mistake Titanic's entrance for his.

Oliver was claiming loss of profits, so his case was against the landlords with whom he had a contract and nothing to do with me, but he dragged me into it anyway and I became a defendant. Why? I think Oliver thought I wouldn't like the bad publicity and would therefore put pressure on Granada to settle. Granada did in fact want to settle and I don't think Oliver wanted it to go as far as court. They could have had a nice easy deal if it weren't for me, but I said something like, 'Excuse me, this is costing me to defend this action, even though we're a joint venture. If you pick up my costs then you can go and do your deal with Oliver and that's fine.' However, as they weren't offering to pay my costs I dug in my heels and refused to become the middle man who'd solve the problem.

Oliver's strategy was wrong, in my opinion. I just made things difficult. Thinking like a restaurateur I got a security man with a clicker to stand close to the Café Royal and click his clicker every time he saw a customer going in and out of the Atlantic. Oliver was licensed for 500 but, as the clicker showed, he never had less than five hundred going into his club. Oliver may well have suffered a loss of profit but strictly speaking it was an illegal loss of profit because the Atlantic was in breach of its numbers.

When the *Evening Standard* asked me what I thought of the affair I told them and they quoted me under the headline MARCO REFUSES HIS RIVALS A 'LIFE RAFT' IN TITANIC BATTLE: 'His solicitors asked me to settle, but I refused to. The biggest mistake Oliver made was bringing the action against me. He wanted to play the big boy's game and go to court, but now he's getting cold feet and is crumbling. Oliver isn't asking for more now. If they settle that's fine, but if they go before the judge and say they have no case he will award me legal costs of about £400,000, which makes it a pointless exercise issuing a writ against me. It's a matter of principle that if he brings a court case he should be big enough to carry on with it and stand in the box. He has put us all through a lot of aggravation and I have spent a lot of time on my case.'

It went to court, though I didn't turn up – and was scheduled as a two-week hearing. It was over after a day or two. Granada capitulated and settled with Oliver, which means Oliver must have got something out of it, though I can't remember precisely what. The experience must have battered him, but it also battered me.

Aside from the drugs and the legal fights with Harland and Wolff and Oliver Peyton, Titanic presented a far more serious problem which would finish us off. It was a time bomb, I suppose, and when it exploded Titanic would sink in the murky waters of restaurant history. It's the story of the 850, that number I mentioned earlier on. Granada – or perhaps Forte – had told us we had a licence to allow 850 punters onto the premises. We did not. The licence was actually for 350. Some dobbin at Forte had said 850 and the venture had proceeded on that basis. No one had ever thought to check; there didn't seem the need to. So we opened up this massive restaurant with a glamorous launch and watched the money rolling in, and then we discovered we were in breach of our licence. I would never have done the Titanic deal had I known it was licensed for only 350. Say Wembley Stadium seats 85,000 people but has a licence for only 35,000 – then it's dead, isn't it?

As I said, we carried on unaware of this problem, still catering for large numbers. One night Robbie Williams came into Titanic and he had a problem. The paparazzi had been following him and somehow he'd taken a photographer's car keys and thrown them down a drain. The pap had then made a complaint to the police so Robbie was on the run. It was a silly mess best sorted out the following morning, so I told him to follow me and escorted him through the hotel and out of another door, where he promptly disappeared off into Soho. The next thing I knew the police were in the restaurant, asking to see me. The local copper was called Bob, who was nice and, I think, in charge of the drugs and vice squad.

I took Bob into my office and he said, 'You know what we did with Johnny Depp at your other gaff.'

Let me quickly tell you the Johnny Depp story. Johnny had been for lunch at Mirabelle, and when he emerged from the restaurant he spotted photographers and started chasing a pap down Curzon Street, waving a plank of wood. It remains a mystery as to where

Johnny found a plank of wood in the middle of Mayfair, but he was arrested and later released on condition he autograph the plank for the police.

'Yes,' I told Bob. 'I know about Johnny.' I think Bob was trying to say that my customers were trouble.

'Where is Robbie Williams?' asked Bob.

I said, 'He left.'

'He can't have left. We've been outside and we haven't seen him leave, so where is he?'

I said, 'Do you think I hid him in the kitchen cupboards? He left through the back entrance.' And I explained to a mystified Bob that there was another way out, via the hotel. Bob wasn't happy with me.

About a week later Titanic got busted. I wasn't there that night, but the authorities arrived, saw a sea of 850 (dare I say more) faces – a heaving mass of people who were off their heads – and we were effectively out of business. They said we had a licence for only 350 so we lost our late-night licence and spent the next two and a half years trying to get it back. It drained us. They said they would give us 650, but we could only have a 1 a.m. licence. That was no good as the whole thing was about late nights. The vibe had gone and it would never be the same. We had people queuing to come in, but eventually they started thinking, Why are we queuing for half an hour, and they'd vanish.

You can still see a bit of Titanic at Frankie's in Knightsbridge, which I modelled on it. The way I see Titanic is, it was nice to have had it and done it, but I wouldn't want to do it again.

———

Quo Vadis was another restaurant that produced a headache or two. A lively 120-seater in Soho's Dean Street, it was where I'd worked in the mid-eighties for Italian chef, Signor Zucchoni, the man who couldn't work me out because of my long hair. I was to be a partner with Jonathan Kennedy, the PR man, and Matthew Freud, the PR guru and Damien Hirst.

So that meant there was Damien, the rock-star artist with a wild, rock 'n' roll lifestyle, and me, the rock-star chef known for his temper. From the outset, it had a nitroglycerine whiff about it. There was, however, a big difference between the two of us. Although I was an enfant terrible chef, I was driven by emotion. What I did was not to create effect, it was me being emotional and expressing myself as a person. Damien, however, the enfant terrible of the art world, did everything for effect. He'd make statements or behave in a certain way purely for the shock factor. Anyway, I think I'm correct in saying that he would only do the deal if I was involved, and so that was how it all came about. We had more in common than simply being enfants terribles, though. Damien was a few years younger than me, but he was another Leeds lad and had been to the same school as my older brothers.

We put Damien's paintings on the walls and the restaurant became home to his trademark style of art: on show were two skinned bulls' heads floating in formaldehyde. One day, not long after we'd opened, I got a call from Matthew Freud. He said, 'Marco, we've got a problem. You'd better get over here.' When I arrived at the restaurant I was greeted by 200 animal rights activists, chanting nasty things about Damien, bulls' heads and our restaurant. As I pushed my way through the crowd one of the protesters screamed, 'That's Marco,' and they all started spitting at me. The thing is, the bulls were dead long before Damien did his work on them. What's the difference between a head in a tank of formaldehyde and a piece of meat on a plate? I didn't stop to argue this point with them, though.

Inside, Matthew and I stood with the restaurant's staff, gazing onto the street as the activists continued chanting. I couldn't see where it was going so I said, 'Why don't we just give them some coffee to calm them down a bit?' The show got tedious so I headed off, past the gobbing protesters, and soon afterwards they stormed the restaurant. The maître d' was chinned, the receptionist attacked. There was a full-scale scrap going on and among the protesters were three or four undercover policemen who then waded in, fists flying.

Come into my theatre of cruelty. This picture
was part of an award-winning advertising
campaign.

Furniture was kicked over and telephones were ripped from their sockets. Five of the activists were carted off to Marlborough Street Magistrates' Court. Then the mother of one of the girls who'd been arrested called me to say her daughter was a depressive on tablets. Would I drop charges? I was quite happy to drop the charges but the police wouldn't have it because they treat activists like some sort of terrorist unit. It was a right mess.

Damien's artwork caused further problems and ultimately led to the pair of us falling out. The restaurant had a deal with Damien whereby it paid him to hang his paintings on the walls. If he wanted to take a painting down he was obliged to replace it with another – it's what you call rotating artwork. I didn't like paying the rent for the paintings, it didn't seem right. Then Damien started taking the paintings down because he wanted to put them in his house in Dublin, so he'd take out a painting that was, say, eight foot by six foot and replace it with something that was twelve inches by twelve inches. You can't do that; it's not right. The idea of rotating artwork is that you replace it with something of a similar size, otherwise it just looks stupid.

If you've got a deal where you're being paid an art rent then you've got to respect that. It wasn't in the spirit in which we'd done the deal. I don't know whether it was Damien taking advantage of a situation or whether it was Damien being Damien, but I wasn't going to tolerate it. I asked him to move out all his stuff and initially there was no fall-out. We needed to replace his artwork and I thought I'd do some pictures myself. It was supposed to be a humorous battle but lawyers ended up getting involved at one stage and there were accusations of plagiarism. For me it was all done with an element of fun. I took myself off to the country and did some conceptual art, painting a canvas black, sticking some cockerel feathers to it and then giving it some weird name like Oil Slick. It's quite time-consuming but it's not hard.

You have to get someone to prepare the canvases. Then you put a black acrylic over a big square canvas, put a glaze to it and stick feathers on. It looks fantastic, to be honest, but creating a great meal is harder.

I also tried doing a bit of spot painting and then I'd slash up the picture and call it *Divorce*. So that was me being incredibly playful. Damien had done his famous DNA model, so I made a model with bulls' eyes and called it BSE. There was lots of publicity as the media followed my entrée into the world of conceptual art. Most people seemed to get my point, that you can scribble all over a piece of paper, frame it, put it on a wall and suddenly it's art. We were like a couple of kids having a play fight when it suddenly got out of control and lawyers were involved. Terrible really, isn't it? We were two grown men, not a couple of ten-year-olds.

And do you know what encouraged me to try my hand at conceptual art in the first place? One day, when we were still mates, I'd been sitting with Damien and I'd said to him, 'Do you remember the world we came from? There was always a fake *Mona Lisa* hanging over the fireplace and three ducks on the back wall, just like in Hilda Ogden's house? I think you should make a really sophisticated version and do three ducks flying across the back wall in formaldehyde.' Three months later I picked up the *Telegraph* and there it was: three ducks on the back wall. That's when I thought, it's not that hard really.

Having said that, he is a genius who deserves everything he's got. And that's how I genuinely feel about it. His butterfly paintings were genius, and the spot paintings are fantastic. So you can't take anything away from him. Maybe he just misinterpreted my playfulness.

What was nice about Damien was that while he had infamous problems, he managed to maintain a wonderful relationship with his lovely mother. The pair of them would come for lunch or dinner at one of my restaurants and I was always aware that his mother was very proud of her son. I used to think, maybe he's made his dream come true and his mother has been there to see it, but my mother hasn't been here to see my dream come true.

TWENTY-FIVE

Letting go of status

THIS SLAVE had been a slave for twenty-one years. When I finally made up my mind that I wanted freedom – wanted out – the chains were released pretty swiftly. For a while I'd been thinking about it, contemplating retirement as I continued to spend long days and nights at the stove or by the passe.

Several factors contributed to my decision to hang up the apron. They included the realisation that I had sacrificed everything in order to be in a kitchen, locked away from the outside world. Obviously, I had to give more time to Mati and the kids. Mati was the only person I talked to about retiring, and she was behind my decision, as you might expect of a wife who rarely sees her husband. In the kitchen I had three stars, but at home I had four, Mati, Luciano, Marco and Lettie, my daughter from my first marriage. When I'd get home from work they were asleep: we tended to meet when Mati brought them into the kitchen and they would sit on the passe fifteen minutes before lunch service began. We hadn't had the time to build a proper foundation to our life and relationship. Before we knew what we were doing – less than two and a half years into the relationship – we were two young people with two kids. We didn't go off partying and having fun like most young people do. I just worked and worked and worked, and then slept when I had a day off. And Mati would pop into the restaurants. That was our existence. I didn't question it. I was so obsessed with my work, so tunnel-visioned that nothing else played a part, but I was starting to accept that I would have to give something back to Mati and the kids.

There was another contributing factor that helped me make up my mind to retire as a chef. I had become disillusioned with the industry. My own bosses might have been prone to swear a lot, but aside from that I had always felt the restaurant industry was an extremely romantic one. Romance and restaurants go together, don't they? There were three particularly unromantic episodes, incidents that left a distinctly sour taste in my mouth. The first was my attempt to join Relais Gourmands, the second was the time when my old friend John Burton Race pinched one of my chefs, and the third was the events that led to the end of my friendship with Albert Roux.

The Relais Gourmands shambles came shortly after I won the three Michelin stars in 1995. I had the Restaurant at the Hyde Park Hotel at the time and reckoned that to join Relais would be good both for business and for status. Relais had three players in the South East of England; Michel Roux at the Waterside Inn, Tim Hart of Hambleton Hall, and Paul Henderson who owns Gidleigh Park. I tried to organise a meeting so that I could establish the formalities of joining, but each person I spoke to asked me to speak to someone else until eventually I ended up being asked to go back and talk to the first person. I was going round in circles. Clearly, they didn't want me to join, but none of them went so far as to say, 'Get lost.'

Initially I was quite surprised by their unhelpfulness. Surely Relais would quite like me on board, I thought. The Restaurant was the highest rated restaurant in Britain – we had the three Michelin stars, five rosettes in the AA Guide, three stars in Egon Ronay, ten out of ten in the *Good Food Guide* and 19 out of 20 (no British chef has ever got twenty out of twenty) in the *Guide Gault-Millau*. We had won the Grand Slam of Gastronomy.

Perhaps that was the problem. Were Michel, Tim and Paul frightened that I was going to take business away from them? The last thing they needed was the Grand Slam winner moving onto their turf. I could have pushed it and sought a solution from the big Relais boys in Paris, but in the end I just gave up.

Walking along Bond Street a few years ago, on my way to Sotheby's, I heard a voice shout, 'Marco!' The face was familiar and for a second I smiled, until it dawned on me that I was standing in front of Paul Henderson, one of the Relais players. The memories of my miserable Relais experience came flashing back, but Henderson was beaming.

'Marco, how lovely to see you. These are some friends of mine,' he said cheerily, pointing to an entourage hovering behind him, 'they're over from America.' He put out his hand to shake mine, but I couldn't do it and nodded towards his hand, saying, 'You can put that back in your pocket.' His jaw dropped towards the pavement and I continued on my way to the auction house.

The Relais episode was annoying but not as infuriating as my experience with John Burton Race. We had met in Oxford in 1985, when we both worked for Raymond Blanc. I was at Le Manoir and John, who is about four years older than me, had done a year at Le Manoir before becoming the head chef at Le Petit Blanc. I always liked him, we got on well and as we climbed the ladder we enjoyed a bit of healthy rivalry. We were both desperate to become the first British chef to win three stars, and others in the industry used to say, 'Who will get there first, John or Marco?' By now you know the answer to that question.

He used to come quite often to the Restaurant, and one night he arrived for dinner with a couple of his boys – the sous chef and pastry chef – from his restaurant, L'Ortolan, in Berkshire. After service I came out of the kitchen and joined the three of them at their table. We had a little chat and that was that. About three days later my sous chef handed in his notice. 'Where are you going?' I asked.

He said, 'I'm going to work for John Burton Race at L'Ortolan.' He told me he had gone for the job interview about a week earlier. I thought, hang on, John was in three nights ago and sat there chatting to me like an old friend, all the time knowing that a few days earlier he had interviewed my sous chef. He had poached my chef.

Poaching staff may well be acceptable in other professions, but I had always followed a certain tradition. If a chef approached you for a job you would, in turn, ask him if he had cleared it with his boss. 'Does Raymond/Pierre/Albert know you are asking me?' I might inquire. If the chef said no, then I'd tell him to speak to his boss first.

That is the way the system worked and it went some way to eliminating friction between head chefs. If John had been looking for staff then he could have asked me to help and I would have assisted. For once I forgot about the tradition and in retaliation nicked not one but three of John's staff, just to send him a message. Maybe that's the Italian in me.

And then there was dear old Albert Roux, Gavroche general, good friend, first boss in London, mentor and best man at my second wedding. Our friendship had been a bit unstable ever since I won the three stars. When he phoned it was usually only to ask if I had heard any trade gossip and there was something that made me question his loyalty. We had lunch one day at the Connaught and I decided to check him out. He asked me about a certain issue, which I knew all about, but rather than give him the full story, I told him a little bit of the truth and a few white lies. The following day I got a phone call from a reporter who appeared to know everything I had told Albert, including the fibs. Of course, it's possible Albert may have told someone who, in turn, told someone else who informed the reporter, but I don't think so. From then on I believed, rightly or wrongly, that I couldn't trust Albert.

He was a giant in the industry, a man who helped change gastronomy and take it forward. Albert is revered and his influence immense, but I was very close to him for a while and I saw another side to him.

I used to go to his house in the countryside and one year I went to spend Christmas with him and his lovely wife Monique. Albert and I were fishing for carp when he suddenly turned to me and announced, 'Do you know, Marco, nine out of ten people in the catering industry are cunts?' I was stunned. Here was this figurehead, a man I had put on a pedestal, letting me see what lay beneath the statesman-like exterior.

One day there were a few of us having lunch at Albert's house and over the meal we chatted about the recent death of a renowned French chef, whom it would be unfair to name. I'd never been fortunate enough to meet this particular chef, but his reputation was legendary and others had described him as a fine man. Curious to know what my host thought of him, I asked, 'Albert, what was he like, what did you make of him?'

Albert didn't mince his words. 'He was a cunt,' he said, and in so doing he hushed the other guests at the table. I thought it was quite a strange thing to say about a man who had just been buried.

I was also confused when Albert told me about his planned legacy as we sat at the riverbank fishing. He had once bought a butcher's shop, he explained, but was disgusted when he took it over because he discovered that chefs stopped shopping there because he wouldn't pay them backhanders.

The previous owner, it transpired, had slipped the chefs a few quid to keep the orders coming in, whereas Albert was repulsed by such a practice. He not only refused to continue with the custom but had a little black book which contained the names of the chefs who took cash. 'That little black book will be my leaving present to the industry,' Albert told me, his eyes still on the river in front of him. 'I'm going to expose all those people who took backhanders.'

Our friendship finally came to an end in the late nineties after Albert was invited to be a judge for the Catey Awards, the annual ceremony held by the *Caterer and Hotelkeeper* magazine. I was at Mirabelle when I got a call from Gordon Ramsay, who had a friend at the magazine. Gordon said, 'They're quite disgusted at *The Caterer*.'

'Why's that?'

'They had the judging for Chef of the Year and you were going to get it, but Albert started saying, "We can't give it to Marco Pierre White, it would be bad for the industry to give him Chef of the Year." You're not going to get the award.'

For years I had listened to Albert criticising other chefs and now he was criticising me.

So I phoned him and said, 'Albert, you were judging chef of the year yesterday for the Catey Awards and it has come back to me that you said it would be wrong to give Marco Pierre White Chef of the Year. And you said that Marco Pierre White is bad for the industry. Is that right, Albert?'

Albert came back with, 'I signed a confidentiality agreement.'

'I didn't ask if you'd signed a confidentiality agreement, Albert. I asked if you said those words.'

'Marco,' he said, 'I don't want to have this conversation with you.'

I told him, 'If I had said about you what you said about me, I don't think I'd want to have this conversation either. You saying you signed a confidentiality agreement confirms to me that you said those things, because otherwise you'd say, "I never said those things; it's a lie."'

Before putting down the phone I told him, 'I would respect you more if you had the balls to be honest with me rather than hide behind some so-called confidentiality agreement.'

A little while later in the *Sunday Business* newspaper Albert's son, Michel, mentioned that I had accused his father of having no balls. 'One thing my father's got is balls,' he said, or words to that effect, but the readers would have been mystified because Monsieur Roux Junior failed to explain the relevance of my remark. Somewhere along the way, Albert spoke to Keith Floyd, the Kofi Annan figure who had patched up my various disputes at Harveys. Albert wanted Keith to be the peace-maker but Keith's advice was simply, 'You know what Marco's like. Just give him time.'

I last saw Albert a couple of years ago, when I arrived at the Sofitel hotel in London for a meeting. Albert and I came face to face in the foyer. He looked at me and I looked at him. 'Good morning,' I said. He froze and didn't say a word, then he looked straight at the door and strutted off. He did a lot for the industry and you can't knock him for that. He also did a lot for me, so I have tremendous regret about the way it ended.

Meanwhile, I had lost respect for Michelin. There was an episode which sounds quite silly now but at the time became something of a preoccupation. Derek Brown had left and been replaced as head inspector by his sidekick, Derek Bulmer, who came to see me one day. When I shook his hand and said, 'Hello, Mr Bulmer' he replied, 'Please call me Derek.' He was a charming man and meant it in the most friendly way but I felt myself shudder at the thought of calling him by his first name. It would have been a bit like a pupil being on familiar terms with the headmaster. Just wasn't right. In fact, in my opinion it was completely wrong and the respect evaporated on that day. It started to dawn on me that I had spent my whole career being judged by people who had less knowledge than me, be they restaurant inspectors or food critics. Please forgive the arrogance, but can you see my point?

There were other reasons for me wanting to hang up my apron. The non-stop process of refining dishes and striving for perfection was exhausting. I didn't want to push myself anymore. Even when you have three stars you still have to keep raising your game. People look at you as a three-star chef and their expectations become greater. It's all about taking yourself as far as you can. It can seem never-ending.

In addition to this disillusionment, my brigade, as I mentioned earlier, were ready to leave me and become head chefs elsewhere and I didn't like the look of many of the new chefs arriving on the scene. I suppose what I could have done is what so many chefs do these days: stop cooking but pretend to the rest of the world that they are still at the stove, crafting and creating. But that is tantamount to lying, isn't it? They're simply pretending to be in the kitchen, when in fact they're in front of the camera. And if they're in front of the camera, who is at the stove?

Surely, if you go to a restaurant run by a top chef you can't be blamed for thinking that the chef who has his name above the door is the man who's in the kitchen. Or maybe I'm wrong. Regardless, I am convinced that once chefs win three stars, they become disillusioned, just like I did. Winning becomes a way of life, and once you feel you can go no further then it becomes nothing more than just a job. You see it with boxers. They win the world title and lose their hunger. Why should chefs be any different?

I had lost the passion, so to stay in the kitchen would be the equivalent of lying to myself. By removing myself from *The Michelin Guide*, customers would know that I was no longer the one doing the food. I had lost all sense of direction, but now I was going to do something about it.

Mati was the one who suggested I hand the stars back to Michelin. We had been driving through London late one night when we passed the Hyde Park Hotel and I was reminded of my workload and started grumbling. She said, 'Why don't you return the stars?' I looked at her quizzically and she continued, 'Look, you're not happy and you haven't been for some time. If it is all about the pressure of having the stars, then why don't you get rid of them. No stars, no pressure.'

When she asked if a chef had ever returned the stars, I replied, 'No, of course not.' And then she said, 'You made history by becoming the first British chef to win three stars. Why don't you become the first British chef to hand them back?'

I pondered this question for a couple of weeks. Then it all clicked into place one morning when I took myself out of the kitchen and onto the banks of the River Test for some fishing therapy.

Test Wood pool is on the Petworth estate and is a great spot for fishing, perhaps the finest salmon pool on the south coast of England. You drive through a rough council estate in Southampton and come to a driveway, and when you get to the end of it – bang – you're in a quiet little paradise. I was introduced to it back in the nineties by Johnny Yeo, the artist and a mate of mine, and it remains one of my bolt-holes. Two other anglers use it; one is called Jumbo and the other is a former gamekeeper known as Toad. We sit there, fishing, thinking, talking and at lunchtime Jumbo produces a lunch of fresh crab and lobster with his own potato salad.

It would have been one morning in September 1999, when Mr Ishii picked me up in the Range Rover at dawn and drove me and my rod from London to Test Wood. Jumbo and Toad weren't around that day, but I sat there for a couple of hours fishing with Billy Webb, my friend and the estate's head keeper. I caught two salmon, put down the rod and wandered up to a nearby lawn for a break. I was standing there, drinking a cup of tea and smoking a Marlboro, when I suddenly thought, 'I don't want to be a chef any more. There has got to be more to life than cooking.'

Standing in my waders and looking back onto the calm surface waters of the pool, I fixed a retirement date in my head there and then. My final day in the kitchen, my last day as a professional chef, would be 23 December. It seemed the best day, as that's when The Oak Room was due to close for a two-week Christmas break. Having decided that I would no longer be a chef it occurred to me that it would be wrong to keep the Michelin stars. The stars, albeit hard-earned and cherished, would have to be returned. Mati was right: the pressure would be removed. I finished my cuppa, picked up my mobile and phoned Derek Bulmer at Michelin UK. 'Mr Bulmer, it's Marco Pierre White speaking.'

'Hello.' He was friendly – he didn't know what was coming.

We didn't do 'how are you?' or 'isn't it lovely weather?' I got straight to the point. 'Just to let you know,' I said, 'I stop cooking on 23 December. Please don't include me in your next guide.'

There was silence at the other end of the line. Cooks spend their lives working for a mention in the Michelin bible, this little book that has the power to bestow glory on slaves of the stove. Yet here I was, effectively handing back the stars it had taken a career to win. My dream had controlled me for two decades, but now I was in control.

There was a pause, a few seconds of silence and when Mr Bulmer eventually spoke, all he could say was, 'Oh.' There was more silence. He must have hoped I would provide an explanation. He must have been anxious to hear the rationale behind my statement but he didn't ask why. The only thing I gave him was a very friendly, 'Goodbye, Mr Bulmer.'

I heard another 'Oh' just as I was pressing End Call. And that was it. All done. It was the shortest conversation in history and now I could get on with my day. I put the phone back in my pocket and thought, Glad that's over. There was a feeling of relief and happiness. Happy to be released from my pain, which might sound dramatic but I think I was in pain. That phone call to Mr Bulmer felt like the most honest thing I'd ever done. It was, as they say, the end of a chapter.

TWENTY-SIX

Courting before marriage

WE ALL make mistakes. Failure is often the first part of success. Go to the best restaurant in the world and you might still see failure. A sommelier might accidentally knock a bottle of wine onto the table so its contents spill out and onto your partner. Your beef or lamb might be overdone or underdone but certainly not the way you ordered it. There could be a mistake on the bill. All these things shouldn't happen in top restaurants, but they do. When any of these accidents happen, it's what happens next that decides whether failure is turned into success.

If the maître d' fails to deal with it, then failure prevails, but if the maître d' realises you are upset and dashes over to your table, a look of genuine concern on his face, he has recognised an inconsistency. His worst fear – imperfection – has confronted him. Maybe he'll offer you drinks on the house, or perhaps he'll rip up the bill and give you the meal free of charge. He apologises with the utmost sincerity. He cannot do enough to tell you how sorry he is and hopes that you will not bear a grudge. He walks you to the door and says sorry yet another time. Now, all of a sudden, you start thinking, I'll come back here. The place is great. So what if they managed to pour wine over my wife's new dress? OK, so I asked for a rare steak and it was burned to a cinder, but what the heck? The place is now your favourite restaurant. The maître d' is your best mate. He knows your name and your favourite table. He knows your favourite wine and from now on it will be handled with care. He asks when you'll give him the dry-cleaning bill for the soiled dress but you say, 'Forget about it.' You love the restaurant so much you're back there every week, spending money and helping the restaurant to succeed.

That is just one of the ways failure can become success in the restaurant business. With that in mind, look at what happened when the New York Times published a libellous comment about me. It was just a few words but nonetheless defamatory. The paper said that I had had 'a well-publicised bout of drink and drugs'. I was angry because it was untrue and I asked for an apology. They could have said sorry immediately and turned failure into success. I would have admired that. But they didn't. Nearly two years later I was at the Royal Courts of Justice, in London, with George Carman QC representing me in a historic case of American newspapers being sued in Britain for libel.

I'll start from the beginning. I got a call one day from an American journalist called Florence Fabricant, who said she wanted to write a profile about me for the New York Times, a newspaper I saw as influential and prestigious. I thought it sounded good and suggested we meet up, then on 13 February 1998, she came for lunch at The Oak Room. She brought her husband, who enjoyed my hospitality but by dessert complained of jetlag and vanished. Florence and I stayed to have a chat and a coffee, and she asked me about my life, as you'd imagine, and I talked to her about cooking, restaurants and my personal background. At no stage, however, did she ask me my views on drink and drugs, and if she had done, I could have explained to her that I rarely touched booze and have never taken illegal drugs.

'Why don't you have dinner at the Criterion as my guest?' I said and she took me up on the offer. That night I popped into the Criterion to say goodbye to Florence and to make sure that she was happy and had all the information she needed. My publicist and great friend, Alan Crompton-Batt, also told her that if she needed to check any facts then all she had to do was call him. A few months earlier I had done an interview with the New Yorker's Luke Jennings and before publication of that piece a fact-checker had phoned to run through various points. Unlike British publications, American newspapers and magazines have teams of fact-checkers on staff. I waited for the call from Florence's fact-checker, but it never came. Instead, on 13 May 1998, precisely three months after I'd done the interview, a friend phoned to say something like, 'My God. Have you seen the *New York Times*?' When I got hold of a copy I was horrified. Florence's article wasn't a fair interpretation of our conversation, put it that way, and then there was a line about me having 'a well-publicised bout with drugs and alcohol'. I got on to my lawyers, Schilling & Lom & Partners. I wanted an immediate retraction and apology. A lot of my clients were American, so the piece was unarguably damaging. I was also tied up with Granada, a PLC, and it was publicity they could do without. The *New York Times* didn't respond. Then things got worse – the same untrue and highly damaging allegations were published in an identical article in the *Times*' sister paper, *International Herald Tribune*, a couple of days later.

The whole thing rumbled on, with the *Times* refusing to publish an apology, so then writs started flying. When they filed their defence it was even more astounding. They said they believed it was true and well known that for a period of time I'd lived a wild life, drinking excessive amounts of alcohol and taking illegal drugs. They said I'd lived a decadent and disreputable life for an eighteen-month period, and that during that time, I had worked only occasionally and behaved in a self-indulgent manner, engaging in drink and drug sprees. They had compounded the damage by claiming all their lies were true.

Now it was war. You must never let people bully you; you have to stand up and fight for what you believe in, otherwise people will walk all over you. An injustice had been done and something inside me came out and made me react.

Libel actions can take a while to come to court, but in the meantime the *New York Times* set about trying to prove its lie. It was bordering on farcical. They hired private detectives in an attempt to dig up some dirt, and Gordon Ramsay, friend, protégé and by now an accomplished chef and restaurateur, got a call from someone saying she was a journalist who worked for the *New York Times*. Gordon was in the middle of talking to her when he realised I had recently told him about a defamatory article about me appearing in the *Times*. The penny dropped when the reporter asked him about the period during which he worked for me at Harveys. Did he have a wild time there? That sort of thing. When she referred to 'sex, drugs and rock 'n' roll' he ended the call. Other people I knew also got phone calls. Gordon told me that Stephen Terry, another Harveys protégé, had received a visit from a woman who had said that she was friends with a journalist for the *New York Times* who had written an article about me and that her friend was being sued. Apparently, she said she wanted to prove that some of the stuff her friend had said about me was true and she asked him whether he could tell her any stories about me taking drugs.

As part of its defence, the *New York Times* took quotes of mine from my cookery book *White Heat* and gave them a nice twist in a failed attempt to make it look as though I was into drink and drugs. But in that same book I had been quoted as saying, 'The rest of the catering world think I'm on drugs, but that just proves how narrow-minded they all are. If I was on drugs I wouldn't be able to carry on, and I wouldn't have any ideas. I look the way I do because I'm exhausted, because I'm giving everything I've got, but that's the only way I can work and think.'

A couple of weeks before the case was due to start the two papers conceded that the allegations were false. I wasn't in the mood for settling out of court and as the hearing drew closer they reassessed the grounds of their defence and decided they would argue that the piece, though inaccurate, had not affected my reputation.

The most pleasurable part of an otherwise draining experience was meeting George Carman, my QC for the case. Knowing George was one of the greatest educations of my life; he was a huge influence and had that rare combination of intelligence and instinct. What a great libel lawyer and clever man. Apart from having a good brain he had a way of speaking that left you, and the jury, mesmerised. He taught me how to create effect and I used to watch him like a hawk. He would go straight to people in such a confident way that they found it difficult to lie and I like to think I picked that up from him.

I remember the first time I met him. I shook his hand and said, 'George, my wife Matilda, Mati, sends her best.'

He said, 'I don't know your wife.'

'She said she used to look after you when you used to drink in El Cid on the Fulham road. Spanish but brought up in England. Mati. Good-looking girl.'

He said, 'I don't remember her.'

I said, 'You once took her back to your apartment for a nightcap.'

He said, 'I never touched her.'

I said, 'How can you make that statement George when you don't remember her? I rest my case, George.'

George went bright red and when he walked out of the room my solicitor Keith Schilling turned to me and said, 'That's the only time I've ever seen George Carman embarrassed.'

We gathered at the High Court on 3 April 2000 – two years after the offending article had appeared in print – and on day one I went into the box. By now the two papers wanted to settle and accepted that what they had said was wrong. It is customary for the claimant's QC to question you in a relaxing and friendly manner before the defendant's QC does a nasty cross-examination. So George was there to warm me up, make me feel relaxed and attempt to show me for what I am.

His opening questioning went like this:

Carman: 'Were you brought up on a Leeds council estate?'

Me: 'Yes, I was.'

Carman: 'Did you watch your mother die at the age of six?'

Me: 'Yes, I did.'

Carman: 'Did your father get lung cancer and was given just months to live …?'

He was drawing a picture for the jury, a picture of a boy from humble beginnings who has fought for everything he's got in life and who is a working-class hero, and then here's the *New York Times* trying to run him down, belittle him and destroy his reputation. But I was floored. It was harder answering George's questions than it was being cross-examined by Geoffrey Robertson QC.

Geoffrey stepped forward, keen to tie me up in knots, but I kept saying, 'I don't understand your question,' or, 'Can you please repeat that?' I think the jury quite liked me. There was, after all, a chance that if I didn't understand Geoffrey's long words then the jury might not understand them either. And so I went on, 'Can you clarify ... can you simplify,' so from Geoffrey's perspective, it was like the Nazis advancing on Moscow and getting stuck in the mud. I'd chuck in things like, 'I can't hear you, would you mind speaking a little louder?' Cough, cough. 'Could I have some water, please?' Then proceedings would halt while I had a sip to clear my throat.

I'd answer the question really quietly and he'd say, 'Sorry.' I was driving him mad. He said something like, 'Were you once described as the Jagger of the Aga.'

I said, 'Aga?'

He started telling me what an Aga was and I told him I knew what one was – I had one at home – but what did he say before Aga? Cue laughter from the judge and jury. Our roles were reversed, now it was me asking the questions. For all his education and intellect, he was dealing with something so simple he couldn't get his head round it. He wanted me to answer yes, but because I knew he wanted me to do that, because he was trying to take me somewhere he wanted me to go, I was doing everything in my power to say, 'No, I don't agree.'

When I was being cross-examined, George always used to close his eyes and look down.

And so it went on, Mr Robertson asking a question and me responding with, 'But you just asked me that question, worded slightly differently. I don't understand where you're going. Can you please simplify the question?'

I think it was the judge, Mr Justice Morland, who pointed out that every time the private detectives had asked people if they knew anything about me the allegations had been repeated. The slander had been going on for almost two years.

There were amusing moments, as when Geoffrey Robertson button-holed me one morning to say, 'I dined in your restaurant Quo Vadis last night. I had the most delicious risotto I've ever eaten in my life.'

George's closing speech was everything you'd expect from a genius. His reputation was one of a master orator. George was a short man but as his son Dominic said after George's death in January 2001, 'With his stage as a courtroom and his audience as the jury he was a giant among men.' The court was hushed, the jury undoubtedly excited about what was to come. Sit down with the popcorn, the lights are dimming, the big movie is about to start ...

Ladies and gentleman of the jury, once upon a time there was a bad, bad boy in the kitchen and the bad, bad boy had the infernal cheek to sue two powerful international newspapers, and they were called the *New York Times* and the *International Herald Tribune*. Of course, it was a claim that should never have been brought because it never was a libel, they had nothing to apologise for, they had no damages to pay and they had done him no harm. They had not hurt his feelings and they had, in fact, done him a great favour. The great favour was to employ private investigators, go round amongst his friends and acquaintances, investigate whether he had, in fact, taken any illegal drugs – a criminal offence – and eventually, on 20 March in the year 2000, announced that they were satisfied there was no truth in the allegation. They had done him an immense favour.

Members of the jury, I would invite you all to try and get yourself libelled by the American newspapers concerned because, of course, the end result will be they will investigate you for a year or more, go round all your friends and acquaintances and then say, 'Well, we the *New York Times* and the *International Herald Tribune*, give you a certificate of innocence and you should be very grateful for that because you can use it if anybody else makes the accusation against you.'

... Of course, this is a fairy tale. That is what no doubt the *International Herald Tribune* and the *New York Times* would like to publish about this case, as they would like to publish many things, but we can come to the real world and the real case.

... What do you know about this man Marco Pierre White? I think one thing you must know is that he has worked extremely hard all his life. He has worked, as the phrase goes, all the hours God sent him in order to succeed.

... There is an element of the logic of the madhouse in the approach of the editors of those national newspapers ... to desperately try to defend this case, defend the indefensible and say, 'It didn't do him any harm. It doesn't libel him,' because nearly two years ago they were saying it should never have been published and it should have been checked with him before it was published. The two positions are completely and utterly inconsistent.

... I started off with a fairy tale, 'the bad boy in the kitchen'. Why was that brought out by Mr Robertson? 'You've got a reputation as a bad, bad boy in the kitchen.' Was that intended as some kind of slur that would cause you, the jury, to award him less damages in some way? What does it mean, not just 'bad' but 'bad, bad boy in the kitchen'? It was repeated like you'd say to a small child, 'You naughty, naughty boy. '... It was all about him, Marco Pierre White, bawling out the staff to get the food on the table, which I am jolly sure he does. You cannot say when six people are paying a lot of money for dinner, 'Would you all mind, please, just getting the plates together, to put them carefully on the table there? Would you be so kind as to attend to your duties?' Of course not. Of course he bawls out, with a few emotive words, no doubt. 'Get moving. Get the stuff on the table,' or whatever phrase he uses. He would not be the great chef he has been and is if he was not able to give clear orders and get his discipline operating on his staff. There is the great discipline of the kitchens involved, kitchens in excellence.

He finished his speech, with the rousing words (cue the Dambusters' theme):

I want your award of damages to send a message across the Atlantic to these two great international newspapers that English juries award damages when people's reputations are sullied and damaged and libelled and award more damages when the conduct of the newspapers aggravates and increases the harm and distress they cause. That is the message I am inviting you to send across the Atlantic to the editors of the two defendant newspapers.

So that was the message: we can't have these Yanks pushing around one of our boys.

After an adjournment Geoffrey Robertson had something to say about this when he delivered his closing speech:

Ladies and gentlemen, you left the courtroom a few minutes ago with Mr Carman's rhetoric ringing in your ears, 'Send a message across the Atlantic to these Americans, you a British jury.' Ladies and gentlemen, racism and nationalism are the curses of our age. I am sure you will put out of your mind any suggestion of that. America may be a powerful country, but nonetheless we must deal with Americans who come here to visit us, who come to this court, when they did not have to, to put the matter before you, without any kind of racism or nationalism …

He argued that even if the story was false, had my reputation been damaged?

There is a difference, is there not, between picking up a gun and robbing a bank and being in the thrall, being caught up in drink or drugs, because we speak of people being victims of drink or drugs. We do not speak of bank robbers being victims of the lure of cash but people being victims of drugs … We do not think that they are bad because they have got over, in the past, a bout of drink or drugs … You would not dream of refusing his food or his company after reading this article. You might shrink from his bill, but not from Mr White himself.

Mr Robertson wanted to give the jury an idea of the size of damages awarded in British courts. (Pass the popcorn, please ...)

Of course, if Mr White during his conversation with Miss Fabricant she had somehow got angry with him and cut his hand off, he would get under the current standards, about £45,000. Well, that is a matter that you may think would cause great anger and distress and, of course, permanent disfigurement. That is the sort of money that is the going rate. There is another personal injury matter that I imagine would be very worrying for a chef: if Miss Fabricant had wielded her knife or fork in such a way as accidentally to have stuck it in his nostrils or tongue and destroyed his taste buds so that he could never as a chef smell or taste again, that would get him, on the going rate, some £9,000 to £12,000 ...

Mr Carman said, 'Well, why is he being asked about being a bad boy?' and made some good jokes at my expense, which is always welcome in these cases, but the reason that he was asked was in light of a passage in Miss Fabricant's article which speaks of Mr White saddling himself with notoriety, throwing people out of his restaurants. That is the passage and he accepted, I think, that he asked people to leave one- and two-star restaurants. It was a matter of shouting at the kitchen boy. He has had this bad boy image and we have heard he quite accepts phrases, 'The Jagger of the Aga', 'The Byron of the Back Burner' and now we know he is really the Cliff Richard of the kitchen. He is a good boy, not a bad boy ...

The jury adjourned on Wednesday, 5 April. They were not out for long before returning to announce that they had opted to send George's suggested message across the Atlantic to the editors of the US papers. They awarded me a settlement of £75,000: £15,000 from the *Times* and £60,000 from the *Tribune*. According to Mr Robertson's figures, that was the equivalent of Florence cutting off one of my hands and chopping off maybe a finger and thumb from the other hand. Plus, of course, costs of about half a million.

TWENTY-SEVEN

About time

IT WAS a weird week. On the Monday morning I stood with George Carman on the steps of the High Court, two white knights charging into battle with the Americans. And on the Friday afternoon, 7 April, I was the groom on the steps of the Belvedere, my restaurant in Holland Park, having my picture taken with my bride, Mati.

Mati and I had known each other for eight years. We had two sons, Luciano and Marco, but had never seriously discussed marriage because my life, of course, was work, work, work. One night we were at Mirabelle having dinner with Michael Winner, the movie director, when he raised the subject. I had retired from the kitchen partly to spend more time with Mati and the kids – marriage was the right step to take. I didn't propose, as such. We were in the romantic surroundings of Mirabelle, Michael shooting Cupid arrows, and we ended the meal as husband-and-wife-to-be.

We married at the Belvedere because it is in a beautiful setting and has a licence that enables couples to tie the knot on the premises. Michael was best man and made a very funny speech, from which I cannot recall a single line. I had thought, who could I choose as my best man without offending anybody else? When you say someone is your best man you can hurt someone else's feelings. I chose Michael so none of my other friends would get offended, because although he was a great mate he was out of my regular circle of friends. I never shared him with anybody because he might not like my friends and they might not like him, so I just tended to him alone.

Mati and I finally get married.

The 170 guests included George Carman, my defender in court, as well as Piers Morgan, who as editor of the *Daily Mirror* would be the one to call me the following January and break the sad news, 'It's just coming through on the wires that George Carman has died.' Rocco Forte, Fay Maschler and her husband Reg were there. Gordon Ramsay and his wife Tana were guests, as was Piers Adam, a friend from my days in Oxford. There was also a smattering of aristocrats, which included Lord Coleridge and the Earl of Onslow.

Alan Crompton-Batt had met Mati and a few of her friends to help do the seating plan. When she had asked him, 'What shall we do with the lords? What's the tradition?' he'd replied, 'Easy. You put two lords on each table.' Forty minutes later, when the plan was finished, he stood up, clapped his hands and announced, 'Right, it is now customary for everyone to leave the room and I get to fuck the maid of honour.'

His two-lords-per-table rule did not suit Onslow and Coleridge. They were pupils together at Eton and apparently one day Onslow accused Coleridge of playing badminton with his yellow canary. I am sure Coleridge would never have done such a wicked thing. The two men hadn't spoken since that day decades earlier and it was only now that they found themselves sitting opposite one another and Onslow's uncomfortable memories of being the Birdman of Eton came flooding back. I remember once going shooting with Lord Onslow and after lunch he said, 'Nature calls.' He stepped ten paces onto the grass and got his cock out and relieved himself in the middle of the lawn, facing the trees. He is a beautifully eccentric man and I thought to myself, I wish I had the confidence to do that but do it facing the shooting party, rather than the trees.

Gordon, meanwhile, brought a film crew to the wedding. They were hiding in the bushes, filming Mr Ramsay for his Boiling Point programme. I had no idea they were there until about eight months later when the producers sent me a video tape which contained the out-takes. Mati and I were happily watching it when suddenly we saw the two of us, dressed in our wedding attire, and then there was Gordon, winking at the cameras.

The wedding was a great day and afterwards Mati and I flew off to Venice for a honeymoon. We arrived at the world famous Cipriani Hotel and were unpacking our bags when the phone rang. It was the receptionist and she surprised me by saying, 'Michael Winner is in reception waiting for you.' It's unusual for the best man to join the happy couple on their honeymoon. Some people might be appalled by the intrusion, but Mati and I were touched that he had gone to the effort of keeping it a secret and there were only good intentions behind his decision to join us in Venice. He stayed for just a couple of days and took us sightseeing and to places of historical interest, like Harry's Bar. Our Winner whistle-stop tour lasted forty-eight hours and then he disappeared, leaving us to enjoy the remaining five or six days alone. On the final day we visited an art gallery and were studying the pictures on the wall when the gallery's owner came over to us and started praising the artist. 'But don't take it from me,' he said and he scurried off to his office and proudly returned with a newspaper cutting. 'Look at what the *Herald Tribune* has said about him.' We didn't have time to explain that about a week earlier I had successfully sued the American newspaper, but we left the gallery with Mati telling the bemused owner, 'Don't believe everything you read in the *Tribune*.'

The hotel bill must have amounted to thousands of pounds, but when I came to pay the manager said, 'Mr Winner left instructions that on no account should Mr White pay the bill.' Michael had picked up the entire tab. At least let me pay for the meals. 'On no account.' Then let me pay for the champagne. 'On no account.' May I at least pay for the cigarettes – Christ, I've smoked enough of the things. Again, the response was, 'On no account.'

Why do grooms so often fall out with their best men once the wedding is over? Michael is a very funny man, a brilliant raconteur and very kind, but he gets tetchy sometimes and I think that was the reason we stopped talking back in 2002.

Honeymooning in Venice
(once Michael Winner had gone home).

I opened Drones Club with my friend Piers Adam and Piers decided to throw a party. I didn't invite one person because as far as I was concerned it was Piers's thing. I felt it was too early for a party, the place wasn't ready. I thought, Piers can have his party and I might have one at a later date. On the evening of the party I was due to be taking Michael for dinner at Drones Restaurant, my place in Pont Street, so it was unlikely that I would even show up at Piers's bash. Then I got a call from Michael, who was swearing down the phone and going mad. 'Why wasn't I invited to the party?' he yelled, though I've cleaned up his language. It was a major bollocking and then the line went dead. He had hung up on me.

I rang him back and said, 'Michael, we seem to have been cut off.' Then he started again, ranting away. When I got home I told Mati about the bizarre conversation, if you can call it that, with Michael. I was quite upset by it. He was making a big deal out of nothing. Or rather, to me it was no big deal but to him it obviously was. Mati took it upon herself to write Michael a letter, along the lines of: *Dear Michael, it wasn't Marco's party. He didn't feel Drones was ready. He was going to take you there next week. This is all a silly misunderstanding …*

———

Michael doesn't live far from us, so Mati walked round with Luciano to drop off the letter. She has never received a response. On that day I made a decision never to talk to Michael again and our paths have not crossed since.

As for Gordon Ramsay, I cut the umbilical cord a few years back. There were a few incidents and I just decided I didn't want to talk to him any more, so I stopped returning his calls. He had been a protégé at Harveys and he was always a hard worker and showed tremendous resilience when it came to my bollockings. He never cracked. Or rather, he never cracked until his final night at Harveys. I don't recall what he'd done wrong but I monstered him and he lost it. Gordon crouched down on the floor in the corner of the kitchen, buried his head in his hands and started sobbing. 'I don't care what you do to me,' he said as he wept. 'Hit me. I don't care. Sack me. I don't care.' I was hardly going to sack him; he was leaving the next day – I'd got him a job working for Albert Roux at Gavroche.

Perhaps I created the monster Ramsay, the monster who ended up as a TV personality screaming at celebrities on *Hell's Kitchen*, doing to them what I had done to him.

In the nineties I helped him launch Aubergine and even came up with the restaurant's name. In its first few months his kitchen wasn't right, so my chefs at the Canteen cooked a lot of the food for Aubergine and his boys came over to collect it.

I had given a newspaper interview in which I'd compared chefs to footballers and had wondered whether footballers made good managers, i.e., can chefs be successful restaurateurs. Gordon then gave an interview in which he used the same analogy but against me. In other words, he suggested that I may have been good in the kitchen but was I a good restaurateur? I was annoyed about it but he said he had been misquoted. I'd heard him say that before and I think that there's a limit to the number of times you can be misquoted.

There was another incident when we were pulled up for speeding and the story appeared in the papers. Gordon said his PR people must have placed it, but I wasn't happy and decided my life would be enriched if I saw no more of him. It's unlikely we shall ever know each other again. When I cut, I cut.

Heston Blumenthal says I am extremely sensitive about friendship and perhaps he is right. One Sunday Mati and I went to Heston's restaurant, The Fat Duck in Bray, for lunch with a crowd which included my protégé Philip Howard and Mati's wonderful parents, Pedro and Lali. I wasn't on speaking terms with Gordon, but by coincidence he happened to be in the restaurant on the same day. He arrived on spec with his wife Tana, said hello to Heston and asked, 'Any chance of a spot of lunch?' Heston didn't know that we weren't talking and breezily said, 'Marco's coming today.' Gordon didn't let on that we had fallen out but simply asked where we would be sitting. When Heston said the garden, Gordon asked if he and Tana could have a table inside. Half an hour later I arrived with my mob. I saw Gordon and said to Heston, 'What's *he* doing here?'

Heston was bemused. 'Who, Gordon? He's come for lunch.'

I said, 'You'll have to ask him to leave.' Philip Howard, a very nice man, shuffled uncomfortably and said something like, 'Oh no.'

Heston called Gordon away from the table. 'Gordon, Marco says he's not going to stay if you are here. I think you should have a word with him.' Heston then scurried away into the kitchen to hide, asking his maître d' to keep him informed of developments.

Gordon came into the garden and said, 'Thank you very much Marco for ruining a nice day.'

I said, 'Why don't you sue me for loss of enjoyment?'

He came back with, 'You fat bastard. I've always wanted to call you that.'

I said, 'Is that the best you can do?'

Gordon left. There was silence in the garden. The customers on other tables were gripped by the scene. I think if it had taken place on stage in a theatre we'd have got a standing ovation.

TWENTY-EIGHT

Vegas without the props

AFTER leaving the kitchen I lost direction. I was hooked on the adrenaline of service and it was extremely hard to kick the habit. It was all very well hanging up my apron on 23 December 1999 and retiring as a chef, but the following morning I woke up to the startling realisation that I was unemployed. Incredible though it may seem, it hadn't occurred to me that I wouldn't have a job. I had an income, because I owned or had an interest in a number of restaurants, including Mirabelle, the Belvedere, Drones, Quo Vadis and Criterion, but I felt miserable having deprived myself of that day-long fix of adrenaline. The structure of my life had vanished.

It was cold-turkey time. I escaped for a bit and there were similarities to the way in which I had behaved after my mother's death, going fishing, hunting and shooting. I'd take myself off to the countryside for a day out with those great friends of mine, my thoughts. It seemed strange that I had stopped cooking in order to be happy but now I found it difficult to boost my spirits. I kept telling myself, I want to develop as a person not as a chef any more. Today I feel as if I have resurfaced, filled with the same energy and knowledge that got me three stars, and wanting to use that knowledge, skill and understanding to move forward.

I have the restaurants but am now firmly front of house, rather than in the kitchen. Food is important, of course, but I am more focused on creating a great environment for the punters. You can sit in the most acclaimed restaurant in the world, but if you don't feel comfortable in the environment, then it doesn't matter how good the

Mirabelle, Luciano, Lettie and Marco on a day out in spring 2004.

food is because you're not going to enjoy your evening. It's awful to go to a restaurant where you find yourself thinking that they're making us feel privileged to be here. People have got to enjoy themselves – food and wine are by-products of going out, unless you are one of the few who go to a restaurant purely to taste the food. I have no desire to do another Oak Room, a temple of gastronomy. My new dream, if you like, is to provide good food at an affordable price.

The days of sitting in an environment which is sterile – and sitting there feeling quite precious – are pretty much over. The average person can't spend £150 a head on a meal. There are a lot of people who want to eat out twice a week and they will not be disappointed because the standard of British restaurants is very high. When I was a kid, eating out was a special treat. On my birthdays my dad would take me and my brothers into Leeds city centre and to a restaurant, the name of which I forget, which was run by a man called Johnny the Greek. Johnny served mostly Italian food rather than Greek but I always ordered the distinctly un-Italian gammon and pineapple. But these days many children are whisked off to restaurants a couple of times a month, if not more often than that.

Children were the inspiration behind Frankie's. One night in the spring of 2004 Mati and I went for dinner with my business manager, Peter Burrell, who also represents the jockey Frankie Dettori. Peter wanted me to meet Frankie so I suggested he come along with his wife Catherine. The five of us went to my restaurant Drones and Frankie and I got along very well. He moaned about the starter, carpaccio, and I said, 'Frankie, what do you know about food?' To which he replied, 'Actually, I know quite a lot about food. Being a jockey I need to watch my weight so I'm very specific and fussy about everything I eat.' I took his point.

He then wanted my advice. 'Can you suggest a restaurant where I can go with Catherine and the kids? A place where I can have good food but also feel happy that the kids are eating well.' He didn't want a fast food joint, in other words. I thought long and hard about the question but was unable to answer it. I simply could not think of a single restaurant that would meet his requirements. When I said, 'No, I'm sorry. You've got me there,' he replied, 'Then why don't we open one together?'

This remark was a little too spontaneous even for my liking, but I promised to sleep on it. A day or two later I phoned him to say yes, I was in. That was how Frankie's started. Four months later, in September 2004, we opened Frankie's in Yeoman's Row, Knightsbridge. It's a basement restaurant serving the finest steaks as well as Italian pasta dishes and things like Veal Milanese. Customers come not just for the food but for the buzz. The kids go into the kitchen and help make the pizza. A magician entertains the children on Sundays. Mirror balls hang from the ceiling, mirrors line the walls, there are leather banquettes and good background music.

Then I opened Luciano in November 2005. Romantically, it is on the site of the great restaurant Prunier, in St James's. Even more romantically, it is the first restaurant I have named after a member of my family. Its walls are lined with magnificent paintings and it has to be one of the finest dining rooms in Britain. The food – simple but perfectly cooked Italian – is right, the lighting is right, the look is right and the whole feel is just what you need for a good night out.

Having stepped away from the stove, my understanding of food is far greater. It sounds odd, but when you've been engrossed in cooking you become, to a certain extent, lost in what you are doing. Seventeen or eighteen hours a day in the kitchen not only stunts your growth socially, it can also stunt your growth in cooking terms. You become blinded. You are just working, working, working. Routine. Standards, standards, standards. As I'm no longer under that pressure I find I can look at a dish, mentally dissect it and see a way of improving it far better than I could then. I can sit down and work things out more easily. I reflect well and am better at simplifying, working out concepts and understanding food.

A young chef has a habit of overworking things and it takes great confidence to believe in your produce and yourself. I have discovered that I didn't need to put that much effort in. For instance, in the old days

I would have put a huge amount of effort into designing a dover sole dish, but now that I'm out of the kitchen I know that it should be served plain and simple, with only a little bit of lemon juice and perhaps a splash of olive oil. Delicious. I no longer want complicated food. If I decided to cook again tomorrow I would do uncomplicated dishes. My menu would contain things I like to eat, and if that's whelks with a bit of malt vinegar and white pepper then that's what I'd do. It might be fresh crab, seasoned nicely, with a bit of olive oil and some hot toast. Or red mullet with sauce vierge – olive oil, lemongrass seeds, tomatoes and basil. Perhaps, it would be a top-quality medium-rare steak, hung properly (which is for twenty-eight to thirty days in my opinion), pan-fried and seasoned properly, then served with a great salad.

Of course I like to indulge and eat something quite rich occasionally. I love classical food and adore a big bowl of choucroûte or daube de boeuf. In the summer of 2005 I bought a pub, the Yew Tree Inn, not far from Highclere Castle in Hampshire. Logs blaze in the inglenook fireplace, the ceilings are low, the wooden beams are four centuries old. There are even a few bedrooms for customers who have let the mood take hold of them and don't fancy the drive home. The menu is good. There might be venison (brought in by yours truly after one of my shoots) and not over-hung or overcooked, sliced thinly like roast lamb and with the same texture too. The menu changes daily, but there could be a risotto of local crayfish, or Brixham mussels, roast fillet of brill or maybe a fillet of beef. But the menu also includes one or two dishes that were served at the Connaught during those twenty-six years when the brilliant chef Michel Bourdin oversaw its kitchen until his retirement in 2001.

Michel served the Connaught's old-money clientele a superb dish, Oeufs de Cailles Maintenon, which is on the Yew Tree's menu for three reasons. Firstly, it tastes magnificent – a blanquette of pastry, on top of which is a druxelles (minced mixture) of sautéed mushrooms and shallots, on top of which are five gently boiled quails' eggs, soft and runny in the centre, on top of which is hollandaise sauce. Secondly, it enables you to taste Michelin-starred food that was being

served in the Parisian restaurants of the fifties and sixties, restaurants
where Michel had trained before coming to England. Eating this dish
is a bit like stepping back in time – one mouthful and you are in the
golden age of Gastronomy, the Escoffier style of cuisine. It's fattening,
of course, but if you want to indulge yourself then this is comfort on
a plate. Thirdly, this dish is on the menu as a small tribute to Michel.
I never worked for him but I admired him tremendously. In my own
little way, its presence on the menu says I haven't forgotten the world
that I came from in the same way that he did not forget his roots. He
didn't forget where his passion was born.

———

It was a quarrel. Or at least that's how it started. We were driving
home from Frankie's in Knightsbridge and, before I knew it, the row
had turned into something quite fierce; a domestic, as they say, that
involved the police and led to me being banged up in a cell for
fourteen hours. The ladies and gentlemen of the British press would
draw their own conclusions about that unfortunate incident on
19 January 2005, but the truth of the matter is I didn't hit Mati; she
hit me. And I certainly don't blame her for doing so.

I had been in Frankie's all day and night and Mati had joined me
for dinner before we both climbed into the Range Rover and headed
back to Holland Park, Mati at the wheel. Somewhere between the
restaurant and home, Mati decided to mention Robin Saunders and,
if you don't mind, I shall have to sidetrack now in order to explain the
significance of that woman's name.

Up until 2002, my life had been run by accountants as well as
figures like Michael Caine and Rocco Forte. I had nothing to do with
the business side of my restaurants. Then, one day in Drones Club,
I met this highly intelligent, high-flying City banker called Robin
Saunders. She was a member of the Club and a great regular. I found
her interesting and was flattered, I suppose, that she took me into
her confidence. Robin told me about business deals she was working
on and asked for my opinions. 'What would you do in my position?'

she might ask and then she'd listen intently as I tackled her deals with my mathematical brain. From time to time I would pop into Drones and she would be there, so we'd have a cup of tea. As these little chats continued, I realised that my confidence was growing. Robin was the person who actually started to make me think I was capable of running a business.

Robin had told me that her father was quite ill, and shortly after nine one summer's morning in 2003 she sent me a text message. It said something like, 'Hi, Marco, just got off the phone to my father. Nightmare. Love to have a coffee.' Robin was clearly looking for a listener, though that is not how Mati deciphered the words when she happened to scroll through the messages on my mobile. There were other messages from Robin, which amounted to nothing more than text flirting although I could never respond to the messages because I had yet to learn how to send a text message. Mati concluded that Robin and I were having an affair, which is understandable because Robin was my new best friend, and she adopted interesting methods of dealing with the situation. She typed a message into my phone: 'Marco Pierre White has left his wife and three children for Robin Saunders.' And then – ping – she sent the message to the entire list of contacts on my phone.

Can you imagine it? Scores of my friends and associates received the message – from me! In the wrong hands it would have been dynamite and, inevitably, it did end up in the wrong hands. Among the list of contacts on my mobile were a handful of journalists who must have been overjoyed to receive the news by text. 'I've only ever had a fucking cup of tea with the woman,' I told Mati as the phone calls from anxious friends started coming in. Needless to say, the press lapped it up.

And then, as we drove home from Frankie's, I got another bash from the Saunders stick. 'Why don't you go and live with Robin Saunders?' said Mati, or something like that. Once back at home, she wouldn't let it drop. Usually when Mati is trying to provoke me into an argument I tend not to respond. I will just sit and stare – at a picture, out of a window, at a clock – and won't utter a single word. I close down, just like I did when my mother died. But for some reason, on this particular night in January, I found myself saying something cruel and utterly untrue. 'I am only with you because of the kids,' I told Mati. They were wicked words and ones that sent Mati over the edge. The anger within her turned into blind rage and I don't blame her.

A second or two passed as she absorbed the remark, then she lifted a lamp from the bedside table and threw it at me. I saw it flying in my direction and then, when it was just an inch or two from my face, it suddenly stopped and crashed to the floor at my feet. The lamp was still plugged in at the socket; had the wire been a little longer I would be toothless, or worse, by now.

Mati was not done yet.

I felt a stabbing pain in my bollocks – it was her knee – then she lunged forward and tried to scratch my face. I had had enough. Grabbing her by the arms, I pushed her back on to the bed so she was lying on it and I was above her, holding her down and telling her, 'Calm down, Mati. Calm down.' Again, I should reiterate that I did not hit her.

When she eventually stopped flailing and writhing I climbed off the bed and went and watched TV in the drawing room, and a few minutes later Mati came in and said, 'I want you to leave the house.'

'I'm not leaving,' I told her. 'Why should I leave my own house?'

'Then I'm calling the police.'

Mati answered the door when the police arrived. The two officers were greeted by her saying, 'Take him away, take him away, take him away.' When they asked me to go to the station I didn't resist. One of them nodded at his handcuffs and said, 'I don't think we'll be needing these,' and I climbed into their car and was driven away.

At Notting Hill nick I was asked to take off my shirt. One of the officers was convinced it was covered in blood stains and he wanted the garment to be checked by forensics. I tried unsuccessfully to explain that the mark had, in fact, been caused earlier in the day when I'd spilled hot chocolate down myself. They put me in a cell but left the door unlocked and for the next fourteen hours I lay on a mattress, chatting to the coppers about their lives and jobs. 'We can give you breakfast,' said one of the officers who was aware of my achievements in the kitchen, 'but I wouldn't recommend it to a man like you.' I took his advice.

Meanwhile, Mati didn't realise I was at the police station. When she managed to calm down a little, she had phoned Mr Ishii to find out where I was. 'He's with his solicitor,' Mr Ishii had replied, which she took to mean I had been released by the police and had headed off to see my solicitor, probably to talk about a divorce.

I was taken into an interview room where two plain-clothes officers tried to question me about the dramatic events that had led to me being in Notting Hill police station. 'I'm a big man,' I said, and neither of them argued with that. 'If I had hit my wife don't you think she'd have marks on her?' Again, they seemed to accept my point. 'She's the one who assaulted me,' I continued. My battle wounds included scratches and a bite mark, which I must have suffered while trying to restrain her. They said that Mati had withdrawn her allegations of assault.

It was Thursday morning when I stepped out of the police station. On the journey home I felt depressed, and while Mati was there when I walked into the house, I don't remember talking to her.

A friend of mine in the CID later told me, 'What often happens in a situation like this is the cops drop the guy off at a hotel or a mate's house, but because you're Marco Pierre White they love it. It's exciting for them to have a celebrity in the cell and, if they have contacts at newspapers, they might make a couple of hundred quid selling the story.'

Sure enough the press got wind of it within hours of my release and door-stepping reporters descended on our home and at Frankie's.

I had to confront the situation. I broke my vow of silence and said to Mati that we should go for dinner at Frankie's. I wanted to kill the rumours that our marriage was over because our marriage was certainly not over and we are still together today. If we were to kill the story it was important to be seen out together in public, or rather it was important to be seen together. When we arrived at Frankie's I put my arm around Mati and flashbulbs exploded.

FIERY MARCO IS ARRESTED AFTER HIS WIFE CALLS 999, ran the headline in the *Daily Mail*, with a strapline, 'Riddle of the "row that went too far" at celebrity chef's £3 million home.' The use of the word 'fiery' was a clever one. I am not fiery, but years earlier I suppose it was a good description of me. The inferences and implications were enough for the average newspaper reader to deduce that I was a wife-beater. The story was all the more piquant because a fortnight earlier I had given an interview, lavishing praise on Mati, calling her 'a very special, very rare person' but also saying, 'Mati feels that, by the time I get home, I've given myself to everybody else. I'm exhausted and there's little left for her ...'

———

Mati shared my dream of chasing Michelin stars. I risked my marriage to pursue that dream, and once I had achieved it, I realised how wonderfully supportive Mati had been.

And now I find myself thinking about where my life could have gone seriously wrong. It was back in the days of Harveys, during the recession of the late eighties. The restaurant business was struggling, but my rivals reacted to the dire economic situation in a completely different way to me: they put their prices down. They reckoned that to reduce the price of a meal would bring in the punters, and when that tactic failed they reduced their prices even further. They were searching desperately for the right price to appeal to customers. In contrast, I put my prices up. My rationale was simple: like it or not, fewer people were eating out, but the ones who were going to restaurants were the ones who could afford to pay more. My rivals sank. Their ever-reducing prices took their losses higher and higher. They went bust and chefs disappeared to do God knows what. Meanwhile, I stayed in business and saw out the recession. I went on to achieve that dream and open thirty more restaurants.

However, there must be more to success than seeing out a recession. For instance, without Mati at my side, I don't know how I would have fared. Would the exhausting journey have seemed too impossible to complete? And then there were my staff, thousands of them who have worked for me not just in the kitchens but in the dining rooms, at the bars, on reception and in cloakrooms. I have always said that winning three stars was a monument to my mother, but now I wonder if I could have done it all without my father? Surely, he is responsible for my success. He is the one who made me the person I am, a driven man who keeps on pushing, and that is what won me my Michelin stars. Gambler that he was, the old man managed to turn me into his own thoroughbred and somewhere along the way I had developed that all-important cook's brain.

Cook's brain. I've mentioned it previously – that ability to visualise the food on the plate, as a picture in my mind, and then work my way backwards. There's no reason why domestic cooks can't do the same thing.

For instance, let's just think for a moment about a fried egg. It's not the most inspired dish, but then again if you can't cook an egg what can you cook? And actually, a perfectly cooked fried egg is quite beautiful.

Apply the cook's brain and visualise that fried egg on the plate. Do you want it to be burned around the edges? Do you want to see craters on the egg white? Should the yolk look as if you'd need a hammer to break into it? The answer to all three questions should be, No. Yet the majority of people still crack an egg and drop it into searingly hot oil or fat and continue to cook it on a high heat. You need to insert earplugs to reduce the horrific

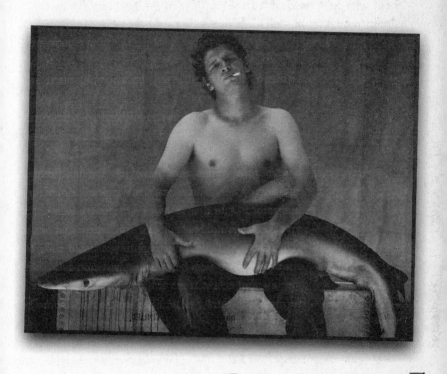

Smoked shark, now on permanent
display in the National Portrait Gallery.

volume of the sizzle. And the result, once served up in a pool of oil, is an inedible destruction of that great ingredient – the egg.

Now let's think about what we really want to see on the plate. We want that egg to look beautiful and appetising because then, when we eat it, we shall all be happy. We want the white to be crater-free and unblackened around its edges. The yolk should be glistening, just a thin film which can be easily pierced by a fork to let the yellowness run out. That's the picture. How do we create it?

Slowly heat a heavy-based pan on a very low heat, perhaps for five minutes, and, once it is hot enough, put in some butter, letting it gently melt. Then take your egg from a basket. I don't keep eggs in the fridge as it only lengthens the cooking process because you are dealing with a chilled ingredient.

If the heat seems too high then remove the pan from the heat for a few seconds to let it cool down. Basically, if you can hear that egg cooking then the heat is too high. Carefully spoon the butter over the top of the egg. After about five minutes there you have your magnificent fried egg – more of an egg poached in butter – just the way you had pictured it on the plate.

If you can visualise the food on the plate before you start cooking it, you can be more precise with portions: how often have you prepared a roast dinner intended for six but ended up creating enough food for a dozen? Picture it on the plate first, and you'll not only get a better meal but save on waste as well.

There were two other men who played a significant role in my life: Alan Crompton-Batt, my publicist, who died a couple of months before I started this book, and Bob Carlos Clarke, the photographer who took those great shots for my first cookery book *White Heat*, and who died as the final pages of this book were being written. Alan and Bob were like my props, supporting me through the rough times.

I met Bob in 1986. My girlfriend Lowri-Ann Richards was friends with him and one day she introduced us. A couple of years later, when I was offered a deal to write a cookery book, I approached Bob to see if he would be interested in taking the pictures. By then he was a well-known fashion photographer. He invited me round for tea and I arrived with a pile of linen tablecloths. Bob thought I was dropping off the laundry but I explained to him how I like to draw on tablecloths and on these particular ones I had drawn pictures of the dishes that would appear in the book. Bob, or was it his wife Lindsay, came up with the title and the book, as you know, was a phenomenal success. There was a time when it was considered Britain's most influential cookery book because it inspired so many young people to become chefs. It was innovative because it contained not only shots of food but also those moody black and white, reportage-style photos of kitchen life at Harveys. *White Heat* was a cult classic, sending out the uplifting message that if I – the long-haired young cook from Leeds – had crossed the North–South divide to find fame in London, you too can do it. A glance at Bob's pictures gave the reader a fascinating glimpse of the haggard, exhausted cooks who produced Michelin-starred dishes, and exhaustion equalled passion.

Bob was one of those friends who pop in and out of your life, rather than being a constant presence. Six months might pass before we saw each other, but when we spoke we could pick up where we had left off. A lot of people in the fashion business found him difficult to deal with, but I never had a problem with him and he was always a dear friend. Shortly before his death we had seen quite a bit of each other and enjoyed a good lunch at Luciano. Then I got a call to say that he had died. Desperately depressed, he had thrown himself in front of an oncoming train.

Although Bob was a big part of my life I can't recall him ever meeting Alan Crompton-Batt, that other influential figure who helped my career. I think I kept them apart, perhaps because I don't know if they would have mixed well. You may never have heard of Alan but there is every chance you will have heard of Jamie Oliver, Gary Rhodes, Gordon Ramsay and Heston Blumenthal. Would you have heard of the chefs, I wonder, if it weren't for Alan? He was the creator of the modern-day phenomenon that is the celebrity chef. He was the Dr Frankenstein who saw the public relations potential of the monsters skulking in the kitchen. His clients did not include Jamie, Gary, Gordon and Heston, but Alan was the man who set the ball rolling back in the eighties. He and his wonderful wife Elizabeth had their own PR business which specialised in promoting the cooks as well as the food. Before then, chefs weren't really discussed in editorial conference or at TV production meetings.

He was the first person I befriended after arriving in London in 1981. Or rather, he befriended me by giving me free beers and coffee. He knew the restaurant business well and had a great palate. While Bob was not a big drinker, Alan was the master of the long lunch. I have never known anyone go into battle like Alan. You could have a conversation with him in an empty restaurant at two o'clock in the morning when he was virtually comatose but he'd still manage to come up with ideas as his eyelids flickered. And the next morning he would be at his desk at nine, putting those ideas into action. He was on the ball.

I remember having an extremely long lunch with Anthony Ellis, chief executive of Carlton Food Network. Anthony and I had enjoyed four bottles of Tiagnello, a powerful Tuscan red, when Alan arrived at the restaurant and bounded up to our table, full of energy. 'That's not fair,' he said after asking how much we'd had to drink. 'You two are well ahead of me.' He was determined to catch up and catch up quickly, so he ordered two bottles of Tiagnello and a burgundy glass which holds an entire bottle. He poured a whole bottle into the glass and downed it in one. Then he got the next bottle, filled up the burgundy glass and demolished that as well. It was an amazing sight. Alan looked at his astonished companions and said, 'I am now on your level.' Though having drunk the wine so quickly he only managed to utter those six words, then he was totally fucked, off the wall.

One day I got a phone call from the Lanesborough Hotel, in Hyde Park Corner. Alan had spent a long afternoon there and staff had had to help him out of the building. On the hotel steps he had clasped on to the railings and wouldn't loosen his grip. Something inside him was saying the evening was not yet over. Staff tugged at him but he hung on like a man dangling from the clifftop, the sea lashing the rocks below.

He was a tortured soul, but he was also immensely clever, and in his youth he had been accepted at Oxford but turned down the place. He could be drunk but still profound and would come out with highly intelligent comments and witty remarks. His memory was faultless and he could recite meals he had eaten decades earlier.

In the autumn of 2004 he went off to stay with a friend in South Africa and that is where he died of pneumonia. I have never cried so much for one person since my mother's death.

Alan may have set out to get publicity for me and my restaurants, but he rarely intruded. He did not drag me away from the kitchen for a photo shoot or ask me to leave the stove because the Beeb had called to see if I would be a guest on a chat show. Alan knew what my priorities were and his encouragement helped me view him more as a brother than as a friend. Food follows fame in the dictionary, but in my life fame has always followed food.

Unlike the jockey it was named after, Frankie's is growing. The first one in Knightsbridge was followed by another in Chiswick. There's a Frankie's in Putney and earlier this year the Criterion, that monster of a restaurant in Piccadilly Circus, became the flagship Frankie's. By the time you read this, there should be a Frankie's in Selfridge's. Then we start expanding across the globe: by the end of this year, there'll be a Frankie's in Dubai and another in Shanghai. P&O wants to put Frankie's in its new cruise liner, *Ventura*.

Earlier this year, in May, I found myself in Las Vegas for the first time. I was there to visit Robert Earl's Planet Hollywood Hotel, a 2,600-roomed number which opens next March. It's going to have a Frankie's in it, you'll not be surprised to learn. The hotel looks very chic, decorated with Hollywood memorabilia, and I think it will be magnificent. Robert put me in the penthouse on the 51st floor – the lift journey is enough to give you jet lag.

As it was, I was suffering jet lag which meant I ended up being wide awake at strange hours of the day. I would stare out at the mountains in the distance, watching the sun rise and set and think about all the people who've watched the sun come up and go down over Vegas. I love the place. It has to be the greatest concept ever created. It doesn't matter whether it's Monday or Sunday, it's business as usual. It doesn't matter whether it's morning or evening, or the middle of the night, it's business. I have never liked the nine-to-five routine and am very happy talking business at midnight, so Vegas and I are well matched. I was fascinated by the Chinese gamblers who would fall asleep on the slot machines which they considered to be lucky. They wanted to glue themselves to it so that no one else could play.

When I was introduced to people in Vegas they often asked if I still get enjoyment from cooking. The answer is, none whatsoever. I cannot stand it. Sometimes I will rustle up meals for the kids – I'll do them simple things like meatballs – but in general I feel like I have done my time with cooking. As you know by now, when I cut, I cut. My marriage to cooking is well and truly over but it's not something that upsets me. At Christmas Mati encourages me to do a roast, partly because she is astonished that I can produce roast turkey with all the trimmings in only one hour (I get two small turkeys from Bresse and poach them before roasting). Though she gets annoyed because I use a pristine white tea towel as my dish cloth.

And I do not envy other chefs. I couldn't sleep the other night so I got up and flicked on the TV. Ainsley Harriott, Gary Rhodes and Antony Worrall Thompson flashed up on the screen. They were appearing in a TV commercial for washing-up liquid. Christ, I thought. Is this what it's come to?

When I was a chef I was wanted in the kitchen eighteen hours a day. I was wanted at the stove, wanted at the passe, wanted in the larder. I was wanted in the kitchen morning, noon and night. A couple of days ago I was talking on the phone to a chef who's a well-known name. It was lunchtime and it crossed my mind to ask how he could find the time to chat to me. Then in the background I heard a voice tell him he was wanted. Was he wanted at the passe? Was he wanted at the stove? Neither. My friend, in fact, was wanted in Make-up.

Stars are still the name of the game. But the way I see it, these days a chef's burning obsession is to become a TV star rather than win three stars from Michelin.

AROUND about the time I started work on this autobiography, in February 2005, Joan Collins held a party at Frankie's to launch one of her own books. I was standing chatting to another guest when I suddenly spotted Shirley Bassey talking to a crowd at a table. *The* Shirley Bassey had walked into my joint in Knightsbridge. When I was introduced to her I said, 'We have never met before, but I grew up with you.' Then I explained to her how my father had been her greatest fan and that one side of a Shirley album was his cure for sadness.

I told her the story of my father's funeral. The old man's widow, Hazel, had considered playing a recording of 'Hey Big Spender'. After all, it was my dad's favourite song. But Hazel decided against it. She reckoned the song was too upbeat and therefore inappropriate for what was supposed to be a solemn occasion. So Hazel picked a sombre number and the mourners missed out on the treat of hearing that Bassey classic.

Shirley sensed I needed serenading and there, in the middle of my restaurant, she launched into 'Hey Big Spender'.

The minute you walked in the joint ...

And bang, I'm back at 22 Lingfield Mount, standing by the front door. 'Off you go,' says Dad and he hands me and my brothers some money to pay for the bus fare into Leeds city centre and the cinema tickets. We're going to see *Diamonds Are Forever*. Dad didn't come with us but I'm sure it would have been his kind of movie; spies, action, adventure, shoot-outs, gorgeous women and best of all, Shirley singing the theme tune.

I don't recall ever going to the cinema with the old man but I do remember a day at the pictures with my mother. During a family holiday, she took me to see *Doctor Zhivago* at the Odeon in Bridlington. The film was released in 1965 which suggests I was about four years old. I curled up on the seat beside my mother and as she watched the classic love story, I slept. I awoke as the final credits were rolling and then, as we were leaving, the cinema manager came up to us with a cheerful smile and handed me a little piggy bank. I was thrilled with the present but what on earth had I done to deserve it? 'That,' said the manager, 'is for being the best behaved boy in Bridlington.'

By now, you know my life story. You know that my behaviour has frequently been questionable. In Leeds I was not the best behaved boy. In London I was not the best behaved boy. In Oxfordshire, when I worked for Raymond Blanc at Le Manoir, I was most probably the worst behaved boy. I was labelled the 'enfant terrible' until I was old enough to be called 'London's rudest chef'. I can think of at least two ex-wives who have issues with my behaviour. I can name at least two US newspapers that had nothing good to say about me. Then there are the former friends and the ex-business partners. Let's not forget the customers I have kicked out of my restaurants in the past two decades after disputes over bills and minks and cheese and whatever. They would all agree on one thing: Marco Pierre White is not the best behaved boy in Britain.

If you raid your piggy bank you might find a penny or even a pound, but look at the treasures you find when you search your memory bank. It was only in Bridlington but there you have it. Long before this mad, mad life happened to me, and when I was with the woman who was my world, I *was* the best behaved boy.

The best behaved boy, Italy 1964.

Index